D0849545

University Research Management

MEETING THE INSTITUTIONAL CHALLENGE

Edited by Helen Connell

ORGANISATION FOR ECONOMIC CO-OPERATION AND DEVELOPMENT

9482/82-1

ORGANISATION FOR ECONOMIC CO-OPERATION AND DEVELOPMENT

Pursuant to Article 1 of the Convention signed in Paris on 14th December 1960, and which came into force on 30th September 1961, the Organisation for Economic Co-operation and Development (OECD) shall promote policies designed:

- to achieve the highest sustainable economic growth and employment and a rising standard of living in member countries, while maintaining financial stability, and thus to contribute to the development of the world economy;
- to contribute to sound economic expansion in member as well as non-member countries in the process of economic development; and
- to contribute to the expansion of world trade on a multilateral, non-discriminatory basis in accordance with international obligations.

The original member countries of the OECD are Austria, Belgium, Canada, Denmark, France, Germany, Greece, Iceland, Ireland, Italy, Luxembourg, the Netherlands, Norway, Portugal, Spain, Sweden, Switzerland, Turkey, the United Kingdom and the United States. The following countries became members subsequently through accession at the dates indicated hereafter: Japan (28th April 1964), Finland (28th January 1969), Australia (7th June 1971), New Zealand (29th May 1973), Mexico (18th May 1994), the Czech Republic (21st December 1995), Hungary (7th May 1996), Poland (22nd November 1996), Korea (12th December 1996) and the Slovak Republic (14th December 2000). The Commission of the European Communities takes part in the work of the OECD (Article 13 of the OECD Convention).

The Programme on Institutional Management in Higher Education (IMHE) started in 1969 as an activity of the OECD's newly established Centre for Educational Research and Innovation (CERI). In November 1972, the OECD Council decided that the Programme would operate as an independent decentralised project and authorised the Secretary-General to administer it. Responsibility for its supervision was assigned to a Directing Group of representatives of governments and institutions participating in the Programme. Since 1972, the Council has periodically extended this arrangement; the latest renewal now expires on 31st December 2006.

The main objectives of the Programme are as follows:

- to promote, through research, training and information exchange, greater professionalism in the management of institutions of higher education; and
- to facilitate a wider dissemination of practical management methods and approaches.

 THE OPINIONS EXPRESSED AND ARGUMENTS EMPLOYED IN THIS PUBLICATION ARE THE RESPONSIBILITY OF THE AUTHORS AND DO NOT NECESSARILY REPRESENT THOSE OF THE OECD OR OF THE NATIONAL OR LOCAL AUTHORITIES CONCERNED.

*

* *

Publié en français sous le titre :

La gestion de la recherche universitaire

RELEVER LE DÉFI AU NIVEAU DES ÉTABLISSEMENTS

© OECD 2004

FOREWORD

In 2000, the OECD Programme on Institutional Management in Higher Education-IMHE launched a project to analyse institutional responses to challenges arising from the implications of the changing education environment on research management, and draw together findings and ideas from current experience. Three international seminars were held and a set of eight case studies developed to illustrate ways in which higher education institutions in quite different settings are confronting **research management challenges**.

The first of the three seminars, *Research Management at the Institutional Level'* launched the project at the OECD in Paris in June 2000. With representation from all major OECD countries, participants mapped three central themes:

- Research management and support within institutions.

- Sources of funding and associated issues.

- Research training and research as a career.

These themes were taken further in the second seminar on *University Research Management: Learning from Diverse Experience* hosted by the United Nations University in Tokyo in February 2001. Participants from both OECD and a range of non-OECD countries in Africa, Asia and South America participated in the Tokyo seminar. In October 2003, the third seminar *Institutional Responses to the Changing Research Environment* with a strong European focus was hosted by the Zentrum für Wissenschaftmanagement (Centre for Science and Research Management) in Bonn.

In addition to the three seminars, *eight invited case studies* were prepared which are included in this report. The case studies focus on aspects of research management of particular importance in the unique setting of each institution. Nevertheless, common themes relevant to the broad field of higher education emerged. Case study institutions were selected to be representative of a variety of national and cultural contexts both within the OECD and beyond. They were also to include both research intensive and research non-intensive institutions.

The IMHE Programme acknowledges with gratitude the contributions of Helen Connell who wrote the summary report (Part 1) and of the project team members and case studies authors: Jean-Pierre Contzen, Lynn Meek, Françoise Thys-Clément, Fiona Wood, Janet Dibb-Smith, Ellen Hazelkorn, Maria Alice da Cunha Lahorgue, Maria Helena Nazaré, Jürgen Prömel, Véronique Cabiaux, Oktem Vardar, Mohammed Yusof Ismail, Mohammed Yusof Haj Othman, Ikram Said.

TABLE OF CONTENTS

EXECUTIVE SUMMARY

In an era when governments are placing unprecedented emphasis on research as a key motor for driving the knowledge society and economy, the effective management of research has become a key contemporary issue for institutions. Whereas university authorities once left academic researchers to get on – or not get on – with their research, now the research 'production' of an institution is crucial to its competitiveness and standing in the hierarchy of universities; it is an increasingly important part of the overall resources that individual institutions have at their disposal. It is research that fires the ambition of the contemporary university.

Several closely inter-related factors in the external environment of universities present new challenges for research management: **changes in funding regimes**; **new societal demands on universities and university systems**; **changes in the practice of innovation and research**; and **expanding research links between universities, industry, commerce, government and the wider community**. Increasingly, also, universities are becoming the favoured sites for publicly funded research. It is not surprising, then, to find that university authorities are showing a keen and growing interest in the overall research profile and research capacity of their institutions, and are seeking ways to best manage research as an essential, or even the key function, of the institution. It is no less surprising that research policies and the management of research are posing severe challenges.

As a way of gaining more fine grained analysis of issues which emerged during the first two project seminars, a number of authors were invited to prepare the case studies presented in Part 2 of this volume on how individual institutions have addressed research management. The institutions selected were drawn from a diversity of cultural settings and higher education traditions, from countries both within and beyond the OECD.

Research universities in a changing national policy context

The study of the **University of Adelaide**, one of Australia's longest established universities and one of its most research intensive, focuses on how the institution has responded to changes over the past decade in the national policy environment which favours research concentration and selectivity.

The **Universidade Federal do Rio Grande do Sul** – the Federal University in the State of Rio Grande do Sul - is a graduate level federal university in Brazil established in 1934. This study illustrates changes in the type of research undertaken within the university consequent on the government's attempt to boost the volume of research funding, by introducing sectoral funds. These comprise levies on the income of privatized sector, royalties and taxes on imported technology funds.

Research in the context of institutional restructuring

Following the national introduction in Portugal of a new research funding model in the mid 1990s, the **Universidade de Aveiro** – University of Aveiro - undertook a major institutional restructure developing multidisciplinary research units alongside departmentally based teaching.

While the **Humboldt Universität zu Berlin** – Humboldt University in Berlin - dates its origins to 1810, its present structure was established during the 1990s following the reunification of Germany. In the broad move within Germany toward increased institutional autonomy, the university has benefited from the ability to test new models of leadership, organisation and financing.

Managing research careers in an expanding research profile

The study of the **Université Libre de Bruxelles** – French speaking Free University in Brussels - serving the French speaking community of Belgium, focuses on the complexity of managing staff research careers in a situation where close to 50% of the institution's research is undertaken by externally funded research-only staff.

Building research from a new or slender base

The study of **Boğaziçi Üniversitesi** – Boğaziçi University - maps the successes and setbacks over several years of a sustained internal initiative to turn Turkey's highest prestige public university into a research university.

In 2001, **Universiti Kebangsaan Malaysia** was designated as one of four national research universities within the context of Vision 2020 whereby Malaysia plans to reach the level of a developed nation and establish a scientific, progressive, innovative and forward looking society. This study illustrates the early stages of the university's well resourced approach to strengthening its research profile.

Not a designated university within Ireland's binary system of tertiary education, the **Dublin Institute of Technology** has, nonetheless, set its sights on building a research capacity. This study illustrates the challenges met by non-university institutions, such as access to lower levels of resourcing, and staffing patterns built around teaching-only commitments.

Issues for research management within institutions:

Drawing on issues that emerged in the course of the project as a whole, Part 1 of this volume is a summary report in four sections:

- The growing significance of the research mission to higher education institutions;

- Strengthening structures and processes for research management across the institution;

- Funding and resourcing university research;

- Nurturing the research career.

The summary report identifies three central clusters of responses and challenges for institutions:

First is the growth of specialisation – professionalisation – of research management within institutions, which involves the appointment of both academic and administrative staff to specific research management positions and upgrading the capabilities of staff throughout the institution to better manage research activities. Institutions have a challenge to construct the emerging research management positions within the institution is such a way as to be able to attract and retain people of quality, experience and vision.

The second area is strategic research planning on an institution-wide basis – a range of issues emerge to which individual institutional responses are quite different:

- Establishing research priorities and developing an institutional research plan;

- Seeking and allocating resources for research;

- Evaluating research quality, both internally and externally;

- Creating an ethical framework for institutional research;

- Deciding how far to commercialise institutional research.

To a great extent this is a departure for most universities where research activities have in the past emerged from the initiative of individual researchers and been undertaken largely in isolation from each other. While individual researcher initiative remains the key, institutions are increasingly seeking to develop a holistic approach to their research undertakings.

The third area is the research career, notably the research career as an institutional responsibility. For many institutions this involves rethinking researcher education, through both initial and post graduate degrees so that students have the appropriate skills to adapt to the greater variety inherent in a research career, including the ability to handle its insecurities. Also – to the extent possible within industrial and other constraints – there is a need to rethink the research career within the institution, to provide continuity, a sense of growth and development in personal capacity (professional fulfilment), and appropriate incentives to encourage quality researchers to remain sufficiently long to make a worthwhile contribution to the individual institutions which employ them.

PART 1

INTRODUCTION

Significance of institution-wide research management

In an era when governments are placing unprecedented emphasis on research as a key motor for driving the knowledge society and economy, effective management of research has become a key contemporary issue for higher education institutions. Whereas university authorities once left academic researchers to get on – or not get on – with their research, now the research 'production' of an institution is crucial to its competitiveness and standing in the hierarchy of universities; it is an increasingly important part of the overall resources which individual institutions have at their disposal. It is research that fires the ambition of the contemporary university.

Several changes in the broad environment of higher education institutions have important implications for how research is managed within institutions:

- The growing significance of research for the knowledge society and economy, which has led to an increased prominence of research policy for governments;

- Changes in the way research funds are available from government and other sponsors, for example competitive allocation, targeting via priorities, performance based funding; there is both a growing competition and a growing pattern of cooperation between higher education institutions with respect to seeking research funding;

- Changes in the way research is undertaken – the scale is large (in terms both of expensive equipment and geographic spread); the type of research problems addressed are increasingly interdisciplinary and problem focused; the basic / applied research dichotomy is of reduced significance;

- Changes in core features of the university: a move toward mass institutions with the increasing proportion of student cohorts enrolling; a questioning of the balance between teaching and research - overall, within the institution as a whole - and within the responsibilities of individual academic staff; move toward greater commercialisation of research, thus a diversification of research activity within the institutional orbit;

- Demand for greater accountability by the broader society: tighter controls over the use of public funds; increased demands for compliance with ethical and legal regulations.

It is not surprising, then, to find that university authorities are showing a keen and growing interest in the overall research profile and research capacity of their institutions, and are seeking ways to best manage research as an essential or even the key function of the institution. It is no less surprising that research policies and the management of research are posing severe challenges. Accordingly, in 2000, the OECD/IMHE established the present project to analyse institutional responses to these challenges, and draw together findings and ideas from current experience.

THE GROWING SIGNIFICANCE OF THE RESEARCH MISSION TO HIGHER EDUCATION INSTITUTIONS

Across OECD countries during the past decade, research has moved significantly higher on all national agenda. National governments have boosted research funding in most countries, albeit in ways which channel research funds increasingly toward national priorities (OECD/DSTI, 2003). With an overall decline in research undertaken in the public research institute sector[1], the bulk of public funding for research is being spent in the higher education sector. While generally from a low base, institutions in a number of countries are significantly increasing research funding from industry sources, often with support from government incentives.

But public research funds available to universities are decreasingly in the form of unconditional institutional grants, and to a growing extent in the form either of competitively attained (often targeted) or of performance based funds, over which the institution has far less discretionary use. At the same time, institutions (society-wide) are required to be more accountable for how they use their public funds.

Towards entrepreneurship and mass institutions

Over its 800 or more years as one of the world's oldest continuous institutions, the university has shown a remarkable capacity for adaptation and survival, no less true now than in the past. The contemporary university is increasingly an entrepreneurial organisation, for which the pursuit of research excellence is a central concern. As the level of core, guaranteed public funding for many universities has dropped in recent years, the institutions and specifically faculties and departments within them have developed innovative strategies to:

- diversify their funding sources;

- develop strategies to improve their capacity to attract competitive funding; and

- generate their own income in a variety of ways including sale of expertise, consultancies, industry partnerships, patents and accumulation of intellectual property and fees.

Universities are searching for new ways to find resources and attract and support high level researchers, scholarships for research students and develop solid research infrastructure.

The changing external environment has stimulated the development of new internal structures and decision making procedures and created accountability and financial pressures. Many of the innovative practices and new structures being introduced are to a degree experimental and even opportunistic. Their analysis and evaluation is a necessary part of dynamic institutional management. Institutions are responding by seeking greater internal efficiency and more effective management, as well as organisational cohesiveness, and strategic direction.

Not all of the innovations have fulfilled expectations, but there is no doubting the determination to push out the traditional boundaries of the research enterprise.

Teaching, research, service to the community

While the research mission is growing in significance for the institution, it should not be seen in isolation from the teaching and service missions of universities. Across OECD countries, teaching and research remain the central missions of the university, but the meaning of both teaching and research is changing. On the one hand, very diverse student populations and the impact of communication technology pose challenges to established conventions in teaching; on the other, research paradigms, which vary by field of inquiry, are changing. Academics are expected – or required – to do research and to draw upon research in their teaching. But their understanding of what 'research' means varies widely and there is debate about just how research intensive teaching can or should be within mass higher education. The service mission, also of growing importance, underscores a growing social expectation that universities will serve their communities and regions. This expectation can significantly impact upon research priorities and funding of programmes.

Teaching students, whether at undergraduate or graduate level, remains core business for higher education institutions. Many universities in OECD countries are becoming large and diversified mass institutions, with a substantial proportion of each youth cohort enrolling in tertiary study, not to mention growing numbers of mature age entrants and those seeking continuing professional development. Universities now need to cater for a student body with a broad range of interests, talents and capacities as well as diverse needs and situations. Universities have in consequence increased both the range of courses offered and the modes of delivery. Managing teaching and learning across the tertiary institution is increasingly complex and costly. National policy initiatives, particularly regarding student places and student funding at the post-graduate level, are of integral importance to the university's research mission.

Research is commonly seen as a key feature differentiating university from non-university higher education institutions in countries operating a binary system. However many institutions resist this dichotomy and in developing their own research strategies are adopting very broad definitions: research not only on a high status/ scientific model, but as many different kinds of structured inquiry, discovery and creative endeavour.

The Humboldtian ideal of the unity of teaching and research as the basis of the university is still widespread within academic life[2]. Nevertheless, strains are now apparent, with a seemingly inevitable differentiation between teaching and research within and between institutions resulting from mass higher education, the increasing specialisation and cost of research, and the growth of private tertiary level teaching-only institutions, including on-line.

Within the large majority of countries, university level institutions are formally accorded an equivalent status (for example standard funding formulae and conditions of employment), while in practice informal status hierarchies among universities are widely acknowledged. Across the very large higher education sector of the United States, however, substantial differentiation of mission among institutions is accepted[3]. In recent years, partly as a result of funding pressures discussed further below, governments in a number of countries have begun to develop policies leading toward growing differentiation of missions among universities. These moves are not uncontested since they affect funding, career opportunities and the internal balance of operations.

University governance and management

Significant changes in the patterns of university governance in a number of OECD countries, particularly in Continental Europe and Japan, have important implications for research management. These changes tend to give institutions greater flexibility and autonomy in key domains, notably administrative and financial. Central authorities are moving from more direct state control of universities, toward varying degrees of state supervision of universities including more stringent accountability measures, output funding and contractual programmes. This model emphasises the self-regulatory capacities of decentralised decision-making units, but within what is often a very firm policy steering framework.

Greater flexibility is also in anticipation of a higher level of consequent innovativeness in the institutions. Decentralised management offers advantages in staff motivation and flexibility; more transparency does not necessarily imply less autonomy for the institution. Granting institutional autonomy has generally been accompanied by strengthened reporting and quality evaluation requirements, and competitive and selective elements in the allocation of public resources. There are mixed messages here and considerable debate within universities about the new balances between 'steering' and 'autonomy'.

The trend in public universities toward greater freedom to define their own priorities and allocate their resources provides a considerable challenge for institutional management – it opens out more options, but also contains more risks. University leadership must be more decisive, to the point of making or orchestrating unpopular decisions. Managerial autonomy, however, is limited in different ways in different countries via various legal, regulatory and organisational procedures in areas such as estate management, personnel statutes, salary scales and access to the university. Risk management and financial accountability weigh heavily on decision making at all levels.

There is, too, a strong traditional culture of collegiality which continues to impact upon decision-making albeit in widely varying ways. It is coming to be accepted that a more professional and a more deliberate approach towards management questions is required by this new environment.

An important consequence is the greater scope which individual institutions are gaining – or taking - to define their own trajectories and to map their strategic directions. This also strengthens the ability of and the interest for universities to seek to influence national policies for higher education and research, often through special interest groupings of institutions.

The university as a place for research

While all universities maintain a strong core teaching function the same cannot be said of research. The level of research engagement of universities is enormously varied on a world scale, as well as within individual national systems, and can vary substantially over relatively short time periods, especially in research-aspiring institutions. This reflects not only the scale of resources available for research within particular countries, but also historical and cultural patterns of research allocation and distribution among universities and as between university and non-university level institutions, whether or not a significant separate structure of publicly funded research institutes exists (as in France, Germany and Korea, for example).

The contemporary university is typically a complex setting for research, housing research in a wide range of fields, undertaken by individuals or by teams, at a variety of levels of detail, over widely varying time frames, and using equipment which may be simple and relatively cheap, or highly elaborate, specialised and costly. Research is most commonly initiated by individuals or teams, and several often competing, research budget centres such as departments/ faculties, and/or defined research centres may have a degree of autonomy in decision-making. Universities increasingly engage in research partnerships with associated institutions of a wide variety of types. While a snapshot may suggest stability, the research environment of the university is in constant flux. Research management in universities is management of change and diversity.

But universities differ in research missions and roles

Differences frequently noted between institutions relate to the *research intensive/ research non-intensive continuum*. Existing research intensive universities frequently have a breadth of faculties with research well spread between fields. Most often, the older and better resourced (and better endowed) universities have a research headstart over newer entrants. In response to the recent intensification of research competition among universities, research intensive universities are likely to act (including collectively) to maintain existing competitive advantages. The new competitive environments do not automatically confer advantage, however; as the case study of the **University of Adelaide** reveals, an existing broad research profile makes prioritizing difficult in the context of a national direction of research concentration and selectivity. Research non-intensive (research aspirant) universities, at an earlier stage in building up their research expertise, have different agendas as the three final case studies show. These institutions may be newly established, they may be former non-university level institutions, or they may be well established universities which have yet to build up substantial research expertise. Issues facing the **Dublin Institute of Technology** in strengthening its research profile, for example include lack of access to traditional resources for research, poor institutional infrastructure, operating on a limited scale without a critical mass of researchers, modestly qualified academic staff, academic workload tensions with regard to research because of high teaching loads, and teaching areas which include new disciplines without significant research traditions.

But how research is integrated within the institution is becoming of increasing significance - *i.e. the research integrated/ research non-integrated* continuum with structures and arrangements more frequently being designed to differentiate the research mission. There are, however, considerable differences in how far and in what ways research is integrated within institutions. **The University of Aveiro**, for example, has developed a model where research institutes and centres are quite separately structured from teaching departments. The study of **Humboldt Universität** emphasizes the teaching responsibilities of all academic staff. But other universities take different approaches to the allocation of responsibilities *vis a vis* teaching and research to individual staff within the institution. For example, not all academic staff may be required to participate in both teaching and research, or to the same degree – and different balances may exist. Universities seem increasingly to facilitate teaching-free periods and contexts for research active academic staff with some new and prestigious categories of academic appointment focused primarily on research. **The Université Libre de Bruxelles** study illustrates a case where a major part of the overall research output of the university is undertaken by research-only staff working on a variety of external contracts. There is the possibility in some institutions of 'buying in' teaching cover as part of research grants to 'cover' for time of academic staff spent on research. With the increasing move toward commercialization of university research, growth of associated industry parks and external research partnerships, significant research activity is relatively loosely tied to the institution. National and university contexts differ on the question of the extent to which academic staff must – or should - perform both teaching and research functions, with a trend evident toward greater flexibility in some systems.

Newer perspectives on research and innovation

The practice of innovation and research particularly in the scientific and technological fields has seen wide-ranging changes. *The once ubiquitous linear-sequential model of research and innovation has been increasingly challenged by newer models in which university research is a partner at all stages, rather than the foundation on which applications are built.* These more recent perspectives see basic and applied science and technology as a single interrelated activity with research taking on a transdisciplinary and more entrepreneurial character, being undertaken in a variety of places and with different external partners - from other universities, government research laboratories or researchers in private industry. Also, greater credibility and prominence within research policies at both national and institutional level is being sought for other paradigms of research than the predominant scientific one.

While cutting edge research is increasingly *interdisciplinary*, disciplinary based structures remain the key organising features of the majority of universities, particularly with regard to teaching. The challenge of how to foster interdisciplinary research in these settings is not new, yet progress remains limited. New stimuli and incentives are needed to create successful trans-disciplinary institutional structures, as well as striking a balance between the need for researchers to commit to interdisciplinary projects and academic institutions being prepared to consider these researchers as suitable candidates for academic promotion, for example to professorships[4]. There are growth points and they need to be fostered, especially in an era when cross fertilisation of different research domains is seen as a key to solving many obdurate problems in society and illuminating previously uncharted or poorly understood areas of the natural and social worlds.

Interdisciplinary research structures operating in parallel with departmental/ disciplinary structures, is one approach, with staffing for centres drawn from disciplinary bases where substantive positions remain. The United Nations University provides an unusual example where the institution as a whole is structured on an interdisciplinary basis. Other institutions provide structured opportunities and fora for researchers from different areas to come together with researchers whom they would be unlikely to meet in the normal course of events. The purpose of such structured contacts is cited as enabling researchers to explore areas of common interest with the express purpose of generating new research questions and new cross disciplinary research teams. This has proved fruitful especially in areas where knowledge is changing quickly, and where certain specialisations are seen to have run their course. To some extent, as Gibbons indicates[5], interdisciplinary research of the mode 2 style has begun to ignore traditional boundaries within the institution: loosely structured networks of researchers (many operating from disciplinary bases), frequently from varied institutions, are themselves taking the initiative at grass roots level to come together for particular research activities. This is a volatile picture of groupings forming, dissolving, and re-forming in different associations, depending on the needs of particular research questions and research undertakings.

As the case studies show, institutions are actively supporting and fostering interdisciplinary research and interdisciplinary researchers through a mix of incentives and structural changes.

Trends favouring big research and global networks

Leading edge research in many fields is growing in complexity, scale and cost. Major facilities for research in some areas of science are increasingly beyond the capacity of individual institutions to fund (for example facilities for researching particle physics, space exploration, astronomy, earth observing systems, deep ocean exploration, studying the human genome). Synergies sought in knowledge creation as well as cost of facilities encourage co-operation between different partners both nationally and internationally. National policy orientations encourage these trends, for example centres of excellence (whether as whole institutions, as specialized centres based at a given institution, or as co-operative centres shared between several institutions) and major national or international investments in large facilities with shared public access[6]. With the useful half life of knowledge at the cutting edge of some fields at around five years, drawing in and retaining high level researchers and providing up-to-date facilities (or access to them) are significant concerns for institutions. Start-up funding (for example to equip laboratories) which universities need to provide to attract young scientists as much as distinguished senior scientists is now a major expense for top American research universities.

Extensive networks needed for research on global issues (for example atmospheric, environmental and oceanographic research) increasingly involve collaboration between partners across wide geographic areas and disciplinary fields. While e-science and informatics is a very costly frontier to invest in, it is persuasively argued that such investment is needed in order to exploit the enormous amounts of information currently yielded by existing tools already developed (currently orbiting satellites for example). Extensive data banks are increasingly being drawn on in social science and humanities research – fields where expensive facilities (libraries excluded) are not generally seen as a research requirement.

Major management issues emerging in the train of these developments include *ownership of intellectual property, the increasing ability of research 'stars' to act quite independently of their employing institutions, the creation of large research 'empires' including purchase of whole research teams and their transfer across national and regional boundaries*. The distribution of costs and income is but one of the growing challenges to research management.

Impact of national research priorities

Given that resources which can be put into research are not unlimited, declared national research priorities and agenda have become practically universal within OECD countries. Policy makers across the OECD are influenced by public pressure to respond to societal needs, to maximise returns on public investment and to enhance accountability (DSTI, 2003). National priorities, both thematic and structural, are commonly used as the focus for targeted competitive funding programmes. While frequently using new monies, sometimes governments are using national priorities as a means of reallocating research funds. National priority setting – and funding – can lead to considerable dislocations within and among institutions. Institutional managers must be highly alert to trends and realities to make positive responses.

Structural research priorities identified by a number of OECD countries concern increasing research funding, strengthening university research, promoting basic research, and organisational features of the research enterprise, such as multi-disciplinarity, and partnership with industry. Broad thematic challenges or disciplinary areas include women's participation, sustainable development, and marine sciences; and specific technology areas such fields as ICT and biotechnology. The remarkable convergence of thematic areas internationally has major implications for universities, particularly for those which do not have a broad profile or where research emphases are of relatively recent origin.

Major areas of student enrolment (humanities, education, social sciences, business and management) frequently show a poor fit with those thematic areas where research is being fostered. That is, there are potentially conflicting areas of demand: by students for courses including higher research degrees, and by governments and specialist staff, for certain kinds of research. This situation brings into question the view that higher education teaching should be research based or related. Does this mean some vague idea of teaching that draws on research (mostly of others) or that all teachers in higher education should be actively feeding into their teaching the procedures and fruits of their own research? There are further issues, including training sufficient numbers of researchers for the thematic areas currently favoured, and also for sustaining research and scholarship in those areas which students are currently favouring, but to which research funding is not being targeted.

At national level, authorities are increasingly defining research priorities for the country as a whole and, as outlined earlier, in some countries questioning long-held views that all universities should be funded for research on an equal/ equivalent basis. Thus there is a need for many institutions to reposition themselves within a fast evolving landscape.

STRENGTHENING STRUCTURES AND PROCESSES FOR RESEARCH MANAGEMENT ACROSS THE INSTITUTION

The challenge within institutions is not just to be alert to a changing policy environment and to foster a strong research climate. It is to show a capability to design and operate new structures and processes for stimulating, guiding and managing research.

Decision-making processes and structures

The ideal of collegial decision making remains strong in many universities as a way in which academic staff both belong to and make decisions within the institution. The spirit is unquestionably important. What is currently at issue is how it can best be expressed in the university today when so many forces impinge upon the institution, coherent policies and clear cut decisions are required.

Universities have increasingly adopted managerial approaches which vest authority for action in specific position holders at the level of central administrations. As institutions have grown in size and complexity, as they face growing demands for accountability and as they establish closer linkages with external organisations, including business and industry, universities have recognised a need for what are often perceived to be radical changes. These changes, moreover, have often been divisive. An underlying tension between the collegial and the managerial approaches to decision-taking remains a feature of many universities. Resolving the tension, or rather, finding the best settings to build on both approaches, is a continuing challenge.

Patterns of consultation and the balance between collegiality and managerialism vary within different institutions. It appears that the balance is moving away (though not entirely) from the university as a self-governing community of scholars, and towards the expectation that institutions will perform according to external requirements, and that individual departments and groups will have the freedom to forge alliances and enter partnerships whether or not these have the backing or even the understanding of the collegiate community as a whole. The increasing dependence of institutions on project funds and non-core grants highlights this issue.

Locus of research decision-making by level

The university has multiple centres at which research decisions are taken each exercising a degree of autonomy and initiative in research matters. Four key levels are shown below.

Institutional governance – responsible for broad policy directions of the institution and accountable to the stakeholders (public/ government funding organisations). Governing bodies see research within the institution as a whole; the institution as a player on the regional/ national/ international scene.

Institutional executive – responsible for successful management of the institution and its programmes. While institutional leaders see research in relation to the broader teaching and service functions of the institution, centrally located specialised positions have been emerging with respect to institution-wide aspects of research management in recent years. The growth of research management as a specialised and professional field of activity over the past decade has been striking. Not only do institutions increasingly have a full time senior executive responsible for research (*e.g.* Vice President Research), this position is increasingly supported by a centrally located research office with institution-wide responsibilities, as illustrated in each of the case studies. Research management emerges as a separate function from management of the university's commercial arms, technology transfer office and industrial parks, although the two benefit from close liaison.

Faculty/ department/ research centre - budget centres which are responsible for research within discipline/ fields of research and for teaching and graduate studies. Overall there appears to be a move toward appointed positions rather than elected positions for deans, and research centre directors, although these may be for fixed terms. Heads of Department, however, appear most commonly to be elected – and in the case where this concerns headship of relatively small groups, sometimes virtually by rotation. **The University of Adelaide** study highlights challenges this arrangement holds for research management, arguing that the tasks increasingly being required of Heads of Department are now more onerous and specialised than can effectively be managed through an elected position. Consequently, this level of research management could benefit from further attention.

"Academic capital" accumulation modifies the relative weight of disciplines – hence particular favoured departments/ faculties/ institutes within the university are wealthier and have greater access to public funds to finance research. Well-funded departments, as shown in a study of US institutions[7], are increasingly autonomous and may as a result have weakened relations with the university's central authorities. This is another challenge to the classical model of collegial consensus.

Level of separate research activities – responsibility for different projects/ programmes – may be individual researchers or research teams; they can be cross-disciplinary, and cross-institution. At this level, institutional allegiance is frequently weak, with stronger allegiance being shown to colleagues, the professional network and discipline/ research field. Considerable independence has traditionally been exercised at this level; with academic freedom valued particularly in the selection of research questions. Responses to increased central involvement in research management can frequently be negative unless openness and responsiveness are maintained. The boundary of the institution is raised especially in cross-institutional work.

Committees are an important and widespread part of the collegial structure of university decision-making, and these may operate at any of the above four levels, whether for providing advice or for taking decisions. They are an important element in stakeholder involvement in decision-making throughout the institution, and efforts to streamline need to ensure that genuine participation is not lost. Several committees within an institution commonly have responsibilities relating to aspects of research, as illustrated in the study of the **Universiti Kebangsaan Malaysia**. While collective responsibility plays an important role in legitimating various management decisions, there is need for an expedient balance between the often time-consuming and time-demanding committee procedures, and the need to act swiftly on occasion. There is a definite trend toward the positional authority of the university's senior executive team, with specialisation through a high level research manager cum academic.

The extent to which the institution is governed as a single entity rather than as a collection of parts has important consequences for how these different levels operate and to what extent they pull together, pull apart or merely operate independently of each other. Different traditions are important here, notably the Continental tradition of strongly independent faculties and weak central administrations, which is now widely questioned. An important challenge for university leadership is how to tighten the links and create a firmer form to the institution but without losing the energy and initiative at the level of researchers/ grassroots.

Balance between central and decentralised decision-making

Increasing institutional autonomy, especially in Continental Europe, has increased the capacity of the institution to make meaningful research decisions at governance and executive level, and therefore for the institution as a whole.

At issue, increasingly, are the relationships across and among these levels. Each level has a degree of autonomy in decisions, and a degree of initiating action. How far autonomy goes and how well interactions are managed, depend on individual structures and arrangements, and often depend on the strength of the *personalities* involved. Clearly the interactions have to be addressed as a management function but ways and means differ considerably.

Of key importance is the way in which the institution establishes its research management structures, the way in which positions are designated and criteria used for selecting people to those positions. Formalising and staffing *centrally located research leadership positions* with institution-wide research management responsibilities is of relatively recent origin for most universities, considerable variation in structures exists. Key institution-wide tasks commonly include:

- establishing an environment conducive to research (research culture);

- fostering flexibility in research focus and practice in the context of the major recent changes in the external environment;

- setting and maintaining quality standards; facilitating and supporting research activities among staff (being well informed about the policies and priorities of external research funding agencies);

- attracting to the university – and holding onto – outstanding and entrepreneurial researchers who have extensive networks.

But institutions differ in what mechanisms they have available with which to address these tasks, as the case studies illustrate, for example:

- the capacity of the central research office, its staffing and its authority;

- the size of discretionary funding and allocation procedures through the research office;

- incentives and disincentives available for encouraging faculty to participate in research projects;

- the nature of the interface between research management and the academic structure;

- how to balance students' educational and career interests with their role as research workers.

Achieving good articulation between those academic and administrative staff with research management responsibilities is extremely important.

Research management emerges as a multifaceted activity, for which the role description is neither clear cut nor limited. The role is currently being created by growing numbers of both academic and administrative staff in widely varied settings, some of whom have specialised expertise (for example in legal and accounting fields). Its essential purpose is to be facilitative of the growth and development of the institutional research undertaking, focusing both internally on the relationship with researchers and externally on the links to funding agencies and other bodies including university businesses.

Characteristics of value to those exercising these positions clearly include:

- Entrepreneurship – seeing opportunities and building creatively on them;

- Ability and willingness to work in a capacity which supports and enables researchers;

- Administrative and organisational skill;

- Strategic thinking and planning ability – forward thinking, mapping and linking activities;

- Networking skill – creating and supporting linkages among people;

- Resourcefulness – seeking resources where these are not obvious and making good use of what exists;

- Good understanding of the research process and the requirements of researchers;

- Research leadership capacity – vision, ability to enthuse others;

- Good understanding of relevant legal and accounting fields, constraints on action and compliance requirements;

- Communicating well with the university's public constituency – informing about institutional research achievements, maintaining trust and openness about research challenges, engaging public interesting in research.

These abilities are very wide ranging and of a high order. Many people who have moved into research management especially at the higher levels, themselves have successful research backgrounds. An important question is whether people of such calibre will continue to find research management a satisfying activity (whether full or part time). Much depends on how research management positions are structured and the scope given to individuals who occupy them. As the **University of Adelaide** study notes, if the positions become too dominated by routine compliance focused and administrative work, the more enterprising people may find it less attractive.

A study of strategic management in some twenty European universities[8], showed consensual decision-making emerged as the ideal, even if in practice budgetary incentives were used. Procedures in use for appointments, promotions and implementing wage policies often serve in practice as means to impose decisions or reinforce institutional priorities. A mix of top-down and bottom-up approaches was seen to be needed to preserve some kind of balance between institution-wide projects defined at the highest level (and taking external constraints into account), and more local or particular interests whereby discipline-specific opportunities and constraints are taken into account. The result is often an uneasy compromise. Without the active participation of faculties and departments, strategic initiatives cannot be really successful, as resistance or deflection will be engaged in to empty initiatives of substance. The most successful central strategies identified in this study tended to persuade rather than impose; coercion envisaged only in extreme situations of crisis.

Whatever the structure, the *personalities* of those responsible for its operation make a difference[9]. The interplay between people and structures brings a certain degree of art or randomness into the management process. In these circumstances, abstract notions of consensus and collegiality are of little value. In the interplay between customary practice and innovative management structures and practices, the values – or the ideal – of consensual decision making by the community of scholars has become seriously fractured. There is a challenge to institutions to find new ways of collective decision taking at the institutional level which are both responsive to their own staff views and well attuned to the scale and pace of change in the wider environment where research priorities are increasingly set and funding allocated.

Confident leadership which commands the respect of the research community and is grounded in the intellectual values of that community is a more fitting model for contemporary university research management than either command models or a tortuous maze of committees. Yet these must be legitimate structures.

Areas for strategic research decision-making

The increasingly competitive environment of the modern university places a premium on shaping a distinctive and well integrated institutional profile. With universities in increasing competition for both researchers and for research funds and research in many fields becoming increasingly costly to sustain, achieving high level research across all areas is unrealistic for most institutions. Institutions are faced with the need to select research priorities, and to develop appropriate strategic research goals. The challenge is to set priorities whilst acknowledging – and supporting - staff not working in these priority areas. There has been less success in this last regard than in defining missions, setting priorities and acquiring resources to match them.

Research management, according to Contzen, is a very complex activity requiring a lot of creativity in devising solutions which should be flexible enough to cope with a highly dynamic environment. His framework of critical components for governance identifies key elements which need to be taken into account.

Critical Components for Governance

Governing a complex adaptive system such as research within the university implies acting on an institutional process composed of *Assets, Skills and Capabilities.* Good governance means:

- *Owning the right assets:* knowledge; rights (IPR); human resources; financial resources; facilities; organisational capital; evaluation.

- *Providing the right skills:* adapting to change; anticipating change; generating change.

- *Enhancing the right capabilities:* relationships; networks.

[Contzen, 2003]

Establishing research priorities and developing an institutional research plan are a first major set of decisions. Depending on the national system, institutions vary in the degrees of freedom within which they can operate. The boundaries are shifting in two directions: more scope for partnerships, alliances, cross border collaboration and more encouragement to innovate. But at the same time, national (and international) priority setting and public funding procedures are defining the field of action and shaping institutional decision-making. As noted above, the strong international movement of devolution of responsibility to the institutions combines strategic oversight at the national/ state level with enhanced institutional autonomy and accountability.

Key questions for institutions in this environment are:

- *How to articulate strategic decision-making at the institutional level with public research priorities and industry sources when so much of the bidding for grants and contracts and efforts to develop alliances and links is at the level of the individual or team of researchers:* Institutions are addressing this in different ways, for example through senior research management appointments, committee procedures and elaborate filtering procedures. While there is an obvious need, there can be considerable costs and delays. There is something of a counter move, to accept the risks of more adventurous entrepreneurship or to authorize institutional leaders and research 'stars' to take initiatives. Such moves can at time result in significant changes of direction in institutional research profiles.

- *How to formulate research priorities and plans which build on institutional strength and engage productively with the local region, whether metropolitan, provincial or rural.* This issue is particularly important for newer institutions and those seeking to orient their mission toward their more immediate environment. 'Location' can be a way of establishing a research profile which is not dependent on declared national research priorities or can use them to mobilise local support for institutional growth.

- *How to balance competing pressures* – for example between basic *vs.* more oriented research; maintaining breadth in research activity *vs.* concentrating on limited areas; supporting existing activities *vs.* responding to emerging possibilities; tried and tested *vs.* high risk undertakings.

- *Ensuring that the institutional processes through which priorities and plans are formulated are widely inclusive and representative, including a productive balance between university governance and university management.* Equally, a balance needs to be struck between the apparatus of central planning and decision making in the institution and faculty/ departmental roles and responsibilities. Central plans, when they are not carefully negotiated and kept under constant review, can come to resemble a rather formalistic ritual rather than serving to point directions and stimulate action.

- *The increasingly onerous impact of reporting demands in the model of central steering.* It is a nice question as to whether institutional autonomy has decreased rather than increased. Certainly it has changed in character.

The consequences of the priorities universities adopt in pursuing research missions themselves give rise to a variety of management issues, for example commercialising the university's intellectual property, maintaining breadth in the institutional research profile, fostering relations with enterprises.

A second area for strategic decision-making is *allocating resources for research* within the institution in such a way that broad and productive engagement in research activities is encouraged across the institution, while maintaining support for existing centres of research strength. Not all bids for support will succeed, and this can be highly de-motivating, especially in institutions seeking to boost their research profile. Earning capacities differ between research fields, and as fashions change. A pool of discretionary funding can be useful for supporting particular institutional priorities, such as research in unfashionable areas. It is important for institutions to have their own start-up funds.

Allocation needs to be made on the basis of institution-wide directions for research. For example, as the case study of the **Dublin Institute of Technology** shows, given the tightness of funds for research, important choices are faced: in recruiting or growing their own researchers; whether to develop a research culture, or a culture of scholarship; whether funds should be targeted to selected niche research fields, or used like seed-corn, used as universal funding across the institution.

A third area of strategic decision-making is evaluating research quality, both internally and externally. Institutions need their own internal systems for evaluating research quality in the light of institutional strategic planning, and several case studies illustrate these. Such mechanisms should be transparent, fair and formative in effect. Performance targets against internal strategic plans are one example. However, this can be a delicate matter, especially when dealing with the activities of highly specialist, expert researchers and teams whose membership extends beyond the single institution.

In the context of the widespread growth of external quality assurance agencies, an issue of growing importance is that the research needs and priorities of countries and regions do not always mesh well with institutional priorities, especially those institutions seeking to establish or strengthen their research profiles. Different evaluative criteria can be operating at the different levels, systems and institutions.

The mechanism of *peer review* is widespread, well established and well accepted within universities and research funding bodies, for making judgments about the quality of research. Peer review uses expertise as the basis of judgment, and assumes disinterested merit-based assessment. While well respected within academe, it can be time consuming and costly, leading, for example, to unduly lengthy cycles for research applications, and considerable delays between the submission and the publication of research papers in refereed journals. Tensions can be seen with the increasing need for swifter decisions. Increasingly standardised and transparent processes are now being brought into peer review.

How the performance of those responsible for research management is assessed is a further important issue. The balance between those in positional authority for research management and the institution's committee structure and operations is crucial.

Decisions about *research ethics* concern both the integrity of research conducted, and those areas which the society will allow to be researched. Attention is commonly given to these questions through university ethics committees which draw in a range of stakeholders. Institutions operate within different national and regional parameters: public debate is encouraged in some countries, and is channelled through various institutional settings (public inquiries, technology assessment organisations, for example); a number of conventions are widely respected, and various agreements exist amongst countries. But important differences exist, such as tighter restrictions on animal experimentation in the European Union than, for example, in Canada; and restrictions on the importation of certain GM products from North America into Europe (with implications for research in Europe). Nor should it be forgotten that on most topics there are community concerns and, in places, highly organised community interest groups. Ethical concerns about research are at the interface of institution- community relations.

Those fields relating to the integrity of living matter (medicine, biology) appear to attract the greatest controversy. Strong public interest exists, for example, in new developments in human cloning, genetic modification of food, the potential use and misuse of the human genetic code, nuclear energy and waste disposal, human fertility treatment, biological warfare, and experimentation on humans and animals. There is evidence that the educated public is becoming more critical and less supportive of ethically controversial research.

Current closer links between university research and commercial development reinforce the need for attention to the integrity of research conduct, given the potential both to falsify experimental results to support the commercial interest of the research sponsor, and to speed up research results for academics under pressure to publish in a competitive environment. Fraud in the administration of research grants - misapplication of funds - has been reported over recent years in a number of highly publicised cases. Accountability for research funding and compliance requirements regarding research methodology have increased in many systems in recent years. A key question is what sanctions are effective against those who do not abide by acceptable limits and standards?

Decisions about how far to seek to *commercialise university research* involve complex legal issues and requirements, as a number of case studies illustrate. Intellectual property is an issue of increasing importance not only in research but, with the emergence of virtual universities and other on-line providers, in the teaching role of universities. While large profits can be at stake for universities, these have generally been realized by the few, rather than by the many; there are also considerable costs for institutions involved in seeking to commercialise their research[10].

Until recently, individual academics in most institutions had the freedom to decide whether and how to exploit any research in which they were involved, including freedom to file for patents and individually reap rewards from these, to engage in external consultancies and keep the payments, and to publish books and keep the royalties. For most staff, the sums involved in these additional earnings were not large. But with the recent push by universities to diversify income streams, the institution's rights to ownership (in whole or in part) of intellectual property developed by its employees and using its resources, have surfaced.

A consensus seems to be emerging that the best system is that where the institution holds the intellectual property rights, with royalty revenues commonly shared between the researcher and institution, and in some cases, the division or unit in the university where the research was conducted[11]. But such distribution of rights and royalties are not always easy for institutions to manage. Institutions face significant and complex legal issues in their exploitation of IPR.

The patenting system, of central importance to research in the life sciences, treats knowledge as essentially a set of discrete elements which can be packaged and treated as property. Difficulties emerge in complex fields increasingly dependent on integrated systems of knowledge, for example biotechnology.

Potential conflicts may exist if background intellectual property rights and 'reach-through' provisions are pushed to their logical limits. Also if growth in research tools or utility patents is linked with exclusive licences, current intellectual property arrangements could have an inhibiting effect on research and technology transfer and on freedom of inquiry and the exchange of ideas, knowledge and information[12].

Other complexities exist. Where industry has helped fund graduate study, students may have accepted an obligation to release the results to industry before publication, but, where results have commercial potential, there is pressure to delay publication, possibly for a period long enough to affect career prospects for the students, and to risk others publishing first.

With regard to licensing agreements for university owned patents, Slaughter noted that universities have acted similarly to any commercial organisation concerned to maximise its own profit.

Universities do not seem as yet to have laid claim to a share in consultancy monies earned by staff members, but this could come onto the agenda. Neither has copyright ownership for research publications loomed large to date, mainly because the potential income stream from academic publications is not large. But with the growth in on-line and off-campus learning, universities are showing a strong interest in the copyright for potentially lucrative teaching materials, and a subsequent spill-over effect could happen.

The need to develop institution-wide policies regarding both research ethics and legal issues and requirements with regard to commercializing research are increasingly important as universities develop closer contacts with the community and with the commercial world. These areas are highly complex and can require detailed technical expertise.

FUNDING AND RESOURCING UNIVERSITY RESEARCH

Of central importance for research management is the impact of the more competitive funding environment on universities and ways of minimising the harmful effects of market competition. Priority setting means gains for some, but losses for others.

External funds follow priorities

As discussed above, external funding bodies are seeking increased control over how their funds are spent, using a variety of mechanisms and approaches. Although researchers and research managers do their best to maintain institutional and research team priorities, these funding sources and strategies are having a major impact. The outcome is the emergence of a competitive research and development environment with a reduced availability of non-competitive funds and a growth of compliance measures some of which are very onerous.

The growth in defining *priority areas for funding* has led to the disproportionate favouring of fields of research with perceived strategic importance for economic growth and with obviously 'useful' – frequently commercially significant – application. Life sciences, medicine and IT continue to absorb huge funds as do military research in several countries. The less fashionable fields, such as the arts and non-commercial languages, and newly emerging research fields, are frequently under-funded, at least from the institutional perspective. This poses a challenge to those institutions which aim to achieve a diversity of research within the institution. Most important, perhaps, there is a serious distortion occurring in intellectual culture and in the fundamental mission of the university as a major source of values and disinterested inquiry. One approach is for institutions to achieve a sufficiently wide range of resources such that adequate discretionary funds exist to support a good spread of institutional research – but, as a number of the case studies show, it is becoming increasingly difficult to build up and maintain discretionary funds. A second approach is for institutions to provide assistance to researchers in less fashionable fields in their bids to external funding bodies. There is scope for cross-funding, but this can be unpopular.

Concentration of research in particular fields *into a small number of centres of excellence* has clear benefits, yet it creates an imbalance in the distribution of research intensity within national systems. In order to maintain a structure of strong regional institutions, both within particular nations and within broader regions (such as the European Union), the onus is on the funding bodies. Scope exists for them to be more varied in the criteria they use in the allocation of at least a portion of their funds.

Growth of performance-based funding by external agencies means that, in some countries, a growing proportion of universities' base funding has become dependent on achieving defined outcomes. In addition to excellence in past performance (the dominant criterion for most funders), some measure of research capacity or of the potentiality for reaching excellence could be used which would enable new universities or new groups of researchers to have an opportunity to become established. This provides a period of grace before their results are judged on a par with established groups. Newer institutions or those developing a research profile are actively seeking modification in this respect.

Funding bodies are increasingly supporting only part of the cost of research – institutions may be required to provide or seek matching funding as a condition of the grant. This can be a deliberate strategy of leveraging on the part of funding agencies, such as the Canada Foundation for Innovation which seeks to get both provincial governments and industries more involved in funding Canadian research. A separate issue is that not all funding bodies provide or provide adequately for overheads, although this is an issue currently being addressed. The converse of this is that institutions do not have a good record on determining the full cost of research; even though some may set standard figures for overheads, these may be seen more as what the market will bear than what the true costs to the institution are. The Transparency Review in the United Kingdom established that, taking a full economic cost approach to university research, the overwhelming majority of university research programmes recently reviewed in that country were unsustainable over the long term as insufficient provision for maintenance of infrastructure was made under marginal cost funding. Changes to the UK funding system are now being planned to rectify this[13]. Also, in over 200 top US research universities, the costs of research are increasingly coming out of internal university funds[14].

These findings raise serious questions for institutions about how much as well as what sorts of research they should be supporting under current funding arrangements. An institution can absorb research costs for a certain time – and institutions in some countries are able to cross subsidise (if controversially, in the case of from tuition fees), but it is unlikely to be a sustainable long term approach. A rethink in costing and funding practices is clearly required, and is an important focus for research managers at all levels.

Short and medium-term research projects (particularly those based on contract-based funding) are, with some notable exceptions, being favoured by funding bodies over long-term research, in the interest of economic payoffs. Both institutions and funding agencies need to consider appropriate provision for longer-term research in particular for blue skies or curiosity driven research. The external funding environment is not generally favourable to these longer-term perspectives and institutions need to be aware of the consequences this can have for their overall research profile, as illustrated in the case study of the **Universidade Federal do Rio Grande do Sul**.

Overall funds are increasing but so is the complexity of allocation

The overall level of public funding available for research is increasing in most, but not all, OECD countries. But new channels to institutions are emerging, the balance between channels is changing in some countries, and the allocative mechanisms are trending more towards competitive modes. Core grants are reducing and targeted funds increasing. New sources of public funding are being explored in some countries, for example the sectoral funds in Brazil (as outlined in the case study of the **Universidade Federal do Rio Grande do Sul**), paralleled by an industry levy for fisheries research in Norway; new foundations for research established with windfall public monies (Norway, Canada, Germany). As mentioned earlier, industry is proving an increasing source of funds in some countries – notably for particular fields of university research (for example engineering).

All of these trends indicate that while the overall reservoir may be filling, there is a less certain pool of research funding for any given institution; it can no longer be assumed that resources for research will keep coming steadily from any given source; sustained institutional effort is increasingly needed to secure research funding, and a strategic approach is important for institutional success. Hence the need for institutions to monitor research institution-wide, and to take a thoroughly pro-active stance in developing and sustaining the institution's research profile.

Decisions on how income from external research grants or contracts is to be allocated within the institution, once procured, have proved complex. What proportion should remain with the research team, with the department or institute, and with central administration as overheads? Certain fields of research have a much higher earning capacity than others, as earlier indicated – how should enterprise in these fields be rewarded? How far should these researchers contribute to supporting other areas in the institution with lower earning capacity? These are among the decision-making and allocative issues that need to be made at the level of each individual institution.

The allocative process must meet several criteria:

- enable the wealthier budget centres to retain sufficient funds to reward entrepreneurial spirit and productive research, and to ensure continued research growth in those fields;

- encourage continued and new research activity (new groups, interdisciplinary activities, young researchers) in priority areas for the institution;

- provide appropriate/ sufficient support for productive researchers in non-priority fields and fields for which external resources are limited;

- through suitable mechanisms (*e.g.* drawing overheads from contracts, earmarking a percentage of base funding), retain a sufficient sum centrally to ensure a coherent institution-wide research management and research identity (a centripetal force to help balance inherent centrifugal tendencies in the institution).

Responses which institutions are commonly making to these changing circumstances, as illustrated in the case studies, are first, to seek to diversify their sources of research funding, and second, to enhance the capacity of researchers to access external funding.

Filling the institutional pool

While universities in some national systems still rely largely on public sources for research funding, institutions in other countries have been vigorously diversifying their sources of research funding. US institutions have long led the way here, but they are no longer alone. Institutions are increasingly:

- Moving to a merit and seeding approach as an investment – building capacity not only to do research but to find means to pay for it;

- Generating their own research funds, *e.g.* from commercial developments, IP, etc.; cross subsidies from teaching fees (a controversial move);

- Accepting the principle of soft monies – generally project based funding, for a fixed period of time; research staff appointed on contract; range of sources from public, private non-profit and private for-profit;

- Sharing resources and facilities in order to gain not just research strength but economies of scale – with implications of variable budgeting and considerable flexibility in use of resources.

Not all researchers see it as part of their responsibility to seek funds from different sources; creating a new, more enterprising orientation towards researching is a challenge faced in many traditional institutions.

In those countries which retain binary or mixed systems, institutions in the non-university sector do not generally have core funding for research or at least not to the same level as universities; also they may not be eligible for major competitive sources of research funds through research councils. Pressure by these institutions has led to a number of changes, for example the Research Council of Norway has established a new pool of competitive funding specifically for the non-university higher education sector[15].

University- industry linkages

The stimulus in the US of the Bayh-Dole Act of 1980 allowing universities to patent and exploit their faculty's intellectual property has led to the development there of the most extensive set of university-industry links among OECD countries. A large number of US university- industry relationships, in areas such as chemistry, take the form of a 'complementarity' model: large firms look to university research to complement their own internal R&D. But university- industry linkages in the biosciences appear quite different because the distinction between basic and applied science has largely dissolved; scientific parity rather than division of labour exists between industry and academic researchers; patenting plays a central role[16]. Information technology, pharmaceuticals and computer graphics appear to be research fields exhibiting a similar pattern of university-industry linkages to the biosciences.

Issues such as secrecy, publication delay, conflict of interest, and the danger that industry funding may taint academics' reputation for disinterested evaluation, not to mention ideological opposition, have in their time given university-industry links a controversial edge.

In US experience, research-based relationships with small entrepreneurial firms or start-ups have posed greater complexities for universities than contacts with large firms in the view of Geiger.[17] Lacking the financial resources to support overheads for internal R&D, small firms tend to focus on applying research findings to developing marketable products. They seek direct involvement of university scientists and, lacking cash, pay with equity. University staff relationships with small firms tend to be closer and more intense than is the case with large firms – they also generally include a financial interest. Conflict of interest is endemic where staff hold equity, and the field of commercial law is complex. A further issue is that findings with commercial potential may remain unpublished. And relationships with small firms can command a great deal of faculty time while yielding few synergies with either teaching (at the undergraduate level) or basic research.

Despite such difficulties, however, and somewhat paradoxically, universities continue to encourage links with small firms – subsidising associated research parks and business incubators – as the key and most effective means of commercialising university discoveries, as well as contributing to national and regional economic growth. In the absence of relationships with large firms, for example in the case of regional and less prestigious research universities, such small and medium firms often provide the best outlets for industry links.

Research-based spin-offs are widely seen as an attractive outcome of science-industry relationships because they offer:

- an avenue for quick commercialisation of new knowledge generated outside the business sector;

- they create high-skilled jobs; they are flexible and dynamic, giving birth to novel fields and markets; and

- they are often a critical element in high technology clusters, acting as a two-way bridge between the public and private sectors[18].

It is clear that these new developments in university- industry linkages have brought universities into a complex and varied set of new relationships with their external environment. Gibbons posed the question of where the university ends and the external environment begins[19]. The more entrepreneurial the university staff, the more permeable the boundaries are becoming.

NURTURING THE RESEARCH CAREER

Much of the discussion about institutional issues in research management is directed towards structures, processes and funding. However, people management is crucial. As research becomes more conditional on a complex array of factors external to the institution, the career of researchers has emerged as a major issue for management.

Research and researchers in an evolving context

Just as there is no single model of research, neither is there a single model of the researcher. There are many types of researchers, depending on their field, their individual skills, character, training and trajectory, as well as on the type of institutions and environments in which they work, and on the way in which research monies are allocated to them.

Researchers at universities are performing more diverse roles than in the past. Besides the researcher-teacher, there is the researcher as manager of a business, the researcher as entrepreneur, the researcher as consultant[20]. Extensive networks and collaborative work with researchers in other parts of the science and innovation system are now common-place, and institutional allegiance may be weaker than ever for many university researchers. Mobility between the public and private sectors has increased, albeit in some systems more than others (North America more than in Europe). Industry is an important employer of researchers, often through joint appointments, secondments, opportunities for doctoral and post-doctoral personnel and so on. The growth of trans-disciplinary and multidisciplinary research makes the research career more complex, and individuals work increasingly as part of teams rather than as individual researchers. However, people still write books and articles based on their individual expertise and studies. And there are significant differences among disciplines, and management should not presuppose a single model or best way of doing research. Also, doctoral and other research students are a major element in the production of research outcomes.

Academic careers have, in most institutions, combined teaching and research responsibilities. Today there is an increasing number of research-only staff in universities, often employed on a temporary, contractual basis. The problem posed to career continuity by the growth of contract employment for research staff is not a new issue, but remains unresolved.

An important consequence of changes in the overall research environment is that the *output of the research career is changing*. Publication in refereed journals is no longer a sufficient measure of successful and productive research – but there is a lag in the recognition accorded by institutional management and others (including funding bodies) of what is accepted as quality research output, particularly for external performance measures. Adequate recognition is needed for such outputs as: collaborative work which may solve problems but which may not be published in the usual channels; policy advice; consultancy reports; successfully initiating and managing spin-offs.

University reward structures commonly favour career progression within a disciplinary framework. To signal their support for *interdisciplinary research*, universities can provide better opportunities for career progression for researchers who have shown the initiative and taken the risk to move beyond the discipline and engage in research in new areas, so that they have not 'lost out' from their home discipline. This is not straightforward, as publication opportunities are more limited and other ways of presenting research findings through meetings, conferences, etc., have their own established boundaries.

From the foregoing, it is clear that it is not only the research – its funding, costs, operation, linkages and results – that has to be managed, but also the researchers, including the researchers' career lines. To the issue of the individual career dependent on a succession of 'soft money' contracts, must be added the rethinking of the education of researchers for roles both within and outside academia, joint appointments with industry and other contractual variables and the recognition – and reward – of a very diverse range of research and research-related activities.

Why and how research?

Why do people choose to engage in research? The motivation for individual academic researchers is the result of many factors which integrate the researcher's own personal history with particular competing and interrelated influences[21]:

- intellectual challenge - some problem or issue considered important but of which very often only a fragment may be amenable to being researched[22];

- recognition by the peer group as expressed through journal publications, invitations to meetings, etc.;

- recognition by academic institutions as expressed through promotion, and grant allocation; and

- recognition by institutions outside academia as expressed through contracts, or affirmation of social and economic relevance.

While much is rightly made of the multidisciplinary research team in various areas of scientific, engineering and medical research, with its dependence on frequently expensive laboratories and equipment, there are still substantial areas not only in the humanities, social sciences and creative arts but also in the natural sciences where research is an individual or small partnership pursuit, not dependent on expensive external support. Productive as some of this research may be, these latter areas are not generally those currently favoured (and funded) by governments as the cutting edge of research designed to boost national economic growth. They do, however, raise important issues for institutional management and are often of interest to non-government funding bodies and organisations. They need to be taken into account in a broader overview of institutional management and funding. Imbalances which are a function of goal priorities (which themselves change) do not sit comfortably with older ideas of research arising either from curiosity and the imaginative pursuit of ideas, or from grander notions of the advancement of knowledge in all fields of human endeavour. Since the university's mission does embrace these wider perspectives on knowledge, institutional research management cannot be responsive only to prevailing public policy interests and dominant funding sources. The needs of the whole research community and all the institution's researchers must be addressed.

There can be a certain tension between the life of the research group and that of the individual researcher who is self-directed in inquiry, and for whom the freedom to choose research problems is important. Despite the many benefits of collaborative work (scope and size of feasible projects, social and psychological support, definition of common goals) it is not uncommon to find researchers who will remain individualistic, wanting at some point to work independently, to pursue different intellectual directions from those of the group, or to seek individual recognition for work undertaken. Much, of course, depends on the way in which research groups are structured, how research goals are established, and how credit for achievements is awarded - in other words how they are managed.

The prima donna is a well known phenomenon among researchers. A researcher can be extremely jealous of his own 'freedom' in research; not wishing to be overshadowed in collaborative work. Professional jealousies can lead researchers to prefer to collaborate with distant colleagues, even when a local collective effort would significantly increase the visibility of the university. And a researcher 'can easily fool himself by thinking that he is unique and the most knowledgeable in a tiny corner of knowledge, and refusing therefore any hierarchy.'[23] These are important points for management at the level of the research team, as well as the department, faculty and institution.

The question of to whom or what the researcher is loyal has long been debated. Are researchers more concerned with the development of the university (which employs them), or of their discipline (from which they gain their stature) or their research network (the colleagues with whom they have closest contact and which may be international in spread)? What is the balance? There can be no conclusive, embracing answer to these questions, since researchers have professional relationships at all of these levels and a degree of loyalty to all – and to the more abstract ideals of truth, inquiry and the enlargement of knowledge. Nevertheless, the questions persist and in respect of the careers of researchers and especially career formation and development, the answers they receive, whether for individuals or institutions, have both operational and ethical implications.

Research active (and inactive) staff

In most universities there is an *expectation* that academic staff will be research active, and while this may be written into the terms of employment, sanctions against research inactive staff have commonly been either lacking or ineffective[24]. It is commonly the case that the bulk of research at an institution is undertaken by a relatively small group of staff. With the growth of performance funding, some national systems have begun to impose sanctions against the less research-active and reward the more research-active institutions (as defined by selected criteria). This has had the effect in those countries of focusing attention within institutions on the level of research activity of individual staff, teams and departments. In 2000 the UK undertook the fifth cycle of its four yearly Research Assessment Exercises. The exercise has been credited with considerably raising the research output of departments in UK universities, but there have been costs – some analysts believe a point of diminishing returns has been reached, and a re-evaluation of the RAE process itself has been undertaken. This sharpens the issue of academic performance and appropriate ways of evaluating performance.

There is also the question of *binary or diverse systems*, where the distinguishing feature of the university sector has traditionally been a research orientation with funding provided on the assumption of research activity, whereas in non-university institutions employment contracts and expectations of academic staff either make no mention of research or give it a lesser role in workplace requirements, as illustrated in the case study of the **Dublin Institute of Technology**. This is changing as increasingly non-university level higher education institutions are pushing to be formally recognised (and funded) as research-active institutions, generally with a focus on applied research in the first instance (*e.g. Fachhochschulen* in Germany, Institutes of Technology in Ireland). This trend raises difficult management issues since many staff are either inadequately qualified or uninterested in research roles – or both. There is, on the other hand, a strong sense of frustration on the part of research-minded staff in these institutions who believe they are severely disadvantaged by comparison with staff in research-intensive institutions.

Attracting and retaining quality research staff

The study of **Humboldt Universität zu Berlin** argues that for a successful research profile, an institution needs to ensure quality appointments in the first instance. The **Humboldt Universität** benefited from a highly unusual circumstance where in the mid 1990s in the context of the reunification of Germany, the appointments of all staff were terminated and staff appointed from scratch – some (not all) were re-appointed, some newly appointed. While this is obviously not a model for all institutions, it emphasises the value of quality new appointments in helping to raise research standards and also to develop new fields of research.

Attracting high calibre research staff who are able to command high salaries is not easy for those institutions where salary constraints hold. Salary packaging, providing attractive conditions, notably for research can help tilt the balance, and are increasingly looked to by public universities. The increasing costs of attracting research high flyers are a growing challenge.

Retaining research staff, particularly in the face of international mobility deserves more detailed consideration. Making conditions attractive for research include attention to pay and conditions, and providing an appropriate environment. For Continental universities, time spent by researchers in the United Kingdom and United States is seen as important for mastery of English, as the international research language (as German once was, particularly in the sciences). But post-graduate study in the United States has frequently led to students staying on. The question of creating an environment to which it is attractive for researchers to come and stay may be beyond the capacity of individual institutions acting alone, it needs attention at national and regional level – a collaborative approach. Canada has given a major boost nationally to institutional research infrastructure (through the Canada Foundation for Innovation) and the establishment of 2 000 new research chairs over a 5 year period; the European Union Framework Programme has defined a European research space. A judicious balance between retention (retaining good staff from the institutional perspective) and mobility (from the perspective of the researchers) needs to be reached.

What sorts of research education do today's students need?

Many governments are showing a heightened interest in research education and its role in the nation's future wealth creation. Until recently, university-based research education assumed a research career largely in academia or in specialist research institutes. While these are still major avenues, a broadening may be occurring, notably to industry; consequently, the purposes of research education are being widely reassessed: how broadly should research be defined in the contemporary university? New course structures and curriculum changes for initial researcher training have occurred in many countries. Professional masters courses now commonly parallel research masters degrees. And new coursework elements, shorter programmes alongside a focus on reducing completion times, work experience in trans- and multidisciplinary teams, a conscious vocational orientation with work experience in teaching as well as industry, characterise a range of alternative doctoral programmes introduced in different countries. While this has added considerable complexity to institutional post-graduate offerings, it begins to address the more varied needs of the greater number of post-graduate students coming through tertiary institutions. Research of different kinds and levels is spread across these programmes. Many countries particularly in Continental Europe have initiated significant changes in the way research degrees are organised and structured. Following the Bologna Declaration, there have been moves to shorten first degrees, and develop a bachelor, masters and doctorate sequence. Different structures for research study are emerging, for example the development of graduate schools in the Netherlands and Germany.

Beyond their research expertise, there are a number of *specific research management skills* needed by existing staff throughout universities as much as by newly trained researchers. There is a question over the most effective ways to foster, for example: the ability to attract research funding; the management of transdisciplinary research and partnerships with outside organisations; business management skills, in the light of commercial ventures; understanding the possibilities and hazards regarding intellectual property; evaluating research performance – both their own and others. It is also very important to encourage and motivate people, especially younger academics. Not all are self-starters and many lack confidence despite their own academic records. The case studies draw attention to ways in which institutions are addressing these needs both for all researchers and those moving into specialised research management positions.

The research career in its various forms needs to be an attractive option both for young people and for staff in mid-career. The perceived lack of interest by young people in some countries in pursuing careers in certain fields of science and engineering remains of policy concern. The university's ability is further challenged to provide adequate rewards and incentives to retain those researchers whose entrepreneurial talents take them outside traditional academic boundaries.

Supporting early career researchers

The early career phase following completion of the doctorate is seen as problematic in a number of jurisdictions, and in some countries is the subject of specific policies at both institutional and national level. Their aim is to ease newly qualified researchers into a career which otherwise may not retain them and their talents.

Promotion of Junior Researchers in Germany: Restructuring the post-doc-period

Weaknesses of the German science system:

- Long qualification period

- Lack of scientific independence

Institutional responses:

- Federal government: Junior professors

- Deutsche Forschungsgemeinschaft (DFG): Emmy-

- Noether-Programme, funding for one's own position

- VolkswagenStiftung: junior research groups

Source: Prömel, 2003.

National level policy changes in Germany over the past decade have sought ways to enable researchers early in their career to pursue their own research interests independently rather than, as in the traditional academic research structure, remaining part of the research team of an established professor until able to be appointed to a chair. The establishment of junior professorships has been a major national initiative in this respect, providing promising researchers in their early thirties with a five year posting (renewable once) enabling them to establish their own research teams.[25] **Humboldt-Universität** is one of the institutions which has adopted this new structure and aims to establish a balance of one junior professor to four professorships within its overall research profile. The German experience illustrates the impact of internationalism on institutions. Of the large numbers of foreign students who until this year have been attracted to the United States for doctoral research, a number seek to stay in the United States on post-doctorate fellowships which enable them to continue their independent lines of research. Other countries, then, are challenged to find ways of providing equivalent possibilities.

Other initiatives to support early career researchers are drawn out in the case studies of **Humboldt-Universität**, **The Université Libre de Bruxelles**, and **University of Adelaide**.

Research-only contract staff

With the growth of externally funded project-based research activity there has been an increase in research-only staff appointed on contract within universities. The management issues for universities raised by significant numbers of such contract staff are discussed in some detail in the study of the **Université Libre de Bruxelles**.

Management issues are extremely complex because of the variety of funding sources, research time-frames, and contract provisions. Issues include: equivalence to and relationship to academic staff; entitlements of different categories of contract staff (*e.g.* conference attendance); continuity of employment through successive contracts; university obligations to staff who have worked for many years at the institution on successive contracts, and are now in the older worker category (*i.e.* those who have made a career of contract research work) (*e.g.* severance conditions). The **Université Libre de Bruxelles** has taken a strong equity-based approach to the needs of research-only contract staff, in which one can find pragmatic as well as moral reasons.

Building a research orientation in research-poor institutions

The central theme in developing a research orientation among teaching staff at higher education institutions is to engage them in doctoral studies – to upgrade the qualifications and research expertise of the overall staff. While it is not generally the case that universities can require existing staff to complete higher degrees, they can create a range of incentives which make it both easier and attractive for staff to pursue research qualifications.

Beyond the doctorate, institutions develop a range of incentives for staff to engage in research, as illustrated in several case studies.

The challenges to be met in order to increase research activity, as perceived by staff at the **Dublin Institute of Technology**, include:

- inadequate physical environment, such as research facilities;

- insufficient funding and high teaching loads;

- inadequate time for research;

- unfavourable balance between research and teaching;

- change from promotion via seniority to meritocracy;

- changing conditions: workload, holiday.

The **Universitii Kebangsaan Malaysia**, encourages and rewards staff research efforts in a number of ways through:

- short term grants to new faculty;

- research awards and scholarships;

- post doctoral attachments;

- sabbatical leave, research leave;

- lead scholar programmes.

- participation in exhibitions (local and foreign)

At **Bogaziçi Universitesi**, incentives offered to staff for research, include: seed money allocation, travel funds to conferences, matching funds, infrastructure support, and encouragement of multidisciplinary projects. Annual Academic Incentive Awards were initiated to recognise research active staff and have absorbed a major portion of the institution's discretionary funding for research. Progress towards increasing research participation across all faculties has been steady, though unspectacular, and not without setbacks. In a setting where research is still largely seen as the responsibility of the individual, there was seen to be a need for leaders, teamwork and champions to lead to a sustainable research momentum.

CONCLUSION

The heightened significance of research for governments – in particular the link between research and wealth creation in the knowledge society and economy – has been a key factor in raising the profile of the research mission within higher education institutions over the past decade. Other factors converge to reinforce this trend.

Universities have proved true to their long history as successful adaptive institutions, and have met the challenge of managing a growing research emphasis in a variety of ways. Despite the enormously varied scale, missions, national and cultural contexts of universities within and beyond the OECD, several common patterns emerge in how institutions have shaped their responses and in the challenges they face. The experience of this project draws attention to three clusters of responses and challenges.

The first concern the growth of specialisation – professionalisation – of research management within institutions which involves both the appointment of both academic and administrative staff to specific research management positions and upgrading the capabilities of staff throughout the institution to better manage research activities.

Institutions have a challenge to construct the emerging research management positions within the institution in such a way as to be able to attract and retain people of quality, experience and vision.

Institutions have increasingly been establishing centrally located full time senior academic research management positions with supportive offices. While the detailed arrangements of such centrally located research offices vary, their importance is increasing within the institutional settings; they provide support to researchers across the institution as well as providing a point of focus and articulation for linkages external to the institution. The challenge is to establish productive relations with the faculty and departmental levels such as to enable creativity at the local level, while achieving institution-wide research goals and to work in ways which achieve a productive balance between the collegial and the managerial.

The second area is strategic research planning on an institution-wide basis – a range of issues emerge to which individual institutional responses are quite different:

- establishing research priorities and developing an institutional research plan;

- allocating resources for research;

- evaluating research quality, both internally and externally;

- creating an ethical framework for institutional research;

- deciding how far to commercialise institutional research.

To a great extent this is a departure for most universities where research activities have in the past emerged from the initiative of individual researchers and been undertaken largely in isolation from each other. While individual researcher initiative remains the key, institutions are developing a holistic approach to their research undertakings – an overview, a stock-take, a new direction; institutions are looking to develop greater synergy between areas of research, and to provide assistance and support to potentially research active staff members. But this is within an overall framework of research activities shaped by the needs and priorities set by institutions (which do not suit all staff) and within institutional means – or within means they believe they can attract.

The third area is the research career, notably the research career as an institutional responsibility. Whereas in most countries and institutions a clearly defined academic career track has existed, for a variety of reasons, this has come under stress over the past couple of decades, for example, in a number of countries the number of permanent tenure tracks has been cut and academic staff are increasingly being appointed to fixed term positions. While this promotes mobility, it also creates considerable instability within the academic career which has lost some of its attractiveness, at the same time as salaries have not kept pace with salaries which researchers in the private sector in certain fields can attract. As it is increasingly difficulty to secure academic posts, so people are moving into serial short term research positions.

At the same time as the academic career is under stress, increasing numbers of research-only staff are being employed by universities on soft money (external contracts) under widely varying conditions and time frames. In some universities, these staff are responsible for a considerable amount of the institution's research output. While some of these researchers may be 'in waiting' for an academic post, and may well secure one, a considerable number are remaining in serial contract employment, creating essentially a new type of research 'career' within the university setting. This raises many questions for the institution, such as the relationship to academic staff (parity on what relationship, at what level/s), continuity of employment and superannuation provision, contribution to the teaching/ supervision of students at the institution etc. Policies in this field are needed, but nascent.

Specific points of the research career are receiving particular attention by institutions:

- Changes within graduate career training programmes;

- A variety of support mechanisms directed to early career years;

- Questioning the balance between teaching and research in academic appointments; universities appear increasingly to be seeking ways to create research-only positions for academic staff, or at least to provide extended periods of research-only space;

- Staff development in research management tasks;

- An increasing number of researchers are now employed in private industry, and mobility between the sectors as well as internationally is valued;

- Academic researchers are undertaking a much wider array of tasks as part of their normal business;

- Support for building a research orientation in research poor institutions;

- Interdisciplinary research careers are not only more common, but are widely fostered – interdisciplinary career development remains difficult in most institutions.

Two key challenges emerge for institutions. First, rethinking researcher education, through both initial and post graduate degrees so that students have the appropriate skills to adapt to the greater variety inherent in a research career, including the ability to handle its insecurities.

The second is – to the extent possible within industrial and other constraints – to rethink the research career within the institution, to provide continuity, a sense of growth and development in personal capacity (professional fulfilment), and appropriate incentives to encourage quality researchers to remain sufficiently long to make a worthwhile contribution to the individual institutions which employ them.

REFERENCES

OECD/ Institutional Management in Higher Education (IMHE) (2000) IMHE experts meeting on Research Management – Paris, June 2000.

OECD/IMHE – Report of the experts meeting on Research Management.

Issues papers prepared for the experts meeting: imhe@oecd.org

Contzen, J.P. "Background Elements for the Discussion on Sources of Funding and Associated Issues".

Geiger, R. "University-industry research relationships: trends and issues drawn from recent US experience".

Henkel, M. "Research education and research as a career".

Background papers presented at the meetings:

Baez, B. and S. Slaughter (1999) "Academic Freedom and Federal Courts in the 1990s: the legitimation of the conservative entrepreneurial state".

Gibbons, M. (1997) "What kind of university? Research and teaching in the 21st century". Beanland Lecture 1997, Victoria University of Technology, Melbourne, VUT.

Hernes, G. and M. Martin (2000) "Trends in the management of university-industry linkages: what are the challenges ahead?" IIEP/S.188/Background Paper, Paris, International Institution for Educational Planning, UNESCO.

OECD (1998) Redefining Tertiary Education, Paris, OECD.

OECD/ Directorate for Science, Technology and Industry (DSTI) (1998) University Research in Transition, Paris, OECD.

OECD/DSTI (1999) "Benchmarking industry-science relationships and research-based spin-offs", Committee paper DSTI/STP(99)25, Paris, OECD.

Slaughter, S. and L. Leslie (1999) "Commercialization of the faculty tripartite role: teaching, research and service" in G.D. White (ed.): Corporate Power in the Ivory Tower, Westwood, Ct. Greenwood Press.

Slaughter, S. and G. Rhoades (2000) "From endless frontier' to 'basic science for use: social contracts between science and society", Tucson. Center for the Study of Higher Education, The University of Arizona.

Slaughter, S. (2000) "Intellectual Property and Academic Freedom" Appellate court cases, 1989 – 1999.

Slaughter, S., T. Campbell, M. Holleman and E. Morgan, (2000) "The 'traffic' in graduate students: graduate students as tokens of exchange between academe and industry", Draft paper, Tucson, Center for the Study of Higher Education, The University of Arizona.

Stahle, L. (2000) "Research training and research as a career", Stockholm, National Agency for Higher Education".

OECD/ IMHE (2001) Research Management at the Institutional Level.

Experts meeting on: "University research management: learning from diverse experience" at the United Nations University, Tokyo, February 2001

Papers prepared for the experts meeting

Connell, H.M. "Issues in Research Management".

Kondo, E.K. "(2001) Research Management in Brazil".

Maass, G. "Steering and Funding of Research Institutions – The Role of Governments".

Martin, M. "Managing university-industry linkages – an IIEP research project".

Meek, L. and F. Wood "Research Management in the Asia-Pacific Region: Australia".

OECD/ IMHE (2001) "University Research Management: Learning from Diverse Experience", report of the meeting OECD/IMHE-ZWM

Sifuna, D. "University Research Management: The African Experience and Challenges".

Thys-Clement, F. "Research Management in the European Union Universities".

Tzang, A. "Research management in the Asia-Pacific Region – Hong Kong Polytechnic University".

Wang, Yen Kyun "University Research Management in South Korea".

Weill, G. "The Perspective of the Researcher".

Papers available for discussion at meeting:

Hernes, G. and M. Martin (2000) "Trends in the management of university-industry linkages: What challenges are ahead?"

Martin, M. (2000) "Managing university- industry relations. A study of institutional practices from 12 different countries". "Improving the managerial effectiveness of higher education institutions", IIEP research and studies programme, Paris, UNESCO International Institute for Educational Planning.

Thys-Clement, F. and L. Wilkin (1997) "The Strategic Management of Universities: teaching and research" in Higher Education in Europe No.2 – Section Tribune – UNESCO Office of Bucharest- CEPES.

Van Ginkel, H. (1995) "University 2050: The Organization of Creativity and Innovation" Higher Education Policy Vol.8 (4), pp.14-18.

Van Ginkel, H. (n.d.) "Variety and impact; differences that matter", Tokyo, United Nations University, Mimeo.

Conference on "Institutional Responses to the Changing Research Environment", Wissenschaftszentrum Bonn, October 2003:

Avveduto, S. "Institutional autonomy and impact of contractual research".

Banda, E. "Do you need new structures?"

Contzen, J.P. "The growing contribution of research to the societal role of the university and its impact on university structures".

Goldman, M. "Biomedicine in the European research area: How to promote translational research?"

Krull, W. "Opportunities and problems in a new European research area"

Maass, G. "Governance of public sector research".

Prömel, H.J. "Institutional approaches to structuring and enhancing the research career: The promotion of young scientists the Humboldt-Universität zu Berlin".

Takeda, S. "Japanese new challenges to change her research culture".

Winckler, G. "New Demands – Old Rules"

Additional References:

Clark, B.R. (1995) Places of Inquiry, Research and Advanced Education in Modern Universities, Berkeley, University of California Press.

Ehrenberg R.G., M.J. Rizzo and G.H. Jakubson (2003) "Who bears the growing cost of science at universities?" (www.ilr.cornell.edu/cheri/wp/cheri_wp35.pdf)

OECD/ DSTI (2003) Governance of Public Research. Toward better practices, Paris, OECD.

Westbury, D. (2004) "The costing of research", paper presented at the European University Association/ OECD/IMHE workshop on "The Challenges of Research Management", Barcelona, June.

PART II

A QUESTION OF SCALE AND FOCUS AT THE UNIVERSITY OF ADELAIDE, AUSTRALIA

Trends in Research Management and Support at the Institutional Level

Fiona Q. Wood and V. Lynn Meek,with the assistance of Janet Dibb-Smith and Edwina Cornish

Adelaide University's mission is to advance knowledge, understanding and culture through scholarship, research, teaching and community service of great international distinction and integrity. It is committed to producing both researchers and graduates recognised world-wide for their creativity, knowledge and skills.

Its major research management challenges can be summarised as:

- a need to shift the culture of Adelaide University (AU) to one which is more responsive to the changes in the external environment (policy; funding; community expectations; and the demands of a knowledge based economy);

- to encourage staff to take ownership of the University strategic and operational plans in positioning the University to fulfil its mission;

- to recognise that multiple career paths outside universities are more likely to be the reality for today's Higher Degree Research (HDR) students than a university academic position and to set in place research training plans, structures and programs that support this;

- to maintain the vitality of the institution's core business whilst it is re-positioning itself to meet external policy and funding challenges;

- to respond to ever increasing legal and ethical compliance issues regarding the conduct and commercialisation of research and to develop risk management strategies that can deal with these;

- to be a key contributor to the development of a knowledge based economy within South Australia; and

- to promote interdisciplinary linkages both in terms of projects and higher degree research student supervision.

Background

Established in 1874 AU is one of Australia's oldest and most prestigious universities. It has produced two Nobel Prize winners and many Rhodes scholars. Adelaide is a comprehensive University, encompassing a broad range of research activities. While not a large institution, the quality of Adelaide's research is such that it attracts one of the highest levels of per capita research funding in Australia in terms of national competitive grants and other public sector funding. It is home to four nationally designated Centres of Excellence and a participant in fifteen Commonwealth funded Cooperative Research Centres (CRCs). The University has an important tradition of working with industry and other organizations to ensure that research expertise is translated into tangible benefits for the Australian community.

Internationally, Adelaide is known for its strengths in the biological sciences, especially agriculture, medicine and molecular biosciences/biotechnology; the physical and earth sciences, engineering; information technology and telecommunications; environmental sciences and management; and social sciences, especially Asian studies, international economics and human geography.

Adelaide's research activities are conducted within five Faculties: (i) The Sciences; (ii) Engineering, Computer and Mathematical Sciences; (iii) Health Sciences; (iv) Humanities & Social Sciences; and (v) The Professional Schools (including Law, the Graduate School of Management, Commerce, Education and Architecture). In 2000 the University employed 2 253 staff, including 720 teaching and research staff and 435 research-only staff. Of the total student population of 12 885, 1 221 (or 9.5%) were higher degree research students.

Research sites

Research activities occur over four campuses. The main university site is at **North Terrace**, which conducts research in the basic sciences, health sciences, engineering, the arts, humanities and social sciences. The University has capitalised on the proximity of this campus to other South Australian research institutions by developing cross-institutional research programs that are internationally competitive and nationally relevant. In the Biological & Health

Sciences, the University has long-standing links with the Commonwealth Scientific and Industrial Research Organisation (CSIRO) Division of Health and Nutrition, which is headquartered on the North Terrace campus, and the major health services in South Australia, including the Royal Adelaide Hospital, the North Western Adelaide Health Service, The Women's and Children's Hospital and the Adelaide Dental Hospital. The biotechnology company GroPep Ltd, which was recently listed on the Australian Stock Exchange, was founded on collaborative research between CSIRO and Adelaide University. The University, the Institute of Medical and Veterinary Science (IMVS) and the Royal Adelaide Hospital (which are collocated) have a long-standing relationship through their support of the Hanson Centre for Cancer Research. There is increasing co-investment by these institutions with the University in research infrastructure to consolidate this precinct as one of Australia's significant biomedical research clusters.

The Waite and Roseworthy campuses have the largest concentration of research expertise in sustainable agriculture, cereal breeding, dryland farming, wine research and land management in the southern hemisphere. On both campuses the University has established strong synergistic relationships with collocated partners. On the Waite campus there is wide-ranging collaboration with several CSIRO divisions, the South Australian (SA) Department of Primary Industries and Resources (PIRSA), the Australian Wine Research Institute and the SA Research and Development Institute (SARDI). The Waite campus is widely recognised both nationally and internationally as one of Australia's most effective research precincts with respect to agriculture; is headquarters to three Cooperative Research Centres (Viticulture, Molecular Plant Breeding and Weed Management Systems); and home to the new Plant Functional Genomics Centre of Excellence jointly funded by the Australian Research Council, Grains R&D Corporation and State Government. The Roseworthy campus focuses on sustainable cropping systems and animal science research programs, and supports a growing education and training program in conjunction with Technical and Further Education (TAFE) and the animal industries. It is the hub of information transfer, communication, learning and new technologies for the rural community.

The University's commitment to effective interaction with industry is demonstrated by its investment in **The Adelaide University Research Park (Thebarton Campus)**. The Research Park is home to the University's Office of Industry Liaison, commercial tenants, research centres and some 22 spin-off companies of staff and graduates. Commercial and industrial tenants are encouraged to participate with the University in cooperative education and in postgraduate student programs, to become involved in joint research activities with university staff members and to provide work experience for students. In return, tenants have access to University facilities and expertise. There is an on-going Enterprise Education Group for undergraduates, graduates and others interested in starting their own business or working within the small to medium business sector. There is also a Graduate Entrepreneurial program, where students are placed within an existing business to develop a business idea outside the company's mainstream activities, or to develop an idea to the stage of commercialisation. Thebarton, now designated as a State Biotechnology Precinct, is also home to BresaGen Pty Ltd which grew out of the University's pioneering gene technology research in the 1980s to become the first university-linked biotechnology company listed in the Australian Stock Exchange.

Institutional research management case-study methodology

The case study undertaken as part of the IMHE project on institutional research management was facilitated through discussions and assistance with the Director, Research Policy and Support, and the Deputy Vice Chancellor (Research) (DVC(R)). To progress the case-study, a two day intensive site visit was undertaken during mid-February 2002. The main components of this were in-depth interviews with key staff associated with the development and implementation of the University's research management policy and strategy and a familiarisation with the various campuses.

A number of key informants were identified prior to the site visit. However, in view of the complexity of the study and time constraints, it was agreed to focus on a core set of informants and to interview others selectively as specific issues arose. Those interviewed during the site visit are listed in Appendix 1 and their willingness to support the project and share in detail views about research management policy, issues and challenges for the University is greatly appreciated. Prior to the site visit, prospective key informants were sent a thematic overview of the OECD/IMHE case study. To provide a framework for discussions during the site visit, a comprehensive list of 11 issues and questions was prepared (see Appendix 2). This framework was prepared in relation to the suggested themes identified by the IMHE project team. In addition to interviews, a substantial amount of key internal and external documentation (reports, working papers etc) of relevance to the case study was provided (these are listed in Appendix 3). Interviews with the Director, Research Policy and Support were taped and the resulting transcripts provided an important source of detail for this case study report.

The remainder of this report addresses the key issues arising from the interviews and document analysis. The discussion commences with an overview of key changes to the policy and funding environment for research in Australian higher education. This is followed by a review of AU research management structures and processes. The next two sections report on two new organisational units designed to enhance research management: Adelaide Research and Innovation and the Board of Research Education and Development. The report then examines research performance monitoring and staff development, followed by a review of approaches and structures to research funding. The problems and challenges of research only staff is the subject of the next section, which leads to a discussion of research management processes and responsibilities at the faculty and departmental levels. The report then identifies a number of cultural impediments to research concentration and selectivity. The conclusion briefly outlines the major issues that the University will need to address as it continues to evolve its research management plans and strategies.

Overview of key changes to the policy and funding environment for research in Australian higher education[26]

Most operating resources provided by the Commonwealth to the higher education sector are allocated by the Department of Education, Science and Training (DEST) as block operating grants based on student enrolments. For well over a decade, however, federal governments have encouraged competition amongst institutions, particularly with respect to research funding. The 1988 White Paper which formed the basis for the present Unified National System stated that 'concentration and selectivity in research are needed if funding is to be fully effective'. The then Labor government's policies were put into effect in a number of ways. First, at the system level, an increasing proportion of recurrent grants was 'clawed back' from institutions and given to the Australian Research Council (ARC) for competitive re-allocation. This included the ARC Large Grant scheme funded directly by the ARC and the ARC Small Grant scheme funded in proportion to the institutions' success in winning ARC Large Grants and administered by the institutions themselves. Second, individual institutions were compelled to formulate research management plans for the competitive allocation to academic staff of research funds available within the institution. Third, institutional research performance was competitively assessed for funding purposes through the so-called Research Quantum (RQ). The RQ, representing about 6% of total operating grants, was based on quantitative performance indicators: number of competitive research grants attracted (80%), publications (10%) and postgraduate completion rates (10%). Fourth, institutions are provided with Research Infrastructure Block Grants (RIBG) on a formula-base with allocations reflecting the relative success of each institution in attracting competitive research funds.

With the intention of increasing competition over research funding even further, in June 1999 the Liberal coalition federal government released a discussion paper on research and research training entitled *New Knowledge, New Opportunities*. This discussion paper provided the basis for extensive community debate about the policy and funding framework for university research and research training.

The paper identified several deficiencies in the current framework which were considered to limit the institutional capacity to respond to the challenges of the emerging knowledge economy. These included: funding incentives that do not sufficiently encourage diversity and excellence; poor connections between university research and the national innovation system; too little concentration by institutions on areas of relative strength; inadequate preparation of research graduates for employment; and unacceptable wastage of resources associated with low completion rates and long completion times of research graduates. A particular concern was with research training and the funding of PhD and research masters students.

The Government released its policy statement on research and research training, *Knowledge and Innovation: A policy statement on research and research training* in December 1999. Major changes to the policy and funding framework for higher education research in Australia were identified in the policy statement. The principal ones were:

- a strengthened Australian Research Council and an invigorated national competitive grants system;

- performance-based funding for research student places and research activity in universities, with transitional arrangements for regional institutions;

- the establishment of a broad quality verification framework supported by Research and Research Training Management Plans; and

- a collaborative research program to address the needs of rural and regional communities.

The policy statement re-introduced the requirement for formal submission to DEST of Research and Research Training Management Plans. Core elements that institutions are expected to report on annually include: research strengths and activities; details of research active staff; graduate outcomes both in terms of attributes and employment; linkages to industry and other bodies; and policies on commercialisation.

These changes have been put into effect by two new performance-based block funding schemes. The approaches are intended to 'reward those institutions that provide high quality research training environments and support excellent and diverse research activities'. The Institutional Grants Scheme (IGS) will support the general fabric of institutions' research and research training activities. The Scheme absorbs the funding previously allocated for the Research Quantum and the Small Grants Scheme. However, infrastructure funding through the Research Infrastructure Block Grants (RIBG) scheme has been retained.

Funding under the IGS is allocated on the basis of a formula. The components and weighting are as follows: success in attracting research income from a diversity of sources (60%); success in attracting research students (30%), and the quality and output of its research publications, through a revised publications measure (10%). The Government considers that institutions are likely to be more outwardly focused in their research when research income from all sources is equally weighted, unlike pre-2002 arrangements which gave greater weight to Commonwealth competitive research grants schemes.

Funding for research training is allocated on a performance-based formula through the Research Training Scheme (RTS). Institutions attract a number of funded HDR places based on their performance through a formula comprising three elements: numbers of all research students completing their degree (50%); research income (40%); and the revised publications measure (10%). The values for each element will be the average of the latest two years' data. The key aspect of the RTS is that it is essentially based on *quantitative criteria*.

The RTS replaces the Research Higher Education Contribution Scheme (HECS) Exemptions Scheme. It provides Commonwealth-funded Higher Degree Research (HDR) students with an 'entitlement' to a HECS exemption for the duration of an accredited HDR course, up to a maximum period of four years' full-time equivalent study for a Doctorate by research and two years' full-time equivalent study for a Masters by research.

Because of the significance of the impact of these new arrangements on Australian universities it is worthwhile to explain the RTS at some length.

Research Training Scheme[27]

The number of RTS places to be Commonwealth-funded at each institution in 2001 was based on each institution's share in 2000 of the then 2 500 HECS-exempt places plus the "gap" places each institution had committed to the RTS. "Gap" places are those additional HDR places offered by institutions in excess of their HECS-exempt allocation. The total RTS funding provided to the sector in 2001 has established the base for future years.

There is a "funding pool" into which funds freed up by net separations each semester will be placed, and from which reallocations will be made on a relative performance basis each semester. Institutions may provide research training on a fee-paying basis to students not granted a HECS-exempt RTS place.

Since 2002 the RTS assigns the total funding for net separations of students across the sector to the funding pool. Students lodging theses, withdrawing from or suspending their studies, transferring between institutions and exhausting their maximum entitlement contribute to the count of net separations. The funding pool is then re-allocated through the RTS formula which reflects each institution's performance as specified above.

Weightings of 1:2.35 for low/high cost course completions and 2:1 for Doctorate by research/Masters by research completions is applied. The formula is applied twice a year since the first semester funding allocation in 2002.

The net separations load for each institution is converted, using the institution's own funding rate per HDR student place and reflecting the balance between low cost and high cost places, to derive a dollar value. These funds are placed in the funding pool for re-allocation to institutions on the basis of the formula at a sector average rate per HDR student place. To minimise initial adverse impacts on institutions of the RTS, an adjustment package, comprising capping and regional protection, applies during the transition period set for three years from 2002 to 2004.

Gallagher (2000, p. 12) succinctly summarises some of the consequences of the new funding formula:

> For many institutions the crucial matter has been the determination of their starting base in 2001 for the application of the performance-based funding formulae in subsequent years. Most recognised how exacting the formulae would be in rewarding shares of the composition of national performance and the rapidly spiralling character of the rewards. If an institution starts in a position it cannot sustain, by exposing to contestability a level of resources above which it is unlikely to win (unless having some transitional protections) and subsequently declines in its performance, then the outcomes will be harsh for it: relative under-performers will contribute more to the national pool and gain less from its redistribution. A higher ratio of

student separations to completions flows through the formula into fewer commencers; and a relative decline in the national share of research income similarly reduces commencing student allocations which, in turn, dilutes research strength and reduces attractiveness for investment.

Commonwealth changes to research funding has required Adelaide University to rethink much of its approach to the management of research and research training. High on the agenda has been the need to identify priorities, concentrate research effort and to develop a set of performance indicators and research management information system that will allow the University to know how well it is performing in its priority areas.

Concentration and selectivity

Concentration and selectivity remain the key issues in research. This means that AU like other universities has to identify strengths and make hard decisions about allocating resources to these areas and not to others. A discussion of this process at AU is provided later in this report.

Under the new research funding formula for research students, the University earns income not only through student load but also through rate of completions. This presents particular difficulty for faculties in the humanities and social sciences that have a large number of research students who traditionally study part-time, take considerable time to complete their degrees and have low completion rates compared to other disciplines. Some of these students are women who have breaks in their candidature for family reasons. While absorbing a large amount of initial RTS load allocation, these areas may lose the University load in the future if completion rates are outside the formula guidelines. This situation presents the University with difficult decisions and highlights the complexity of priority setting and concentration in the area of research. If the RTS were strictly and immediately applied in certain areas it would devastate the research training programs in those areas and limit access to research training to those in a position to study full-time. On the other hand the University must protect its overall share of the national research student quota.

The challenge introduced by the RTS is for the University to closely examine how it can provide the best quality environment for research students and ensure that they have every support to complete in minimal time. A clear implication entailed in the RTS for research managers is that there is a shift in load from areas with relatively poor HDR completion rates to other areas. The allocation of scholarships could be a tool for shifting load or in supporting areas of strength. Again the challenge is to reach a balance between ensuring sustainability under the formula and ensuring that the educational objectives of the University and its mission as an institution are maintained. This is particularly difficult for a strong research university such as Adelaide, where all academic staff have the expectation of conducting research and supervising research students.

How the University is attempting to successfully meet the challenges imposed by an increasingly difficult and sometimes demanding external environment in the management of its research enterprise is the subject of the remainder of this report.

AU Research Management

The planning process at Adelaide University, which guides resource and management decisions, comprises a long-term strategic plan, a rolling five-year operational plan, and a suite of area and special purpose plans, including a research and research education plan. The University is continuing to invest in the improvement of its planning processes, support systems and databases, and has recently implemented "ResearchMaster" as one of four integrated management information systems to improve the efficiency of research management activities and reporting.

Responsibility for overseeing the development and implementation of the University's Research and Research Education Plan and related policy rests with the Deputy Vice-Chancellor (Research). The DVC(R) and the senior research managers meet regularly with the Executive Deans and Associate Deans (Research) and Associate Deans (Commercialisation) of each faculty. The ADRs, together with other senior research leaders comprise the University Research Committee, chaired by the DVCR. The individual meetings ensure that faculty-based strategies are in place to deliver on the research performance objectives of the University and to monitor each faculty's progress against their specified targets. The collective meetings provide an opportunity to monitor research trends and identify the most effective strategies of each faculty in supporting research and research education initiatives. These strategies are being reinforced by a series of training initiatives to raise awareness of commercialisation opportunities and by the development of promotional "tools" to promote the University's capabilities to industry, in Australia and internationally.

The DVC(R) recently reviewed the operation of her portfolio and the University's commercialisation company (Luminis Pty Ltd), and has subsequently made some structural adjustments to better address the University's key research objectives. These include:

- the co-location and better integration of activities of the University's Research Branch with most of the functions previously undertaken by Luminis. The rationale behind this merger has been to provide a "one stop shop" for University researchers requiring support for any of their research, consulting or commercialisation activities. The combined operation is also intended to facilitate better capture and management of intellectual property and identification of opportunities for attracting industry investment in research. It will provide a focal point for marketing the university's research capabilities nationally and internationally and improve access by industry to University researchers. The new entity became fully operational at the end of 2001 and is known as Adelaide Research and Innovation (ARI); Luminis has become ARI Pty Ltd. Other major restructuring initiatives include:

- the establishment of a Graduate Centre responsible for ensuring that research students have the resources they require to undertake their research and receive the highest quality of supervision and support for professional development;

- the establishment of the Board of Research Education and Development (BRED) to provide advice to the DVC(R) on the University's research education training policy and processes and oversee the development of the university's early career researchers ;

- the creation of a Graduate Scholarships Committee - responsible for providing advice to the DVC-R on research scholarship policy and allocations;

- expansion of the role of the Dean of Graduate Studies (now the Academic Director of Research Education Policy) who becomes a member of the University's senior management group;

- the appointment of a Commercial Director; and the appointment of Business Development Managers to increase the University's revenue from industry sponsored research and University IP; and

- the planned establishment of a Commercial Advisory Group - to provide advice to the DVC(R) on commercialisation strategies and monitor the operation of the University's consulting and contract research activities.

Two of these new organisational units - ARI and BRED- are discussed in more detail below:

The role of the Adelaide Research and Innovation

ARI – Research (Research Office)

The Research Office plays a vital role in university research management at AU. Whilst part of its functions are concerned with administrative and compliance issues a key priority for the Office is its partnership with researchers – in particular the value-added support it provides to the departments/faculties/centres. This means that the Office initiates a wide range of activities aimed at helping to build and maintain strong collegial rapport with the researcher community. Examples include: ensuring that new department heads and professors understand the research system at AU; providing strategic planning advice and counselling to faculty research leaders and individual researchers; assisting research fellows to develop career plans; and ensuring that research and research management issues are addressed in the context of other University plans and developments (*e.g.* Information Technology, Human Resources, Finance, Marketing, International).

Other activities reflecting this team approach between the researcher and the research administrator include: engaging with academics pre- and post-research grant award; helping them understand how to fully cost their proposals and put a value on the work they need to do; providing them with the tools that will ensure that they don't compromise themselves – for example in relation to intellectual property; making it easier for researchers to comply with grant conditions so that they can concentrate on the research activity itself (*e.g.* through the use of ResearchMaster software which automatically emails grant recipients 6 weeks in advance of reports being required by external agencies). Within the new policy and funding environment with a much greater emphasis on competitiveness, the Office is also increasingly involved in helping researchers to interpret this environment, try to decrease anxiety, and help ensure success. The relationship between the Research Office and external funding bodies is particularly important in this regard. Specifically, where a Research Office Director has a strong professional network with outside bodies it is often the case that senior officials from these organizations will use the Director to sound out proposed policy and procedure changes.

An important component in performing this relationship building and partnership role with researchers is to have a diverse team of professionals with different perspectives and skills but who overall have a strong service orientation and also have the personality and confidence to go with that orientation. In this regard the Office looks for people with particular kinds of discipline backgrounds as well as organisational, communication and strategic skills in order to effectively address the University's mission and stated Office goals. Staff development is very important to the Office. However, in the last few years the basic administrative load of the Office has substantially increased. This is in part due to the increase in the number of grants applied for and awarded but also due to the increasing pressures regarding compliance. Such pressures inevitably result in the Office having to give up on some income generation and of value-adding activity, which carries with it the risk of the Office increasingly becoming a "back room". This in turn impacts on the team that has been built up with a "service ethic" and range of complementary skills and attributes which make a difference to the type of research support provided to the University, and to the high reliance of researchers on their services. In practical terms, there is a limit to which it is considered reasonable to ask staff to stay in jobs that have become re-defined to a substantially narrower and less creative set of activities which constrains their interaction with researchers.

A trial has been undertaken at AU involving the development of a complementary research support/management unit between the Research Office and the Faculty of Health Sciences. This Faculty has hundreds of clinical affiliates working in hospitals and numerous complex research management issues. An experienced member of the Office was targeted to lead this initiative and is working closely with his former Office colleagues to ensure the Faculty unit complements, supports and extends Central activities rather than duplicating them. This trial also enables a more detailed understanding by the Research Office of what researchers in this Faculty are doing, of the research management issues faced by the Faculty, and the kinds of value-added support to researchers that best can be provided to the Faculty.

There is a strong appreciation at AU that those involved in research management require training in these roles and the context within which they are expected to operate. This view is not restricted to administrative staff whose positions are dedicated to research management. Others who require some form of training include many of the academic staff who serve leadership roles with respect to research, such as Faculty Associate Deans Research, Associate Dean Commercialisation, Research Centre Directors and others with important strategic or administrative research management roles at Faculty and Departmental level. Postgraduate Coordinators are fairly well briefed and meet regularly, but for many others serving research management roles it has been largely an uncoordinated approach based on learning by doing.

ARI - Commercialisation (ARI P/L)

Intellectual property relationships need to be managed appropriately – particularly in terms of legal liability and risk management. In this regard it considered essential to involve the researchers in the IP management process as there is a danger that in not involving them they will still undertake the work anyway without the necessary background briefing about what is entailed in agreements with outside bodies. Compliance issues are a challenge at AU as indeed at other universities. Like the Research office, ARI P/L pays particular attention to the skill sets of its staff, particularly in terms of legal and accounting skills.

One of the big questions regarding IP and IP management is whether these are legitimately part of a university's core business and particularly that of individual academics. In this regard it is considered extremely important to educate academics on policies and procedures. This requires taking to them a suite of tools/activities and key learning experiences.

Issues for places like AU include: the stage at which you fund IP/technology transfer; budgets and mechanisms for capturing IP; the roles and responsibilities of staff and management regarding IP and technology transfer; and the lack of flexibility for staff in terms of employment arrangements – i.e. being able to move outside the university to set up commercial ventures and then be able to move back again without penalty. Another issue is that the policies of outside funding agencies need a lot of processing by the universities. There is also the problem that when academic staff leave to set up commercial ventures the research effort moves out as well.

An issue identified for Australian universities in general relates to the low level of venture capitalist investment. In the US, for example, the level of funding for start up companies begins at approximately USD 10 million whereas the view was that Australia engages in similar activities basically on a "shoestring" – i.e. in the hundreds of thousands rather than millions. Another issue for Australian universities in general identified by the Commercial Director at AU, was the lack of an appropriate and workable model of university/commercial linkages.

With numerous business units and 4 companies (two of which have been listed on the Australian Stock Exchange), the IP unit at AU is one of the most successful in Australia (though it should be noted that the commercial side of

AU is not currently funded directly by the University). Nonetheless, there is still some way to go before innovation and technological transfer are firmly placed on the South Australia political agenda. This is in contrast to some other states, such as Queensland and Victoria, which have recently been investing relatively heavily in knowledge-based industries.

With a view to bringing more commercialisation awareness and capacity within the University, AU offered 5 subsidised enrolments to University staff to undertake a Diploma course in Commercialisation of Science and Technology in 2001. The Diploma is a subset of the Masters of Science and Technology Commercialisation Course run jointly with the University of Austin in the US. The initial feedback is that whilst it is an incredibly demanding course there is real value in the skills being acquired, particularly as the students are using genuine workplace issues and problems in the course.

BRED and its Working Parties

The Board of Research Education and Development is responsible for providing advice on the University's research education and training policies and processes. The Board currently has six working parties which provide advice on priority issues. They were set up to examine specifically: Doctoral Education; Professional Development for Early Career Researchers; Quality Issues for Research Education; Research Infrastructure; Students Matters; and Graduate School.

These working parties were given fairly demanding briefs following the introduction of the RTS. For example the Doctoral Education Working Party has been examining a broad set of issues including: the current rules for PhDs; what the university should do to make the Adelaide PhD more accessible and attractive to the best students; and retention and completion issues. It has also been discussing such fundamental questions as: what does a PhD mean at Adelaide; should a PhD be offered on the basis of publication; how can the Adelaide PhD be better promoted; and what attributes does the University wish to ensure that its PhD students acquire?

The activities of the Working Party on professional development for Early Career Researchers (ECR) have been similarly broad reaching. Of particular concern has been the professional and career development needs of ECRs and how the University might best meet these as well as identifying ways of enhancing career opportunities and job security and mobility down the line. One of the recent surveys that the University has conducted regarding the needs of PhDs and ECRS has shown that these groups still have fairly traditional expectations regarding careers – *i.e.* they see it primarily in terms of an academic career and focus on issues such as writing for publication and grantsmanship. However, from an institutional point of view it is considered that many of AU's PhD graduates will not necessarily be going directly into traditional academic roles where writing for publication will be the most critical skill and that other skills (project management, team development, commercialisation, IP etc.) might more effectively prepare PhD students for alternative career paths.

The University provides some training centrally and some departments/centres also are quite advanced in this skills training and active mentoring. However, from the Committee's point of view a big question is what you make mandatory. At an undergraduate level some departments are already providing IP training in their courses because of the awareness of staff who have strong industry links and recognise the importance of having commercialisation/IP exposure. But an important issue which the University is addressing is what sorts of activities in research management should be undertaken at the departmental/faculty levels. There are some departments that have very active programs in these areas and this raises the question of how to most effectively extend such practices across other departments. These issues are discussed in more detail below.

Research Performance Monitoring and Staff Development

Monitoring of Research Performance

The DVC(R) undertakes an annual profile of the research performance of all departments. This profile identifies those areas of the University that are performing well in relation to the Commonwealth indicators (income, completions, publications) and those that need to improve. It provides a basis for identifying strengths and weaknesses, developing research plans and setting priorities at Departmental, Faculty and University levels. The University's Planning & Development Office, established to monitor progress against both faculty and university-wide objectives, provides support for this process.

Benchmarking

The University has compared its overall research performance with other Australian universities for the last eight years and has consistently ranked highly on a *per capita* basis, particularly in terms of its ability to win National Competitive Grants to support its basic and strategic research activities, and in its publications output. Additional research performance indicators are currently being recommended (and justified) by Faculties and mechanisms put in place to collect the required data. These indicators will be incorporated in a new agreed set of indicators and evaluation instruments being developed as part of the University's new quality framework.

Incentives to Reward Research Performance

Research performance is a key criterion for promotion at most Australian universities. Executive Deans at Adelaide University are able augment salaries, where they are able to levels that will attract good researchers to the University and retain those that are already employed. However, in a highly competitive environment, leading researchers can become targets for "poaching" by other research universities keen to strengthen existing areas, or by weaker research universities who 'buy in' leading researchers as a means to quickly enhance their research profiles. Those universities that have the capacity to entice people to research only leadership positions and provide them with significant resources make it difficult for other universities which need their senior researchers to undertake substantial teaching and administrative duties as well. Recently, Adelaide has had senior researchers poached by other universities because it has not had sufficient discretionary funds to match these offers in many instances. A particularly vexatious problem is not having sufficient discretionary funds to offer research only positions. Concentration and priority setting at the national level is likely to exacerbate this situation.

The University seeks to encourage its staff, where appropriate, to carry research through to commercial application. Accordingly, it offers staff a significant share of the financial benefits that are derived from successful commercialisation of intellectual property arising from their research. Once direct initial costs have been recovered, income is shared equally between the inventor(s), the department(s) and the University.

Support for Staff Development

With the establishment of the Board of Research Education and Development the University extended the focus of University policy covering research education beyond research students to also include early stage career researchers. As part of this initiative, additional programs supporting the professional development of researchers are being developed at University level and, Departments with good programs being encouraged to make them more widely available. Short courses in commercialisation have been trialled. As mentioned above, the University is also sponsoring several staff to undertake the University's Diploma in Science & Technology Research Commercialisation.

Approaches and structures to research funding

The University's budget process aims to reward excellent performance, while ensuring flexibility to support new ventures and to develop new research fields. All Research Infrastructure Block Grant (RIBG) funding and 50% of the Research Quantum is allocated to faculties according to the proportions in which it is earned. The remaining 50% of the RQ is retained centrally and is used to fund the salaries of central research management and support staff, certain research infrastructure, such as the library, and various research initiatives (*e.g.* special studies program, postgraduate scholarships, contributions to Commonwealth funded centres, contributions to the salaries of Commonwealth Research Fellows who are not fully funded, start up funds for new professors, postgraduate scholarships, and until recently an internal research grant scheme).

The RIBG is passed in total to the Faculties in proportion to which it was earned. Faculties are expected to allocate infrastructure funding to support areas of strength from which it was earned, in accordance with general guidelines set by the Commonwealth, and have been required to report how they have allocated their proportion of the RIBG to support Faculty priorities.

In contrast to the RIBG, faculties have had more flexibility in how they allocate their proportion of the RQ. For example, faculties may choose to use some of the funding to support emerging research areas or Early Career Researchers.

In the last three years, a proportion of the RQ retained by the Centre has been used to fund the "salary differential" of Commonwealth funded fellows (ARC, NHMRC, etc). This situation is a direct result of the introduction of sector-wide Enterprise Bargaining in the mid-1990s which allowed every institution to set their own salary scales. The Commonwealth government research grant funding agencies subsequently decided to set their own rate for the salaries of research personnel supported under their various fellowship schemes and not the institutional rate – thus leaving a salary gap which each institution has had to cover from their own funds and representing a form of 'penalty' for the more successful research universities.

This funding decision has had a particular impact on a university like Adelaide which as a strong research institution attracts a substantial number of research fellows of various types but is small and has fewer discretionary funds. Commonwealth funded fellows are by definition of international calibre and represent key resources for the university adding critical mass in key areas of research priority. However, having a large number of competitive

Commonwealth funded research fellows on its staff has meant that Adelaide is effectively penalised for being a strong research institution. How the differential is covered in practical terms is that the University provides half the salary short fall and the departments the remaining 50%, which also means in a sense that successful departments who attract nationally and internationally recognised research fellows are also penalised. Because of the increasing funding difficulties, at both the centre and faculty/departmental levels, it has become increasingly difficult to maintain any sort of discretionary research fund.

With the change to formula funding under the IGS/RTS scheme the University is re-examining its funding allocation principles, but will continue to ensure that research excellence is rewarded and research students are supported. This is discussed in more detail below.

The new funding regime

The White Paper is a challenge but not all negative. The general principle of attempting to focus research training resources in areas of strength is supported by the University and the sector generally. But as several senior managers noted, "the devil is in the detail". As discussed earlier, with respect to funding there are some major ramifications for the University of the Federal Government's Research White Paper. Treating competitive research grant income the same as all other research income for the purpose of calculating the IGS and RTS particularly disadvantages a University like Adelaide. The University has formally expressed its concern to the Commonwealth that this policy effectively subsidises industry research and thereby is contrary to the spirit of 'competitive neutrality' legislation. The University has excelled in attracting national competitive grant income which with respect to the RQ was weighted double other types of grant income. Under the new regime, the University does not have the same advantage and consequently may not have the same level of resources to support infrastructure and other aspects of research. This may mean that research infrastructure will have to be increasingly subsidised from other sources.

A priority from management's point of view is to ensure that the academic community understands the new funding situation and its implications for AU. In relation to research projects, staff need to realise that a more realistic and professional approach to the funding and management of projects must be adopted. This includes better costing of projects; a willingness to go to a wider range of funding sources for research project support; a better understanding of the potential value of IP and how best to capture it; and enhanced relationships with industry and the community in general.

UNIVERSITY RESEARCH MANAGEMENT: MEETING THE INSTITUTIONAL CHALLENGE –ISBN-92-64-01743-7 © OECD 2004

The expectation by government is that higher degree research students will go where the strength (as defined by their set measures) is both within and between institutions. However, at Adelaide there are some areas which have small numbers of staff who while not producing large numbers of publications do not require much funding either. In some areas in the social sciences and humanities, there are large numbers of students studying part-time and who therefore take a longer time to complete.

In their research management plans universities are required to identify their research priority areas along with research active staff based on publications, research grant income and number of research students supervised. Application of these criteria to departments and faculties has alerted Deans and HODs that not all staff are as research active as often presumed. In several instances it can be demonstrated that a considerably large proportion of the research activity (grants, publications and supervision) is the product of a relatively small proportion of the staff. Under a strict regime of concentration and selectivity, this immediately raises the question of differential allocation of resources and workloads between research and other areas.

With the introduction of the RTS, the University is confronted with a situation where it is funded on size and value in *quantitative* terms. Therefore, it has to: (1) ensure that it does not jeopardise future RTS requirements; (2) increasingly divert support to areas of strength; and (3) address the question of exactly what sort of university AU wants and related to this, for example, the question of the role of the humanities and social sciences. Responses to these questions are an evolving process. However, it is clear that AU will need to gradually redirect RTS funding to areas of strength and the faculties are currently engaged in evaluating their performance statistics and re-defining their strengths and priorities for research training.

The need for budget transparency

Until recently, each Faculty has handled the RQ/RIBG funding differently. In science/agriculture there has been a central research fund and a range of ways it could be used – some competitively based. However, in the Social Sciences and Humanities there hasn't been much money to give away so the issues have not been as focused. In Engineering the faculty believed it knew what was wanted in terms of research activity so the funding was allocated to those areas. In the health sciences the issue of subsidised staffing is a problem. Other faculties have found it increasingly difficult to maintain discretionary funding or to ear-mark funding for specific needs.

Until recently, the issue of transparency was complicated by the way in which the University budget process is conveyed to the research community, making it difficult for researchers to understand how RQ money comes into the university and how it is distributed to the faculties and the centre. This led to incorrect assumptions and allegations by staff of cross-subsidisation.

A further complicating factor has been that until recently the presentation of the University's budget had not clearly distinguished between *discretionary* and *fixed* allocations amongst faculties and between the faculties and the centre. This created an impression that the University had a greater degree of flexibility with its funding than it was the case in reality. The Faculty of Science, for example, brings in quite substantial funding in directed research grants every year and would, on this basis, appear to be fairly wealthy. But these funds are predominantly from competitive research grants, where nearly all of the funding has been earmarked in the grant application. Related to this is that few projects receive the total amount requested and virtually none of them include infrastructure and other over-head costs, resulting in the fact that it actually costs the University more than it receives to conduct research in many of these areas. Very few grants recognise staff in-kind commitments. These realities are often not fully appreciated by the research funding community.

Thus one of the major achievements for the University during 2002 was recognising the importance of transparency to reflect how resources are being strategically channelled. In particular, each area within the university needs to know how it is resourced to undertake research and research training activities to a certain standard, and be assured that they are not cross-subsidising some other area of the University. *The more blurred the budget process is, the more difficult, if not impossible, it is to effectively manage at each level.* It is recognised that academic leaders of the institution need to know how the budget works so that they can effectively contribute to the many challenges confronting the institution – *i.e.* be a part of the solution.

Furthermore, it is now expected that faculties will be more transparent about how the money they receive under the IGS, RIBG and the RTS is allocated to support their research activities. Questions put to faculties include:

- To what extent is the IGS supporting their areas of research strength and other research related activities?

- To what extent is the RIBG truly supporting areas of strength as identified in faculty plans?

- Particularly with respect to the RTS, how are the faculties allocating the funding they receive to support research students and the work of their supervisors, and what are the principles adopt in making these decisions.

Also as part of the new approach to the budget the DVC(R) has become "gatekeeper" for IGS and RTS funding. One of the roles of "gatekeeper" is to recommend how research money is channelled to faculties. Another role is to address the issue of RTS and load shifts and how the capacity to continue to earn RTS funding can be safeguarded. The DVC(R) has made it clear to the faculties increasing attention will be paid to the following: shifting resources to areas of demand, strong HDR completion and research strength. Each faculty has been asked to identify their areas of research strength and will need to be more transparent in how they support research in their revised plans. They will need to show how they are using funds and also be explicit regarding the principles used to allocate these funds.

Explaining the budget is an iterative process involving a wide range of staff and committees. For AU there has been the added complication that a new finance system was only recently introduced which prolonged access to the needed detailed management reports until it was functioning properly. Nevertheless, staff at all levels have appreciated the new transparency.

Problems and challenges of research only staff

For many universities, due to the smallness of numbers, research only staff (staff whose duties are primarily research rather than teaching and research, such as post-doctoral fellows) would raise few significant problems. However, because AU is a research intensive university it has significant numbers of staff in the research only category. Until recently, there has been some confusion regarding the rights and privileges (*e.g.* access to conference travel and study leave) of this category of staff.

An advisory committee on research fellows identified two distinct categories of research only staff. Category A fellows are those who bring in their own salary from external funding sources. They are accorded the same right and privileges of other academic staff. Category B fellows are those employed on another staff members externally funded research grant. These staff do not have all of the privileges of the first category, thought they have been extended some privileges, such as support for attending overseas conferences. Clarifying the rights and privileges of the two types of research only staff has greatly improved industrial relations in this area.

The Adelaide Research Staff Association was founded in November 2000 to represent the interests of those Adelaide University staff whose primary function is to conduct research. It provides an integrated, supportive network for the University's research staff and plays an important role in setting priorities for future professional development programs for researchers, as well as a source of feedback on policy matters. As indicated previously, the need for such an association is peculiar to research intensive universities such as Adelaide. The RSA has a positive relationship with the DVC(R) and has recently agreed to assume responsibility for awarding a new annual 'research prize' for an Early Career Researcher.

Research management processes and responsibilities at the faculty and departmental levels

The department is the base organisational unit on which the rest of the University's structure is grounded. It is here where most of the research activity originates and/or takes place. Thus the new funding climate is increasingly making the role of Head of Department (HOD) a demanding one indeed. While the University has appointed Deans with executive responsibility, HODs remain elected positions. But increasingly demanding skills, responsibilities and expectations are being placed on them, including human resource management and financial planning. As one informant put it, the HOD position can no longer be considered as a role shared amongst colleagues as a 'good citizen chore', with the unwritten expectation that no decisions are made during the period of tenure that may prejudice other colleagues. However, the University now needs HODs to take on very active roles in managing their staff, assigning responsibility for postgraduate coordination and making sure that a quality job is done, that certain programs are in place, that budgets are effectively managed to support them, that staff are counselled about using their skills to best effect, and to promote staff development. The issue of appointed HODs is further complicated by the fact that it is seen as an industrial matter and which so far has not attracted union endorsement.

The faculty is the principal financial unit, responsible for allocating resources between departments and supporting strategic initiatives that operate across departments. The faculties are now required to address the Universities strategic research priorities in terms of their own research and commercialisation intentions. Based on departmental input, the faculties are developing their own new research and research training plans. Clearly, the government's White Paper has made the faculties much more aware of the need for rigour in the planning process and raised their awareness with respect to the training needs of both HDR students and early career research staff particularly in terms of commercialisation and working with industry. The faculties and departments are beginning to evaluate such issues as the need for more structured PhD programs, mentoring of early career researchers, peer support for grant proposal writing, and the involvement of industry in research and research training. Some departments which are particularly advanced in this area are being encouraged to share good practice amongst themselves.

Increasingly, departments and faculties will need to be much more explicit about what they are doing, how they are doing it and why. For example, while Adelaide's higher degree policies have been regarded as models by other universities, the way in which departments structured their research training programs was rather ad hoc with little consistency or monitoring across the University. Built into the culture of a university like Adelaide, with its long research tradition, is the unquestioned assumption that at the departmental level the individual supervisor and the department supporting them is providing the right intellectual environment, related infrastructure support and is complying with university protocols for HDR students. Such assumptions can no longer be left to chance.

The proposal now being investigated is that there should be common standards of practice across the university on the structure of departmental based research training programs with certain minimal elements prescribed (such as the code of practice including specific departmental and faculty responsibilities and an induction program). The re-established Graduate School through its web site will maintain information for current and prospective students on the nature and content of the structured research training programs offered by each faculty and department. Until recently, there was no central data source for such information. A centralised data source will also assist departments in benchmarking amongst one another as to best practice with respect to the programs they offer their HDR students.

In terms of evolutionary change the University is moving towards a situation where the centre must increasingly impose uniform policies to respond to Commonwealth government pressures, replacing to some extent procedures traditionally the province of departments. Faculties, as cost centres, are also increasingly being asked to play a quality control function vis-à-vis the departments. In addition to faculty plans merely reflecting the ambitions of departments, they now need to ensure compliance with Commonwealth and University expectations, the level of quality, and consistency across their various programs. Given the University's disciplinary diversity, the faculties are best placed to do this.

Culture impediments to research concentration and selectivity

As argued above, concentration and selectivity have been the defining characteristics of research policy in Australian higher education for more than a decade. However, while the 2000 Research White paper increased the financial penalties for non-compliance to the new policies, Australian institutions have reacted differently to questions of concentration and selectivity. Historically, the former CAEs and Institutes of Technology did not have as well an entrenched research culture as the traditional universities, particularly the so-called sandstone universities of which Adelaide is one. The newer universities have put considerable effort into building a research culture but have had neither the resources nor the motivation to build a deep research culture across all academic aspects of the institution. Sandstone universities have been built on the opposite expectation which presents its own problems with respect to the new research funding regime. Somewhat paradoxically, it may be easier to implement policies of concentration and selectivity in research funding in the newer universities than in the older, more traditional ones.

While not all universities expect to conduct research in all areas in which they teach, this is a tradition of the sandstones. Thus as a result of the new Commonwealth approach to research funding, Adelaide is having to re-examine its approach and its principles, particularly in relation to those disciplines comprising large numbers of part-time students (who tend to have longer completion times and lower completion rates). When considering available resources (through the IGS and RTS for example) faculties may need to decide that some departments will not be highly research active, and will concentrate their effort on professional training at the undergraduate level.

But most universities have yet to adequately discuss these sorts of hard questions at the discipline, the department, the faculty and university levels and articulate what it is they believe to be their core business. These are tough issues, but as discussed above, may be less so for universities without a long and strong tradition of research where not all academic staff have the expectation that they will be active researchers. Their emphasis is predominantly on high quality teaching and scholarship rather than large scale externally funded fundamental research investigations. But at Adelaide and other traditional research universities, people come with the expectation that they will contribute to new knowledge. This is causing some stress in light of the new research funding regime.

Another aspect of the traditional research culture has been that the individual scholars have tended to adopted attitudes that they know best when it comes to issues of setting research agendas and providing the finest intellectual and physical environments for research training. This is another source of tension under the new policy and funding regime which requires much more attention to issues of compliance and accountability, particularly with respect to ensuring that students are enrolled in areas "proven" to provide the appropriate intellectual stimulus; the right standard of infrastructure; and prepared for a diverse range of careers' and complete in a reasonable time frame. These issues and tensions in turn raise fundamental questions about what kind of university Adelaide wishes to be. And in answering these questions, it is no mean trick to simultaneously safeguard the future of the institution whilst engendering a feeling of understanding and acceptance of the issues at the faculty and departmental levels.

Conclusion – ongoing issues

Though AU has put much effort into enhancing its research management structures and strategies, a number of issues will require continued attention. The University's approach to research management is an evolving one and it is well recognised that not all problems can be solved immediately nor all strengths supported at the same level. Also, the complex and turbulent environment in which the University must operate will place new issues and challenges before the institution. About the only claim that can be made with any certainty is that the University will continue to face issues demanding hard choice with respect to concentration and selectivity and the prioritising of funding. A few of the more immediate issues are summarised below.

First, there is the question of to what extent the university should channel funding to the faculties and give them total discretion as to how and where it is allocated. The alternative would be channelling some funds from the centre directly to specific areas of strength, such as particular institutes or centres.

A second question is to what extent the University should centrally control PhD placements to ensure maximum returns through the new RTS formula. Such controls could be seen to be contrary to the traditional situation where an institution's higher degree profile develops as a result of potential students identifying a preferred supervisor and host department.

Third, with the increasing focus on universities and their research partners effectively managing and commercialising their intellectual property, some key research programs are being incorporated into special purpose vehicles, operating as a commercial or quasi-commercial entity, often in partnership with other agencies and with a separate management and governance structure. The University is confronted with the question of how it can maintain control of such core research activities in such a model.

Fourth, while the university wishes to encourage cross-disciplinary team research there is a problem with distributing infrastructure support equitably amongst all members of a team. In the past RQ and RIBG money went to the area where the first Chief Investigator of a grant was located, ignoring other research associate with the grant located elsewhere in the University. In light of the objective both locally and nationally to encourage more multidisciplinary research – research which is at the cutting edge of two disciplines which is where research sponsors are keen to invest resources and where many breakthroughs appear to arise – there is a need to ensure that the incentives are there to encourage people to work in teams.

Clearly, there are many such issues that the University of Adelaide, as a research-intensive institution, will confront as it seeks to maintain and build on its strong research and research training profile and reputation in such a changing environment.

External environment:

- a perception that Commonwealth agencies are introducing programs 'on the run' with inadequate cross-agency/institution discussion

- there have been several major Commonwealth Reviews which will feed into the Backing Australia's Ability 2

- a new State government has been elected and this brings with it a new agenda, and different funding priorities and commitments

- there has been the creation of a State Innovation Directorate and Premier's Science & Research Council and the establishment of a 10 year strategic vision for the State (with associated opportunities for UA to influence this vision).

Internal environment:

- there have been the appointments of new institutional academic leaders (and Faculty structures) with financial mandates

- there has been ongoing debate on competitive/contract research pricing and infrastructure funding

- reconciling cultural tensions between academic focus and commercial realities

- a substantial re-structuring of the Research Branch

Also there have been a range of responses and achievements in relation to these new developments and issues. These include:

Externally:

- active participation in State Government strategies (*e.g.* Premier's Science & Research Council; Office of Innovation)

- strengthened partnership with key collaborating institutions (SARDI, SAM, CSIRO) and 'real' joint achievements (*e.g.* AGT and DSTO Chairs)

- cooperative development of major infrastructure

- establishment of new relationships with Industry Cluster leaders

- growing national/international dialogue and benchmarking between research universities

Internally:

- a continued emphasis on the importance of "Scale and focus in research"

- establishment of URC Executive (Faculty research leaders) to lead strategic change and agree to focus resources

- University financial issues "road show" – to better communicate the actual costs of research

- survey of early career researcher perceptions and career development needs; appointment of a Task Force

- establishment of a Research Finance Team; co-location in the Research Branch

- IP audits conducted in Sciences, Health and Engineering

- framing of new IP policies and protocols (about to be launched with a 'tool kit' to help with understanding compliance and other issues.

REFERENCES

Gallagher, M. (2000) The Emergence of Entrepreneurial Public Universities in Australia. DETYA Higher Education Division Occasional Paper Series 00/E.

New Knowledge, New Opportunities: A Discussion Paper on Higher Education Research and Research Training. (1999) Canberra: AusInfo.

Knowledge and Innovation. A Policy Statement on Research and Research Training. (1999) Canberra: AusInfo.

Wood, F. and Meek, VL. (2002) Over-reviewed and underfunded? The evolving policy context of Australian higher education research and development. Journal of Higher Education Policy and Management. 24(1): 7-20.

APPENDICES

APPENDIX 1

Staff interviewed at Adelaide University February 2002

Professor Edwina Cornish, Deputy Vice-Chancellor (Research)

Mrs Janet Dibb-Smith, Director, Research Policy and Support, Adelaide Research and Innovation

Mr Steve Winslade, Commercial Director, Adelaide Research and Innovation

Professor Ieva Kotlarski a former acting DVC-R and Faculty Dean (Science) and Associate Dean for Research (Health Sciences). Also a leading researcher and very active as a postgraduate/postdoctorate mentor.

Mr Bill Jones, Planning & Development Office, formerly Research Information Analyst in the Research Office; was involved in a benchmarking study of the University against other top Australian research universities; and also responsible for compiling research performance information and conducting training sessions throughout the University to illustrate the potential impact of the Federal Government's two new performance based funding schemes – the Institutional Grants Scheme and the Research Training Scheme.

Dr Gerry Mullins - currently convenor of the Quality Issues working party of BRED and long term provider of training courses and advice to postgraduate supervisors.

APPENDIX 2

Discussion framework for IMHE case study on research management at the University of Adelaide, February 2002.

Issues and questions

1.   The issue of institution-wide co-ordinated research policies and strategies as against a more entrepreneurial, free hand for individual departments and research units.

- To what extent are research activities constrained by institution wide policies?

- How are internal research funds allocated?

- Are there any constraints on individuals applying for outside funds?

- Is team research encouraged and to what degree?

2.   Questions arising in institution-wide attempts to: formulate priorities; attract and allocate resources; establish personnel policies for recruitment and career development of researchers and support staff; evaluate research quality and research capacity; establish a productive relationship between the processes of institutional management of research activity and institutional governance.

- How are research priority areas identified?

- What proportion of overall research funding goes to priority areas?

- To what extent is research training concentrated in priority areas?

- Are there policies that mandate the importance for funding and research student recruitment in priority areas?

3.   Different ways of fostering an environment conducive to research.

- What are the processes through which policies and strategies have been achieved?

- What are the key problems and issues emerging as part of this process?

- What policy approaches have worked best?

3.   .Management structures for research (including research ethics and evaluation): central and decentralised research management roles and responsibilities (collegial/ managerial tensions; remit of chief research officer); research interfaces with external bodies;

- To what extent is research management devolved to faculties and departments?

- What support structures are in place for the individual researcher to manage his/her grants?

5.   How the institution addresses questions of balance between its research, teaching and community missions.

- Can a staff member be promoted on a teaching only profile?

- Can a staff member be promoted on a research only profile?

- To what extent is research important for the appointment of new staff - is this the same across the institution?

6.   Examples of articulated, institution-wide, over-arching strategic plans; difficulties arising. What is the value and usefulness of such plans?

- Is research an important feature of the strategic plan?

- Does the strategic plan actually influence behaviour within the institution?

- How important is the research management plan?

7.   How the institution has experienced/ been affected by pressures and movements at the system level to achieve research concentration both within the institution and regionally;

- To what extent does the University regard the White Paper on research as a threat and/or constraint?

- Is the White Paper changing the institutions approach to research and research training?

8.   Staff selection for and training in research management: approaches; areas of success; problems and difficulties.

- Is this centralised or decentralised?

- Are there staff with research management responsibilities at the faculty   and/or department levels?

9.   How significant intellectual property and legal issues have been for research management at the institutional level?

10.   Examples of how institutions manage the at times conflicting claims and interests of individuals, teams, departments/ faculties and the central administrative and policy apparatus.

- Please give examples.

11.   How has the research enterprise been enhanced by institution-wide management?

APPENDIX 3

Support Documents provided by Adelaide University of relevance to case-study

Academic Promotions Handbook: Human Resources Policies and Procedures, The University of Adelaide, 2002

Agricultural Biotechnology (Glossy Brochure), The University of Adelaide, 2001.

Annual Report 2000 (Glossy Brochure), The University of Adelaide, 2000.

Board of Research Education and Development Project Plan (spreadsheet), The University of Adelaide, 7 February, 2001

Combining cultures to establish Adelaide Research & Innovation - integrating research management services to support both innovation and commercialisation, Dibb-Smith, J., The University of Adelaide, 2001. (paper presented at New Zealand Research Management conference)

Contributing to the Prosperity of Australia and the World: Research and Research Training Management Report (separate booklet, not in folder), The University of Adelaide, July, 2001.

Department Research Profiles (Briefing Note), Jones , B., The University of Adelaide, 20 February, 2001.

Ensuring Timely Completions: BRED (Academic Board Meeting - for discussion), The University of Adelaide, 3 October, 2001.

Faculty Research, Research Commercialisation and Research Training Plans (VCC Meeting - For Discussion), The University of Adelaide, 2001.

Final Report of the Quality Issues Working Party, The University of Adelaide, 2002?

Graduate Centre: Final Report of the Working Party, Cornish, E., The University of Adelaide, 7 December, 2001.

Higher Degree - Research HECS 2002: Report to Research Committee Meeting, McFarland, P., 13 January, 2002.

Institutional Grant Scheme (overheads), The University of Adelaide, 2002.

Medical Biotechnology (Glossy Brochure), The University of Adelaide, 2001

Molecular Biosciences (Glossy Brochure), The University of Adelaide, 2001

Office of Industry Liaison, Commerce and Research Precinct, The University of
    Adelaide, 2002.

Operational Plan 2000 - 2002 - 2004 (Memorandum from Edwina Cornish),
    The University of Adelaide, 28 February, 2000.

Post Docs and Early Career Researchers Resource Site, The University of
    Adelaide, 2002.

Postgraduate Programs 2002 (Glossy Brochure), The University of Adelaide,
    2002.

Quality research (powerpoint presentation on university profile), The University
    of Adelaide, December, 2001.

Research and Community Service: Quality Review Portfolio, The University of
    Adelaide, 1995.

Research and Research Training Management Plan 2000/2002, The University
    of Adelaide, 2000.

Research and Research Training Plan 1998-2002 (including key strategies),
    Milbourne, R., The University of Adelaide, 1998.

Research at Adelaide University (separate booklet, not in folder), The
    University of Adelaide, 2001.

Research Branch, Strategic Plan (July 1999-December 2000), The University of
    Adelaide, 1999.

Research Education at Adelaide University: Report from the Deputy Vice-
    Chancellor (Research) Board of Research Education and Development,
    The University of Adelaide, 5 September, 2001.

Research Funding and Network Opportunities (brochure only), The University
    of Adelaide, June, 2001.

Research Management Plan & Application of 1993 Quality Funds (Supplementary documents), The University of Adelaide, 1993.

Research Management Plan 1998-2000 Triennium (Draft), The University of Adelaide, 1997. Research Management Plan, The University of Adelaide, 31 January, 1997.

Research Staff Association Homepage, The University of Adelaide, 2002.

Research Staff Association: Here for you (brochure only), The University of Adelaide, July, 2001.

Review of the Higher Degrees by Research Programme, The University of Adelaide, November, 2001.

The Research performance of the University of Adelaide by Academic Groups: A Benchmarking study between the Group of seven, Milbourne, R., The University of Adelaide, 1999.

Towards a defining statement for the PhD and related graduate attributes, Academic Board Meeting, Report from the Deputy VC (Research) for discussion, The University of Adelaide, 2001.

University Research Committees, The University of Adelaide, 2001.

RESPONSE TO CHANGES IN RESEARCH FUNDING AT THE UNIVERSIDADE FEDERAL DO RIO GRANDE DO SUL, BRAZIL

Maria Alice Lahorgue

Introduction

The past twenty years have brought much upheaval but also a consolidation of major trends such as the globalisation and universalisation of ICTs (information and communication technologies). After the end of the long period of growth known as the glorious thirty years (1945-1975), governments experienced a growing fiscal crisis and accordingly started to think about reforming the structure of public spending. The impacts that this reversal of expectations had on higher education systems have already been exhaustively documented and amounted to a challenge to Humboldt's ideal of the university on the grounds, firstly, that it was too expensive and secondly that it was too far removed, in the opinion of government leaders in most countries, from society's needs.

By the same token, questions were asked about research - particularly basic research - and its funding. The research effort requires an ever-increasing volume of financial resources due to the speed at which equipment becomes obsolescent and new equipment more sophisticated (high-performance computers are a good example of this trend in that they cost several million dollars to buy only to become obsolescent two or three years later). It was commonplace in the past to think that excellent research would linearly and naturally lead to technological innovations and economic growth. In fact, from 1945 until the 1980s, science evolved in accordance with the "rules" propounded by Vannevar Bush[28]. Under the terms of this "social contract", governments, as a general rule, financed scientific research in the expectation that the findings would have positive impacts on the economy and society, without any deeper assessment of research projects. This proved to be quite removed from reality, forcing decision-makers to adopt new types of rationale. B. Martin (2000), in demonstrating the relevance of science and technology forecasting as a means of lowering the risk of making poor policy decisions, argued that a major change had taken place in the relationship between science and society over the past decade.

The new "social contract", which is still being written, places the emphasis on the mission and strategic orientation of research, as well as on new forms of university governance. This trend reduces researchers' degree of freedom in that financial donors want either to choose the topics of research or to receive guarantees that research will have a successful outcome. There is a certain consensus on the need to continue the funding of basic research, including research undertaken "because the researcher wants to", because it is a prerequisite for advancing our knowledge of the world. And yet it is now almost a rule that priority in the allocation of public funding is given to applied research projects with highly specific objectives and the prospect of an immediate transfer to the productive sector.

In a country such as Brazil, which is in the throes of a major fiscal crisis and which is striving to enhance its systemic competitiveness, research funding policy is to a certain extent radicalising this trend towards "controlling" and choosing S&T projects solely from the standpoint of industrial policy.

In Brazil, the public sector is responsible for practically all R&D and the main actors responsible for the production of knowledge in the public sector are the universities. The government traditionally funds the researcher and his partners (not-for-profit as well as commercial organisations) directly without giving any thought to the impacts of these activities on university institutions. Over the years this approach to financing has created a culture of individualism in which decisions are taken by majority vote within the research group and in many cases solely by the researcher.

The main source of funding for university research is the National Fund for the Development of Science and Technology (FNDCT) at the federal level, and the funds in federated states that are managed by research support foundations. These funds have never provided what might be considered to be an appropriate volume of resources and their tendency was to become sporadic rather than continuous sources of funding.

The federal government decided that from 1999 onwards it would increase research funding in order to resolve the problem of continuity, signalling at the same time its pursuit of a clearer policy towards the development of technology. The outcome was the creation of sectoral funds with substantial resources that are not dependent on the Treasury. The increased funding highlighted the palpable need to change the decision-making process within institutions with a view to improving the balance and relationship between investment (whose current pace sharply contrasts with the earlier sluggishness), staff and expenditure on maintaining the complex of new buildings and equipment.

This paper presents Brazil's experience of these changes from the standpoint of federal public universities. The first section presents a brief history of research funding in Brazil. The second section goes on to describe the features of the sectoral fund instrument and the results that have been achieved. The third section describes the management of research in one of the largest federal public universities, the Federal University of Rio Grande do Sul. The fourth and last section illustrates the challenges that the universities must meet and preliminary reactions two years after the initial introduction of the new form of funding.

Public Funding of Research in Brazil

Efforts by the Brazilian government to develop S&T infrastructure and train highly skilled human resources were given greater impetus during periods characterised by the construction of a nationalist project, which mostly coincided with exceptional regimes. The National Science and Technology Council (CNPq) was established under the last Vargas Government[29], in 1951, at the same as the CAPES scheme (co-ordinated training of higher education staff). These two organisations were responsible for putting in place a large higher degree system which every year awards 6 000 PhDs and 18 000 Master's degrees. Figure 1 below shows the number of PhD's and Master's degrees warded over the period 1987-2000. In the course of this period, the number of doctoral students receiving their degree rose six-fold.

During the 1970s when the military was in power (1964-1986), the Brazilian government undertook a major effort to enable scientific and technological knowledge to be appropriated by nationals in order to gain control over the development bases of new industrial processes and products. The public universities were the sole institutions that could be used to direct this effort, firstly because they had qualified staff available and secondly because the industrial sector was not encouraged to innovate given the totally protected nature of the domestic market. This was the start of a process consisting in the institutionalisation of research through the implementation of a policy tied to an economic project that had become all-determining, a process which gave priority to the universities.

Figure 1. **Awards of PhDs and Master's degree in Brazil**

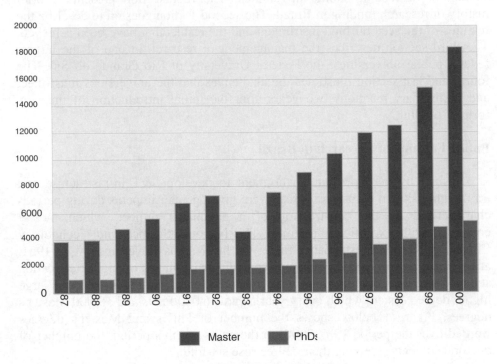

during the period 1987-2000

Source: MCT, 2001.

According to figures produced by the CNPq in 2002, Brazil has some 15 000 research groups. Almost 90% of these groups have been set up by universities, isolated colleges and research institutes. Table 1 illustrates the trend in these numbers over the past ten years, during which, for example, there has been remarkable growth in the number of institutions.

Table 1. **Number of institutions, research groups, researchers and PhD holders, Brazil, 1993, 1995, 1997, 2000 and 2002**

	1993	1995	1997	2000	2002
Institutions	99	158	181	224	268
Groups	4 404	7 271	8 632	11 760	15 158
Researchers (R)	21 541	26 799	34 040	48 781	56 891
PhD holders (D)	10 994	14 308	18 724	27 662	34 349
(D)/(C) as a%	51.04	53.39	55.01	56.71	60.38

Source : CNPq, 2002, www.cnpq.br

The importance of the role played by the universities in the research sector is apparent in the distribution of scientific staff and engineers in Brazil. Approximately 71% of such staff are employed in higher education institutes, 17% in the private sector and 12% in government (MCT, 2001).

The funding of this system, which is dominated by the universities, is provided by agencies such as the CNPq and the Finep (established in 1967) and through instruments managed at the national level, the most important of which being the National Fund for the Development of Science and Technology (FNDCT).

The FNDCT was the instrument used to implement the 1968 Strategic Development Plan as part of the effort to develop science and technology (this national plan was the first to clearly place the emphasis on S&T). The 1970s were a period of plenty. The FNDCT funded major projects, providing support for whatever was required to set up and consolidate a research group, namely equipment, buildings and wages. This support depended upon the quality of projects (agency/researcher relationship) and the way they fitted into institutional policy (agency/institution relationship). This period laid the foundation for research infrastructure in the fields of physics, biochemistry and, *inter alia*, engineering.

The 1980s, the lost decade in Latin America, brought a reduction in the funding resources available to the FNDCT. As a result, the projects sponsored were not as costly as those funded in the previous decade and the new policy direction focused on projects "with a beginning and an end", abandoning support for institutions. In addition, applied research was given precedence over basic research, and "hard" sciences priority over human sciences. The basic research groups set up during the earlier period found it hard to keep going. Laboratories were no longer upgraded and researchers carried out basic research disguised as applied research in order to gain access to the funding available and to finance the running of their laboratories (staff and consumables).

The shortage of funding continued during the 1990s. The instability of financial sources, above all the national Treasury, became the bane of Brazilian research. This aspect of research funding had for some time been viewed not as a sign of volatility but simply as the normal state of affairs in Brazil (Guimarães in Schwartzman, 1995).

Without being able to save the entire infrastructure, the FNDCT and its decision-makers opted for groups of excellence, avoiding the alternative solution of a massive dilution of resources. It was for this reason that the federal government, pending a solution to the problem of instability, decided to launch two programmes which concentrated resources on the most efficient research groups: Pronex, the Groups of Excellence Programme set up in 1996, and the Millenium Institutes Programme introduced in 2000. These two programmes, funded firstly the Treasury and secondly by the World Bank, have similar objectives, namely to support research groups that can compete at world level and that, in addition, are capable of acting as a catalyst for a national network of laboratories. Pronex has approved 206 projects and the Millenium Institutes 3[30].

The projects within the network called for co-operation between groups that had already been consolidated and newly emerging groups, thereby enhancing funding outcomes with regard to infrastructure and the dissemination of research skills. This characteristic was beneficial for the most recent institutions and for those in less developed regions. In contrast, the restriction of funding almost exclusively to academic excellence clearly posed political problems in view of the fact that sectors which had not yet reached the level of excellence defined in the programme, or which were unable to collaborate with other more effective groups, were doomed to stagnation due to the lack of funding and accordingly made their displeasure known. The human and social sciences are a good example in this respect in that only 24 out of the 206 projects funded by Pronex are from that area.

Sectoral Funds

The fact is that the funding provided by Pronex, the larger of the two projects mentioned above, has proved disappointing for the same reasons that the FNDCT had had to face. The funding of agencies continued to suffer from fairly severe budget restrictions. Figure 2 clearly shows the instability of the Treasury as a source of funding for S&T in Brazil.

In 1999 the government launched its sectoral funds. These funds are financed by means of levies on the income of privatised sectors, royalties and taxes on imported technology. In other words, the funding resources are no longer dependent on traditional sources of budgetary revenue. All the sectoral funds, apart from the fund relating to telecommunications which is managed by the Ministry of Communications, are grouped within the FNDCT. Finep and CNPq share the task of managing the funding of projects. Infrastructure and running costs are funded by the Finep and scholarships by the CNPq.

Figure 2. **Federal government expenditure on S&T, 1991-2002**

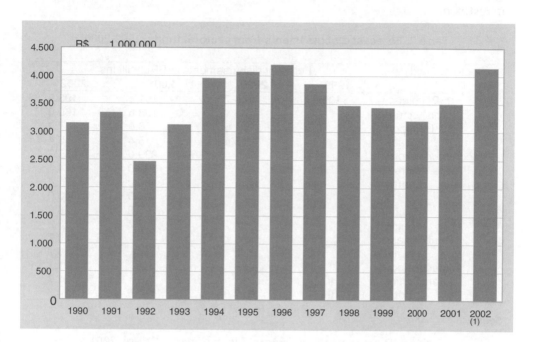

1 – Budget Act
Source: MCT, 2002.

Research and other activities financed by the sectoral funds are aimed at eliminating bottlenecks in the sector from which each fund draws its finance. Funding is allocated on the basis of calls for tender awarded by the management committees of each fund. These committees are made up of representatives of the government, the industrial sector concerned and the scientific community.

Table 2 provides a list of the sectoral funds created and projected disbursements over the period 1999-2000, while Table 3 shows the situation in 2001. Comparison of forecast spending with the sums actually disbursed show that funding revenue had been overestimated. Disbursements by all funds as a whole amounted to slightly over a third of the amount that had been forecast for 2001. More or less the same outcome is expected in 2002 as a result of the recent reappearance of the Brazilian fiscal crisis.

At all events, the sectoral funds have brought a major increase in funding for research. Data regarding the CNPq show that between 1999 and 2000, the amount invested in aid for research more than doubled from BRL 50 million to

BRL 102 million (www.cnpq.br). There was similar increase in infrastructure investment.

Table 2. **Forecast disbursements from sectoral funds, 1999-2000**

Sectoral Funds	Forecast disbursements in BRL millions			
	1999	2000	2001	2002
Petroleum	109.4	245.7	151.1	193.9
Infrastructure		45.1	138.6	160.0
Transport		1.6	8.0	7.9
Space		5.4	5.4	5.4
Telecommunications			239.0	255.3
Verde-Amarelo			192.0	214.1
Energy			80.0	71.4
IT			44.0	40.0
Water			26.8	28.3
Mining			2.7	3.2
Agribusiness				50.7
Health				50.7
Biotechnology				21.7
Aeronautics				21.7
Total	**109.4**	**297.8**	**887.6**	**1 124.3**

Source : MCT, 2002.

Table 3. **Disbursement of sectoral funds (Finep + CNPq), 2001**

Sectoral Fund	Contracts awarded		Completed
	Projects	BRL millions	BRL millions
Petroleum	359	104.4	116.6[1]
Infrastructure	98	157.2	74.1
Verde-Amarelo1	232	152.3	57.5
Energy	316	69.2	52.5
Mining	25	5.6	2.3
Water	123	23.7	20.6
Total	**868**	**512.4**	**323.6**

[1] Includes values for 1999 and 2000.

Source: www.finep.gov.br

Public Universities and Research

The effort undertaken in the 1970s favoured the institutions that were the best prepared to take advantage of the investment. At the time, the public higher education sector accounted for approximately 50% of the student body and almost all doctoral students in the country[31]. This explains why science infrastructure was located in the public university sector where there is a very large group of federal universities.

An analysis of the research groups inventoried by the CNPq demonstrates this dominance. In the latest version of the Directory of Research Groups -- 2002[32], there were 268 institutions and 15 158 groups inventoried (see Table 1). The ten largest institutions, accounting for less than 4% of the total, were responsible for approximately 36% of the total number of groups and 40% of the total number of post-doctoral researchers. Of these ten institutions, all of which are public, three are universities in the São Paolo state system and the others are federal universities.

It is therefore hardly surprising that the public universities were well placed to benefit from the new forms of research funding arrangements, resulting in a concentration of research capacities in terms of both infrastructure and research staff.

The example of the petroleum fund, the CT-Petro, provides a clearer insight into this process of concentration. CT-Petro was set up at the end of 1999 with the aim of maintaining growth in the oil and natural gas sector by raising output and productivity, reducing costs and prices and by improving product quality and the quality of life of consumers. The fund was financed through oil royalties whose payment is managed by the National Petroleum Agency (ANP).

According to the Finep report on disbursements by sectoral funds, in 2001 (www.finep.gov.br) the CT-Petro approved 359 projects, of which 167 under the "order to firms" sub-programme. This sub-programme is intrinsically institutional in that it is directed more towards research groups and laboratories than towards individual researchers. The funding covers operating costs (technology scholarships, laboratory equipment, travel expenses, etc.) and investment in buildings and equipment.

The 167 projects secured funding of around BRL 40 million and involved 30 institutions. Merely three institutions (UFRJ, the Federal University of Rio de Janeiro; PUC-Rio, the Pontifical University of Rio de Janeiro; and the UFRGS, the Federal University of Rio Grande do Sul) were responsible for projects that accounted for 49% of the total funding provided under the sub-programme, which reflects a major concentration of resources at both the inter-institutional and intra-institutional levels given that the Chemistry, Geology and Engineering faculties are those that are best placed to take on projects seeking solutions to bottlenecks in the oil sector.

If we take the two federal universities mentioned above, it may be noted that the funding provided for projects from the CT-Petro fund is almost twice the amount of investment that had been possible in 2001 from budget resources (see Table 4). While these new financial resources are welcome, they nonetheless bring new challenges for institutions in terms of the internal consistency and trajectory of teaching activities and institutional research.

There are therefore new challenges facing the research managers who must now cope with not only a lack of funding but also inequalities between institutions. Better insight into the response capacity of the structures that have been put in place for the management of university research at the institutional level can be gained from a case study of one of the best performing universities in Brazil, namely the Federal University of Rio Grande do Sul – UFRGS.

Table 4. **The three largest institutions in terms of the CE Petrol "Order to firms" sub-programme, their share in total funding and their budgetary investment in 2001**

| Institutions | CT-Petro – order to firms – 2001 | | | Execution of 2001 budget[1] |
	Value – BRL thousand	Share of total --%	∑%	∑ investment[2] -- BRL thousand
UFRJ	9 409	23.66		3 134
PUC-RIO	6 588	16.57	40.23	
UFRGS	3 551	8.93	49.16	4 447
Total	19 548			7 581

1. Data are solely available for federal public universities; PUC-RIO is a private establishment.

2. New buildings and purchases of equipment.

Source: www.finep.gov.br and www.mec.gov.br/spo/custos

Research Management at the UFRGS

UFRGS was established in 1934 through the amalgamation of isolated faculties and institutes into a single institution. The earliest facilities date from the end of the 19th century, such as the Pharmacology Faculty of the School of Engineering. The UFRGS currently has around 27 000 students, of which 19 000 enrolled on Master's courses and 8 000 doctoral students. Over the past ten years growth in the number of doctoral students has outstripped the number of enrolments on Master's degrees. Between 1998 and 2001, for example, the number of Master's degree students has risen by 18% while the number of doctoral students has increased by 27%.

The main sources of information about university research are the Directory of research groups mentioned above and the assessment of CAPES programmes. The latest edition of the Directory of research groups ranks the UFRGS in fifth place with 489 groups and 2 021 researchers, of which over 70% hold doctorates. The breakdown of groups between the major fields of science (natural sciences, life sciences and humanities) is more or less the same for all groups, as it is for those managed by the UFRGS, which shows that there is no particular specialisation within the university in that the distribution of research groups reflects the national average[33]. As a general rule, research groups are integrated into PhD teaching programmes and therefore another measurement of their performance can be found in the assessment of doctoral programme teaching carried out by the CAPES. The CAPES assessment[34] ranks programmes on a scale of 1 to 7, as in the UK system. A mark of 6 or 7 corresponds to teaching which is of an excellent standard and which, in addition, is of international significance. A mark of 5 indicates teaching which is of excellent quality but which does not have any further significance at the international level. A mark of 1 is awarded to new teaching programmes. The UFRGS scores well in this assessment in that out of the 64 doctoral programmes offered by the University, 58% have been awarded scores of 5 to 7, compared with a national average of merely 33%.

Since its founding the University has had close links with regional society. It should be borne in mind that the initial academic units within the University were the Pharmacology Faculty and the School of Engineering, that is to say training courses designed to meet technical needs. Such interaction with the local community has led to the commercial cultivation of oats in the State of Rio Grande do Sul, innovations in the local mechanical engineering and plastics industries and also quality control procedures for exports of chicken meat. Some 300 contracts a year are signed with firms, a large proportion of which relate to co-operative research and training programmes.

This has not meant that basic research has been neglected, however. Technology transfers have profited from feedback from basic research carried in the University's laboratories. Biochemistry, physics, earth sciences and genetics are all internationally recognised areas of excellence[35] within the University.

Two types of organisational structure have been put in place to manage the research activities of the UFRGS. One is a collegial system and the other an executive one. The collegial structure is typical of the governance of the University: there are research commissions in all 27 academic units which make up the institution, the chairs of these commissions meet in the research chamber and representatives of this body are members of the Council for teaching, research and out-reach[36]. This organisational structure is responsible for all internal standards and for the approval of research projects (which must first be approved by the relevant academic unit). While on the one hand the decision-making process is fairly slow, on the other hand the decisions taken are final. The executive is represented by the Vice-Presidency for Research, Propesq[37], established in 1996. Propesq originated in the Research Support Department of the Vice-Presidency for doctoral studies and research, itself established in 1986, which provides an indication of the relatively recent nature of the management of research activities.

Propesq manages research activities through programmes such as the Scientific Induction Programme, the Scientific Induction Salon, the Research Support Programme and the Scientific Journal Publishing Programme. The Scientific Induction Programme and its annual Salon are very important components of the research/teaching system, not only because they bring Master's students closer to the research sector but also because they act as a magnet for new doctoral students. A survey of 1 600 participants in the two Induction Salons and the National Science Induction Day in 1998 and 1999 revealed a high propensity among students to enrol on Master's and doctoral courses[38]. The programme currently has over 1 700 scholarship holders, funded either out of the University budget or by agencies such as the CNPq, the main source of funding, and the Research Support Foundation run by the government of the State of Rio Grande do Sul.

The other Propesq programmes are mainly funded from the UFRGS budget. These activities clearly complement the research projects funded by agencies (Finep and CNPq) and firms. Propesq therefore pursues two lines of approach, one geared towards the implementation of its internal programmes and the other towards encouraging the award of research funding that will allow this activity to continue to develop smoothly.

Propesq programmes play an important long-term strategic role. Even though the funding of such programmes accounts for merely a fraction of total research funding, it makes it possible to identify research talent among scholarship students starting out on their studies and allows provides support for research groups during their period of consolidation or when their sources of funding become precarious. The funding activities relating to the promotion of research consist of theme-based conferences, forecasting efforts and participation in various fora on science, technology and innovation, among others. In connection with the latter activities, Propesq works in partnership with the Secretariat for Technological Development (Sedetec), established in 2000.

Sedetec has the status of a Vice-Presidency and is responsible for all activities relating to the application of research findings and the creation of new enterprises on the basis of university research. Since the early 1990s, the UFRGS has set up S&T nurseries, drawn up internal standards on the supply of services to enterprises and on the protection of intellectual property, and implemented programmes to promote entrepreneurship, among others. Before the creation of Sedetec, these activities were dispersed within the University's organisation chart and, as a result, were not readily visible. Transferring promotional activities to a single unit allows far more pertinent dialogue between research activities and activities relating to the transfer of technology, whilst ensuring that such transfers are not carried out by individuals but by the institution.

The new research funding structure described above requires the UFRGS to revamp its research management strategies, which in light of the results obtained have proved to be highly successful. The creation of Sedetec is part of this redevelopment, which in the short term will necessarily involve the entire University given that the new challenges are far greater now they have ever been at any time in the past.

New Challenges and the Quest for Answers

The introduction of sectoral funds has brought at least three types of pressure to bear on teaching and research institutions: the first relates to unplanned investment; the second to the concentration of funding within a limited number of academic units; and the third to the very management of research.

Decisions regarding which new investment to finance from the fund are taken with reference to each individual research and development project. The sole exception is the infrastructure fund (CT-Infra) which is designed to provide solutions to infrastructure bottlenecks within institutions and whose proposals must necessarily be approved by the university councils.

The increased amount of funding available for research has been matched by a commensurate increase in investment. University laboratories have taken the opportunity to renew their equipment and facilities independently. Unless investment is properly co-ordinated, there is a danger that an institution may be over-equipped in certain areas, thereby generating unexpected operating costs (laboratory technicians, consumables, maintenance contracts, etc.). These costs will arise at the end of research projects, *i.e.* after the average 24 months that projects last, and will have to be met by institutions whose budgets are usually inelastic.

Among the "competitive" universities, *i.e.* those which are most able to give a positive reply to calls for tender, the increased research funding in certain scientific areas offers the prospect, given the sectoral nature of funds, of a consolidation of the trend towards wide differentiation between academic units within institutions. At one end of the spectrum there are wealthy units, *i.e.* those whose capacities put them in an advantageous position with regard to calls for tender, which are in the process of improving their conditions of competitiveness; while at the other end there are "poor" units whose research capacities either have not been dovetailed into the needs of the industrial sectors concerned by the sectoral funds or are not yet in a position to be competitive. Improvements to the material and operating conditions of laboratories in the latter category of university will depend solely on the budgetary resources of the university, given that almost all the available research funding is concentrated within the sectoral funds and that there are no compensatory programmes.

Sectoral funds are typically financial instruments aimed at applied research and innovation. Given that sectoral funds are practically the sole source of major research funding, there is a strong movement towards the abandonment of basic research in favour of applied research. Before, research group used to pass off basic research as applied research in order to meet the conditions of funding. The difference at the moment lies in the involvement of representatives of industrial sectors in the preparation of investment plans and the assessment of projects, which precludes such behaviour on the part of researchers. Research groups financed by sectoral funds, in seeking to improve their operating conditions, will try to do more of the same thing (that is to say applied research on commission) and to do it better, thereby securing more contracts and more funding. Institutions, on the other hand, have to plan in the long plan and on all fronts. Managing university research is now a necessary and unavoidable means of avoiding the dispersal of the capacity to generate new knowledge.

University institutions are started to acquire better insight into the impact that the change in research funding has on their mode of operation. For the time being, reactions are highly mixed. The history of each university brings its full weight to bear on the choice of institutional strategies. As a general rule, the newer universities have a greater chance of having a more institutionalised form of decision-making process, whereas the older universities, formed from isolated faculties and schools, find it harder to draw up an institutional strategy. Given that the older universities are also the largest and most efficient ones (as may be seen in the examples of the UFRJ and UFRGS), and therefore those which have been most affected by the change in funding arrangements, the problem of putting together institutional responses to the challenges posed has become a major concern not only for university managers but also for those responsible for industrial, scientific and technological policies at national level.

REFERENCES

Blanpied, W. (2001) "Inventing US science policy". www.nsf.gov. 15/12/2001, p. 11.

CNPQ. Site www.cnpq.br

FINEP. Site www.finep.gov.br

INEP. Censo do Ensino Superior de 2001. www.inep.gov.br.

Lahorgue, M. (2002) « Le financement public de la recherche et les réponses institutionnelles: le cas du Brésil ». In Conférence Générale IMHE 2002, Paris.

Martin, B. (2000) "Matching societal needs and technological capabilities: research foresight and the implications for social sciences". Sussex: SPRU, 2000. Electronic WP n° 60. p 16.

MCT (2001). Ciência, tecnologia e inovação. Brasília: MCT, 2001. 264 p.

MCT (2002). Palestra do Presidente da República. www.mct.gov.br 30/05/2002.

MEC. Site www.mec.gov.br

Noll, R. (1998) (org.). Challenges to research universities. Washington: Brookings, 1998. p. 217.

Schwartzman, S. (org.). Ciência e tecnologia no Brasil: política industrial, mercado de trabalho e instituições de apoio. Rio de Janeiro: FGV, p. 371.

UFRGS. Site www.ufrgs.br

A HEI WITH ENTREPRENEURIAL ORIENTATION
UNIVERSIDADE DE AVEIRO, PORTUGAL

Maria Helena Nazaré

Introduction

This case study, containing information on research management at the University of Aveiro, Portugal, was developed as a contribution to the OECD/IMHE Project on University Research Management.

The study was developed taking into account the guidelines and issues delivered by the working group in charge of the project. According to those guidelines the perspective adopted for this document should aim to provide an insight to the problems faced by the University of Aveiro, the strategies adopted, implementation plans and unsettled issues.

For purpose of clarity the information was organised as follows: the first section contains a brief presentation of the University of Aveiro, its origins, its organisation and some overall figures, providing the background for the subsequent analysis. The second section is focused on policy and strategic issues on research management, ranging from the definition of main objectives, to the specific organisation for research and to the balance between individual and institutional decision-making. The third section deals with the provision and allocation of resources for research, in terms of research staff, support staff, equipment and funding. The fourth section concerns evaluation of research activities and the use of evaluation results by the institution. The final section deals with research results, their protection, dissemination and exploitation.

The University of Aveiro

The University of Aveiro, founded in 1973, is a relatively new institution. Since its beginnings a strategy of close interaction among teaching, research and response to societal needs, innovation and regional integration has been developed.

Almost 30 years after its creation the mission of the University of Aveiro may be stated in the following terms "To create knowledge, expand access to knowledge, for the benefit of People and Society, through research, teaching and cooperation." (in Development Plan 2000-2006).

One of the most visible aspects of this strategy concerns the areas chosen for education and research. Teacher training, electronics, ceramics and environment were among the first domains developed at the university. The evolution of the university has lead to the development of new areas such as music, new communication technologies, or, more recently, health sciences and social sciences.

The University of Aveiro is organised among Departments, which are the main organic units that carry teaching activities. Internal organisation and management of staff and resources is now based on 17 Departments, of various sizes.

At present the University of Aveiro offers a wide range of undergraduate and post-graduate programmes, in different areas such as engineering, science, arts, business administration, economics and planning, education, communication and fine arts. Research and services provided by the University also involve other domains and competencies.

There are over 8 200 students enrolled in 36 undergraduate programmes, and over 1 000 post-graduate students in 60 masters, PhD programmes and specialization courses.

University missions are carried out by over 710 teachers and researchers, 57% of which have a PhD, and about 440 administrative and support staff (figures from late 2001).

In physical terms the University of Aveiro has been developed as a single-site campus, integrating all the facilities for teaching, research, co-operation and administrative issues.

The University of Aveiro also seeks to promote polytechnic education, and it is one of the few Portuguese universities with an integrated project for this area. The objective is to respond to an increasing demand for diversified courses of shorter duration, geared towards the professional requirements of the region and the country. At present the project includes the Águeda Higher School of Technology and Management (created in 1997), the Aveiro Higher Institute for Accountancy and Administration and the Aveiro Higher School of Health.

The remainder of this document will only deal with university-based research.

Research organisation, policy and strategic issues

The overall goal of the research policy of the University of Aveiro is to achieve excellence, according to international standards, in all the research areas developed at the university.

The current status of research activities within the university is not uniform: some research units already present a high-quality record, while others have not yet reached the above mentioned objective. However, it is necessary to distinguish between mature research units and research units in their early development stages, having different scientific productivity and demanding different resources.

Institution-wide strategies are therefore conceived taking into consideration the specificities of the different research units. Some of the most relevant strategic issues are the definition of research domains, staff recruitment and development policy, the availability of adequate infra-structures and scientific equipment, funding and evaluation.

These issues are dealt with in the following sections.

Research management structure

To better understand the decision-making process at the University of Aveiro a brief description of the research management structure is required.

The organisation of research activities has significantly changed in mid-1990s in response to a new research funding model, implemented nation-wide by that time. It is thus necessary to give an account of the major features of the previous system, the main changes introduced by the new system and the associated motivations.

From the beginning of the University, research activities were primarily organised within the departments and therefore there was a close match between research and education units. Each department organised its own research activities, often through the setting-up of several research teams, each one focusing on a specific area of knowledge. Allocation of resources was usually made by a two-step procedure: global allocation to departments, and intra-departmental allocation of resources. The later was of the responsibility of departmental management and coordination structures.

In mid-1990's there was a reorganization of the public research funding system in Portugal, introducing the concept of research units and the use of external evaluation of research activities for the definition of funding amounts.

A research unit should have well defined research topics and objectives, and should congregate researchers from the fields required to pursue those objectives. Membership to a research unit is, therefore, no longer dependent on institutional affiliation.

The funding model includes periodic (annual) reporting of activities and external evaluation (triennial) of all the funded research units. The panels for external evaluation are organised by major areas of knowledge and usually include a majority of foreign experts, so that quality assessment based on international standards is ensured.

Access to this funding programme is initially based upon proposals from research teams and, thereafter, is based on the results of the evaluation of funded research units. In section *"Evaluation of research activities"* more information is provided on the funding and evaluation procedures.

This model was seen, within the University of Aveiro, as a challenge that must be met in order to secure funding for research activities, but also as an opportunity that could enable a significant change in the organisation of research teams and, indeed, in the overall organisation of research.

Through the analysis of existing capabilities a first set of 15 research units was initially set up, in 1994. Throughout this process, with a very large degree of initiative from individual researchers, choices were made concerning the scientific scope of research units and in terms of individual affiliation to a specific research unit.

The set-up of research teams based upon research objectives promoted, in many cases, the crossover of the traditional departmental boundaries, therefore increasing a multidisciplinary and interdisciplinary approach, key elements for the advancement of many of the areas of expertise in the University of Aveiro, such as the cases of Environmental Sciences and Materials Science and Technology.

The resulting units had no longer a close match with the departmental structure, co-existing units with members from several departments, units where almost all the members are affiliated to one single department and even researchers that develop research activities without being integrated in any research unit. This change in the structure of research teams lead to a situation where education structures are mainly of departmental base while research structures may have both supra-departmental and intra-departmental nature, depending upon the cases.

As a consequence, former research management bodies at departmental level and institution-wide level had limitations in terms of research coordination and management of resources.

The need for a new model for the co-ordination of research activities was acknowledged and a new unit, at intermediate level, was created within the University of Aveiro: the Research Institute. This institute has the role to promote, coordinate and support research activities. Main decisions are to be taken by the Council of the Institute of Research, composed by the heads of the Research Units and the Vice-Rector for Scientific Affairs. This structure thus provides a platform of discussion and striving towards an harmonious development of research and innovation within the University.

Apart from providing guidance on funding opportunities and partnerships, both at national and international levels and providing support to administrative work of the units, the research institute also plays an important role in direct support to research activities through the implementation of internal funding programmes. Furthermore, the Research Institute has functions of liaison with external scientific governing bodies.

Therefore, the current policy and management structure for research includes the Scientific Council, the Rectorate, the Research Institute and the Research Units.

This system, while maintaining a large degree of freedom within the research units, in terms of definition of specific objectives and strategies, enables an overall coordination required to identify and to tackle the most significant common issues, and to optimise the allocation and use of financial and material resources.

Creation of research units and promotion of research is specific scientific domains

As previously mentioned, there has been an evolution of the research areas in the University of Aveiro. Early choices were made based upon perceived needs for education and research in new domains, at national level, and specific needs and interaction potentialities at regional level. In some cases these needs were matched by existing skills in the university staff, while in other cases there has been an active policy to support the development of new areas.

The creation of research units in 1994 was based on previous research expertise and lead to the creation of units in the following areas (named accordingly to the groupings used by national science bodies): language sciences, education sciences, earth & space sciences, mathematics, electronic engineering and computing, materials sciences & engineering, chemistry, marine sciences and physics.

The selection of new areas to foster is the result of an approach combining bottom-up and top-down strategies, meaning that initiatives from teachers/researchers and challenges and opportunities identified by higher management levels both play an important role. As a result of these approaches new research units were created on 1996/97 in biology, arts, mechanical engineering and management.

Another recent development, concerning thematic priorities, was the decision to promote, both in teaching as well as in research, the area of health sciences & technologies. The decision was supported by a feasibility study that put into focus the national need for higher-education specific courses related to health & health technologies, the importance of coupling education activities with research activities and existing know-how within the University in areas such as electronics and instrumentation applied to medicine, physics and biology. This lead to an integrated programme, including the development of a new department and the creation of the Aveiro Higher School of Health.

In 2002 two new research units were proposed. One unit is focused in Optimisation and Control, and originates in the division of the existing unit in Mathematics and Applications. This separation will enable an increase in coherence within the former and the new research unit. Another unit is in Innovation and Competitiveness of the Territory, resulting from changes in the objectives and composition of previously existing units. Both of these changes are geared bottom-up, this is from an internal discussion process of the members of the units.

A piece of legislation in 1999, on the legal framework for research institutions, created a new institutional setting: the so-called Associate Laboratory. The creation of such laboratories requires a high degree of scientific merit, recognized through external evaluation, together with the capability to contribute to the achievement of national science and technology policy' objectives, in a qualified and efficient way. These laboratories will receive long-term funding (up to 10 years), for the attainment of specific objectives under a defined time-frame. Evaluation includes a mid-term assessment of the fulfilment of objectives. These institutions are to be formally consulted by government for the definition of programmes and instruments of national science and technology policy.

The characteristics defined for the Associated Laboratories make them an important strategic option for the University of Aveiro, to secure long-term funding for research, instead of the usual short-term or medium-term prospects coming from project or research unit funding. This will enable a thorough development in terms of personnel, equipment, support and overall research activity.

Taking into account the fact that the network of Associate Laboratories to be created requires high-quality research, and is intended to be geographically and thematically comprehensive, there was a need to decide upon which University of Aveiro research areas could fulfil the requirements.

An internal analysis based on the existing expertise and on the recognition of very high quality level in some domains, such as material sciences and technologies, environment and telecommunications, lead to the submission of three proposals, one in each of the above mentioned areas. The definition of candidate areas and the interaction with the funding bodies was mainly driven by university top management, with support of senior researchers in charge of the detailed planning and internal discussion within each area.

From the submitted proposals two have already been approved. In materials sciences and technologies the Centre for Research in Ceramics and Composite Materials was created. The core of this centre is composed of two existing research units, who were merged to a large extent: the research unit in ceramic materials and the inorganic chemistry and materials centre. The other approved laboratory is the Telecommunications Institute, which groups research teams based on three different institutions from Lisbon, Aveiro and Coimbra.

Resources for research

This chapter deals with the provision and allocation of resources to research activities, including research staff, support staff, equipment and facilities, and funding.

Research and teaching staff

The three main components of the University's mission, research, teaching and cooperation, are largely developed by the same people, since the UA has not a significant body of full-time senior researchers. Teachers/researchers are, additionally, involved in management and coordination bodies.

This fact, although with some value for the integration of research, teaching and knowledge-transfer, presents serious drawbacks including severe time constraints and dispersion of attention into an increasing number of tasks.

Of greater concern is the fact that senior researchers are devoting an increasing amount of time to managerial and administrative functions, instead of an increasing scientific leadership.

This problem is not unique to the University of Aveiro, and is closely linked to the legal framework regarding higher-education teachers and higher-education institutions in Portugal. A need for the revision of the legal provisions has been well acknowledged by all the stakeholders, but the definition and approval of new rules has proved to be a very slow and controversial process. Measures increasing flexibility in staff management, specifically concerning the allocation of teaching and research time, would be warmly welcomed. This issue remains unsettled, and is one of the most significant obstacles for a more efficient management of human resources.

The allocation of teaching and managerial tasks remains primarily a departmental responsibility, without the interference of scientific management and coordination bodies. As has already mentioned been mentioned, research functions frequently cross departmental boundaries, making an integrated staff management more difficult.

Moreover, the recruitment of teachers/researchers is closely linked to the need for teaching staff, based upon alumni/teachers ratios. The proposal for new recruitments is based at the departmental level, and submitted to coordination bodies and to top management for approval. The selection of candidates is mainly based upon scientific merit, but the recruitment process is not essentially driven by research needs.

The creation of a full-time research body might contribute to promote research quality and intensity, but faces severe financial constraints. In fact, while teacher personnel cost is directly met by governmental funding, providing that staff numbers are below a pre-established ceiling, research staff is not funded in the same mode.

To minimize these problems the University of Aveiro has been adopting staff related measures to pursue the defined objectives and strategies.

In order to support the policy for further development of areas of research excellence and to promote the development of new areas, a programme for the attraction and recruitment of researchers with very high qualification was set up in 2000. Under this programme contracts of up to 5 years can be signed.

This programme lead to the recruitment of five researchers, over the last two years, in areas such as materials sciences, earth sciences, bioengineering, Asian studies and higher education studies.

On the other hand, temporary research positions may be allocated by research units, based upon their own strategy and fund management. Some research funds, both internal and external, may be "earmarked" for fellowships. This recruitment by research units is an important instrument for the implementation of each unit strategy, and mainly includes post-doctorate fellowships. The selection process is geared by the research unit, without interference of departmental levels or higher management levels.

Another relevant issue concerning research staff is the creation of the Associate Laboratories mentioned in the previous chapter. The contractual arrangements for the associate laboratories of the University of Aveiro will enable the creation of a stable body of full-time researchers in the specific areas of action of those structures.

Another internal arrangement undergoing discussion is a change on the academic calendar. Proposals for the reduction of the teaching and examination terms may enable an increased concentration on research, cooperation activities or dissemination of results in the corresponding freed time. Such a decision must be taken by the Pedagogic Council, and a consensus has not yet been reached.

Infra-structures and equipment facilities

A significant part of the major equipment was acquired in early 1990's through the national funding program Ciência. At that time, research organisation was still departmental-based and therefore acquisitions were made according to specific departmental strategies. Most of the research equipment of the University of Aveiro remains located in, and is managed by the departments.

The organisational change into research units lead to some unclear or even, at times, conflicting situations between the new units and the departments. Equipment and support staff is still allocated to departments, so that their use requires an understanding between departments and research units.

The use of equipment and facilities is now usually based on formal or informal agreements. In the case of shared interest equipment there are internal procedures concerning availability of operating time and costs associated to the use of the equipment.

Some specific costly equipment of shared interest among research units is managed by a central unit created for that purpose: the Central Analysis Laboratory (LCA). This functional unit provides analytical services for both internal use in the University and to outside customers. The LCA organisation includes a board, administrative staff and technicians which have specialized in the processes and operations related to the installed equipment.

The current problem faced by the University, concerning equipment and facilities, is twofold. On one hand there is a clear need to upgrade the equipment acquired in early 1990s. On the other hand there is a need for new equipment both for the development of new areas as well as for the continuing development of already established areas. This need is especially felt in basic sciences and technologies, and is also closely linked to the need for new facilities specifically designed to accommodate these equipments, and to enable a sound and safe operation.

The renewal of scientific equipment was addressed by the University of Aveiro through an internal funding program, designed in accordance to the specific needs and strategies of the research units. Significant funding was allocated for the purpose of equipment renewal.

Research units must also apply for additional funding for scientific equipment through a competitive national funding programme, in place in 2002.

On the other hand a project for the construction of a "Technological complex", capable of accommodating specific research equipment and activities, was developed and submitted to national funding programmes.

Support staff

Support staff for research activities includes both administrative and management personnel, as well as technicians. The allocation of such personnel is based on the departmental structure while, as already mentioned, research is organised among research units. Therefore co-ordination between heads of department and heads of research units must be ensured.

Technicians are usually in charge of specific instruments and have a technical career. Apart from an initial training period, to acquire the necessary skills specific to the instruments or techniques in use, they may undergo further career development actions. Nevertheless this remains largely to the individual interest and departmental strategy.

Research management functions are allocated to senior researchers. The need for administrative support was recognized by the university and subsequently measures have been taken to tackle this issue.

A specific unit for financial management support was created at central level. This unit deals with all financial matters of research projects, financial reporting included. Work of this unit has proven very valuable, enabling further control and standardisation on financial issues, while diminishing administrative burden on the departmental staff and on the researchers themselves.

On the other hand the informative and support role of the Research Institute is also recognized by the University of Aveiro's scientific community. The institute acts as an interface with external bodies, namely funding organisations, and acts as a local contact point.

There is not a widespread use of staff with specific research management skills. Some research units, especially large ones, could benefit from the use of research management staff. Such personnel, who would work closely with the heads of research units, could contribute to a more efficient and integrated management of research activities, while reducing the time allocated for senior researchers to managerial functions. This issue remains to be addressed.

Funding

Overall funding for research activities has amounted to EUR 20 million in the last 3 years. These figures do not account for most of the research staff, which in reality is also teaching staff, since the salaries are supported by governmental funds. The development of research facilities has not been included in the above figures.

About 80% of research funding comes from external sources. Almost 60% originates from national funding programmes, both from the research unit funding programme and national competitive funding of projects. Most significant programs for project funding have one call per year, opened for all scientific areas. There are also some thematic programmes, on specific priorities defined by the government.

Funding for research units takes into account the number of PhD members of each research unit and the results from the external evaluation procedures, better results meaning increased funding.

Project funding usually consists of two major components: direct costs and indirect costs. Indirect costs are calculated as 20% of direct costs.

About 20% of external funding has been obtained through international competitive funding of research projects, mostly from the European Union Research Programmes. This figure reveals the importance of the internationalisation of research activities pursued by the University of Aveiro.

Internal funding accounts for 20% of the budget used for research activities. Most of this amount concerns funding of research units and is based, since 1999, on development contracts signed between the Research Institute and each research unit. This is part of a strategy to provide units with medium-term funding, to enable them to consistently develop their own research strategy, with the objective to achieve the level "excellent" or "very good" in national evaluation procedures. This is a 3-yearly funding programme based on contracts where general and specific objectives, strategies and resources required to fulfil those objectives must be clearly identified.

Examples of specific programmes developed by the university include post-graduation fellowships, and funding for research projects on health issues.

Evaluation of research activities

While the overall quality goal set for all research units is to achieve the marks of "Excellent" or "Very Good", in the external evaluation, there is also an internal evaluation of research activities.

Both evaluation systems address research as a collective activity, not yet addressing individual research performance.

External evaluation

External assessment of research units is carried out within the scope of the Research Units' Pluriannual Funding Programs. This funding program is a complement to the competitive funding through projects and fellowships, allowing funding at a low, but stable, level. This evaluation process only addresses research work and not the overall academic work of University staff.

Part of the assessment consists of the evaluation of research work for the last 3-year period, concerning scientific achievements, knowledge transfer, training of researchers, organisational aspects, financial and overall management of the research unit. Development plans, projects and funding for the following three years are also considered.

The findings of the research evaluation process are expressed in reports, developed for each research unit assessed, and addressed to the Science and Technology Foundation (FCT), body of the former Ministry for Science and Technology, in charge of the Research Units' Pluriannual Funding Programme.

The reports contain the overall unit rating and the findings that support the evaluation. The guidelines for evaluators state: "Comments and recommendations regarding the Unit activities, research orientation and organisation (extensively explain the Panel's overall judgement of the research unit; make substantive comments and recommendations; address strengths and weaknesses, distinguish sub-areas of activity if appropriate)."

A key feature of the reports is the inclusion of specific recommendations to overcome existing constraints or to further enhance the existing capabilities, enabling the improvement of the research unit development plan. Panel reports and research unit comments are published together and widely distributed.

Results from research units evaluation are used to determine whether or not the unit is eligible for this kind of funding and to determine funding level, better results in the assessment meaning larger funding. The maximum value is allocated to research units rated Excellent or Very Good. Funding is discontinued for units rated Poor.

The top grades, used for the final research unit evaluation are:

Grades	Description
Excellent	Research activities at a high international level, with publications in internationally leading journals.
Very Good	Research activities at a good international level and at a high national level, with publications in internationally leading journals.

In addition, evaluators assess the adequacy of additional Special Programmatic Funding for a restricted number of research units, as a result of specific needs detected during the evaluation process. The main criteria to be used in selecting units to be proposed to this special funding programme are the following:

- Clear needs of operation, maintenance or small equipment funds for carrying out high quality research activity.

- Potential for increased high quality research results and internationalisation.

- Opportunities for increased research performance that could be enhanced by hiring researchers or technicians.

This additional funding must correspond to increases in performance that could not be attained with the funds that the unit has had available in the past or is likely to have in the future. Evaluators' recommendations must include proposals of the appropriate amounts of additional funding, their uses, time span, associated performance expectations and requirements to be included in the corresponding contract.

This evaluation, made usually by foreign experts in the field, has been valuable in assessing the strategy of research units, and their performance according to international standards of good practice. As a result of external evaluation assessments, there have been structural changes in some of the research units of the University of Aveiro, such as merging of former units or splitting into new units, as well as reorientation of research activities and objectives, and the corresponding allocation of resources.

Internal evaluation

Internal evaluation of research consists mainly of the assessment of the execution of the development contracts of each research unit. The main purpose is to enable the allocation of internal funding in order to promote high quality research and to address the problems faced by research units in the development of their own research strategies. The results from the first 3-yearly period are undergoing a thorough assessment.

Previously, research productivity indicators were used, together with research unit size, to allocate internal funding to research units. Such indicators are still used as an input to the allocation of board places to scientific areas.

Research results and cooperation activities

Results from the external evaluation show an improvement in the research performed at the University of Aveiro. In the 1996 evaluation 43% of the research units attained the result of "Very good" or "Excellent" whereas results from the last evaluation (in 1998 for new units and in 1999 for already existing units) showed an increase of the above figure to 69%.

Most of the research results are expressed as papers published in international journals, project reports and seminars. Legal issues concerning intellectual property rights are becoming increasingly important, in particular in research contracts where there are enterprises as partners or end-users. Support is being provided to researchers by a central unit dealing with legal affairs.

Noteworthy is an increase of interest in the patenting of research results in recent years. For that purpose legal and administrative support, concerning the patenting process is provided, and the University provides funding to face patenting costs. GrupUNAVE –Innovation and Services, was created by the University of Aveiro to manage the interaction with the business-world. Support to the patenting process is among the services offered by this institution, which has recently become a regional contact point for theses matters, broadening these activities from university support to private and public sector institutions support.

In spite of the increase in the number of patented results an actual exploitation of this knowledge is still lacking. There is clear room for a more active approach in the dissemination of such results and in the search for partnerships for such exploitation, or for the creation of spin-off companies that could benefit from existing knowledge.

The University of Aveiro is actively involved in promoting cooperation with the private sector on a regular basis for the development of research activities. This activity is not only a supplementary way of financing research but also provides a valuable interaction with society, essential for the development of research and teaching. Cooperation in research and knowledge-transfer depends largely on a bottom-up approach.

RESTRUCTURING AMID CRISIS
HUMBOLDT UNIVERSITÄT BERLIN, GERMANY

Jürgen Prömel

Introduction

Just like the famous scientists Alexander and Wilhelm von Humboldt, the name of Humboldt University, Berlin, is known worldwide. Founded in 1810 as "Berlin University", the institution was called the "Mother of all modern universities". It followed Wilhelm von Humboldt's educational ideal of combining research and teaching. Central to this model is the transfer of knowledge in the spirit of research and the idea of research-oriented teaching. Since then, there have been 29 Nobel Prize winners among scholars who have worked at Humboldt University for part of their scientific career.

Thus, Humboldt University has succeeded in taking a leading position in research performance in Germany. The university's success in continuing or resuming traditional international partnerships and the interest shown by renowned universities from all over the world, clearly show that Humboldt University plays an important role in global scientific exchanges.

The research profile of the university is determined by basic research. It also includes social or ecological questions, and aims towards the economic application of its results. In many areas, research at Humboldt University is internationally acclaimed, for example in medicine, biology, history, cultural and art studies, mathematics, Scandinavian studies and economics.

The quality of research at Humboldt University is not least proven by the EUR 92 million of external funding raised in 2001 by university scientists *i.e.* 20% of the total university budget of EUR 457 million. Although the state continues to be the main source of finance for universities in Germany, third-party funding is gaining in importance: between 1993 and 1999, public funding rose by 2.3%, whereas third-party funding increased by 5.1%.[39]

At present, about 850 research projects at Humboldt University are financed by third-party funding. Of these, more than 120 projects are currently sponsored by trusts and foundations (VW Foundation, German Science Sponsorship Association etc.). Numerous projects have been implemented with the support of the European Union and funding from industry.

Humboldt University's largest sponsor, as for all universities in Germany, is the *Deutsche Forschungsgemeinschaft* (DFG). In its research ranking based on third-party allocation it places Humboldt University 9th of all German universities for the period 1996-1998[40]. The university has been particularly successful in the fields of medicine and biology, where it takes the leading position in Germany. Until now, the largest part of the funding has gone to the Faculty of Medicine – almost 61% of the university's entire third-party expenditure for research in 2001. In the fields of humanities and social sciences, Humboldt University came 2nd among German universities with EUR 18 million.

If these figures are remarkable when considered out of context, they seem almost miraculous when taking into account the fact that this success was virtually all achieved during the last decade. As a university of the former German Democratic Republic, Humboldt University had to struggle for its mere existence after 1989. Starting from scratch, the university had to develop and establish a new profile as a scientific institution as well as start competing for third-party funding.

The following chapter is written as part of an OECD case study project on universities' research management. It aims to trace the policies and measures that account for the progress outlined above and look into factors and concepts that might be applicable in other places. Firstly, the historical settings are outlined, followed by the political, legal and administrational framework that forms the basis of present-day research at Humboldt University.

According to this outline, the four factors on which potential success and future development are based, are discussed in detail: scientists and scientific management, promotion of young researchers, internationalism and university-industry relationships. To conclude, the key factors for research performance are summarised. Conclusions can therefore be drawn from the Humboldt University example for other universities in Germany and around the world.

The Context for University Research

Historical setting

Though one of Germany's most famous universities, Humboldt University is comparatively young. On its foundation in 1810, Wilhelm von Humboldt envisaged a *"Universitas Litterarum"* which would combine teaching and research and provide students with an all-round humanist education. This concept spread throughout the world and initiated the foundation of many universities of the same type over the next century and a half. Wilhelm's brother Alexander pioneered the introduction of many new disciplines in science.

Although the Royal Charity Hospital already existed as a plague hospital in 1710 and later served as the clinical training location for military doctors, a new Faculty of Medicine was set up at the university. However, the proximity, cooperation and competition between these two, and of other medical institutes located in the centre of Berlin, had a strongly stimulating effect on medicine in Berlin. Eventually, the Faculty of Medicine and the Charity merged. Thus, by the turn of the 19th century, the university had developed into a highly productive research institution.

Between 1933 and 1945 the university went through the darkest chapter of German history. The expulsion of Jewish academics, students and the political opponents of National Socialism caused great damage to the university, which had once been renowned as the home of humanitarian thought.

Since 1949, the university has borne the names of its founding fathers Alexander and Wilhelm von Humboldt. Humboldt University was the largest university in the German Democratic Republic to foster intensive research and exchange links with Eastern Europe. Although a number of highly gifted and motivated researchers taught at the university, research and teaching were often carried out under difficult political and financial conditions.

Since the unification, Berlin has maintained three universities. As a result of the problems connected with the unification process, Humboldt University went through an extraordinary process of reorganisation and succeeded in attracting outstanding scientists and scholars from East and West, from Germany and abroad. With the aid of partly external structural and appointment commissions and with much advice and recommendation from groups of experts, Humboldt University developed new academic structures. The content was evaluated, changed and redefined. At the same time, the entire staff was submitted to personal and academic scrutiny. Financial restrictions and structural factors led to a drastic reduction in personnel.

The institutional structure of Humboldt University changed fundamentally in the first half of the 1990s. The university had to close down five institutes. In addition, ten institutes were merged. For example, the Department of Veterinary Medicine was transferred to the Free University of Berlin and the Department of Food Technology to the Technical University. The Departments of Agriculture and Horticulture of Humboldt University and the Technical University were merged and located at Humboldt University. The most far-reaching decision, however, was to integrate the Free University Virchow Clinic into the Charity, Faculty of Medicine of Humboldt University, in 1995.

Following these mergers, the Charity became the largest university hospital in Europe, with about 2 500 beds in 49 clinics, treating roughly 100 000 inpatients and 250 000 outpatients per year with support from 26 theoretical institutes. This merger had a great impact on the character of Humboldt University. It enlarged the medical department to nearly half the university: one third of the university professors, two thirds of the scientific staff and four fifths of other personnel working in the medical department of the university. Within the structure of Humboldt University, the Charity is comparatively independent. It disposes of funds of its own and coordinates its research activities through an independent Division for Research Matters.

As a result of the internal restructuring process, Humboldt University is now made up of eleven faculties and two central institutes. The teaching and research profile of the university covers all the basic academic disciplines in the arts, in social science, cultural science, human medicine, agricultural science, mathematics and natural science. Today, it is more than study courses or course combinations that are offered at Humboldt University. Some courses are new and unique: "The Reformed Medical Curriculum", "Statistic", "British Studies", "Transatlantic Masters", "Master of European Sciences", "Polymer Science", "International Health", "Gender Studies" and "International Agricultural Sciences". 37 655 students enrolled for this wide range of courses for the winter term 2001/02, of which 11.9% from abroad. At present, 417 professors work at Humboldt University.

Political, legal and administrational framework

In Germany, universities are state institutions, *i.e.* they are financially, politically and legally supervised by the state. A federal law (*Hochschulrahmengesetz*) provides the framework for tertiary education at the level of the federal government. Its specific interpretation, however, differs from state to state. It is common for the regional states to claim the right to a say in academic matters, though nowadays there is a tendency towards greater autonomy for universities. For this reason, alternative control mechanisms for the quality of research and study have become an important issue.

The environment for universities and scientific research in Berlin is characteristically very vital and heterogeneous, not only due to the huge number of research institutions in Berlin, but also to the efforts of these institutions. The research ranking of the *Deutsche Forschungsgemeinschaft* reflects this activity. Berlin takes the leading position in Germany with a total research expenditure of EUR 275 million for the years 1996-1998.

The development of Berlin's scientific landscape is closely linked to the reunification of Germany, a particularly palpable process in the formerly divided city of Berlin. Compared to other East German universities, Humboldt University was fortunate to come under the prevailing higher education laws of the western state of Berlin. It was therefore able to start its transformation right after the reunification. Subsequently, reforms at Humboldt University became part of the far-reaching structural reform within Berlin's university landscape in the 1990s. The State of Berlin applied a strict policy of austerity together with the reforms that continue to determine conditions for research and science.

In the course of political reforms, the universities in Berlin were given greater autonomy. Here, two aspects proved to be most important for independent university management.

Firstly, since 1997, universities have global budgets fixed by contracts (*Hochschulverträge*). These contracts are valid for three to four years, the present contract expiring at the end of 2004. Hence, despite the severe public deficit of the State of Berlin, its universities can make reliable mid-term plans. This aspect is particularly important, as public universities in Germany do not have an income of their own through tuition fees.

The second important aspect to autonomy is the so-called "*Erprobungsklausel*", a legal paragraph permitting universities to test new models of leadership, organisation and financing to accelerate decision-making processes and increase efficiency.

Humboldt University seized this opportunity and set up a professional university administration in September 2000. Previously, the university had been governed by a dual system typical to Germany, consisting of a President and a Head of Administration (*Kanzler*), one being responsible for academic and overall matters, the other for budget and administration. In contrast to this, the new system comprises an executive board of management with a full-time presidency: the President and four Vice-presidents. This system is so far unique to Germany, each of the Vice-presidents being responsible for his or her own department: teaching, finance, research and international affairs.

The Vice-president for Research is responsible for all questions concerning scientific progress. He supervises the Division for Research Matters of the university. This central unit provides a staff of about 16 persons to support scientists. It is responsible for research funding information and advice for applications, the administration of the third-party budget for fairs and exhibitions, technology transfer, intellectual property rights, support for start-ups and a quarterly published science magazine.

With its excellent academic tradition and after ten years of structural change both within and outside the university, Humboldt University is now in a position to make use of its full potential. Relative autonomy from the state - in decision-making if not financially - and a supportive structure within the university create a framework for excellent research performance.

Research at Humboldt University: Key Factors

Just over ten years ago, Humboldt University began its scientific life anew from scratch. Today, it can be counted among the most successful universities in Germany. The potential success and future development are based on four factors: scientists and scientific management, the promotion of young scientists, internationalism and university-industry relationships. These four key factors will be outlined in the following chapters.

Quality of research: people and management

Personnel policy

Research, and successful research in particular, depends strongly on the human factor, the scientists. In Germany, demands on scientists are twofold: according to Wilhelm von Humboldt's tradition of combining teaching and research, all professors are obliged to do both. In general, professors have a work quota of eight hours' teaching a week alongside their research projects. Even junior professors have to teach four hours a week thereby assuring the transfer of knowledge in the spirit of research and the idea of research-oriented teaching.

After the reunification of Germany, the university had to decide whether to keep or to dismiss former university personnel and the opportunity was seized to make a completely fresh start in science and research. In an attempt to attract the best scientists, the university wanted to ensure a high scientific standard and to be competitive within the State of Berlin as well as in the whole of Germany.

Two additional reasons stood behind the renewal of personnel at Humboldt University: the economic constraint of a decisive reduction in staff as well as the need to replace ideologically influenced areas of research. In an unequalled upheaval, the university dismissed all its academic employees, in order to hire them individually anew.

In December 1990, Structure and Appointment Commissions were set up to work out the new organisational and personnel structure of the departments and to prepare future appointments. In 1992, the commissions were also entitled to evaluate all the scientific staff. Taking professional qualifications and personal integrity into account, the commissions had to formulate recommendations for further employment.[41]

Thus, in the years between 1990 and 1994, 6 000 persons left the university (for very different reasons), whilst 2000 new academic staff were hired. By 1995, the number of staff was almost halved.

This personnel reform was the beginning of the university's scientific future. The large-scale recruitment of new heads of department laid down the foundation for new synergies and methods of interdisciplinary research that account for the progress in research performance. The renewal took place at a time when the mobility of university professors was low in other areas in Germany.

Since then, Humboldt University has fostered this tradition of excellence in personnel. The central issue in the university's personnel policy is still to appoint the best scientists and, naturally, to keep this scientific elite at Humboldt University.

At present, an important initiative to recruit the best scientists is the Harnack Programme for female professors. In Germany, only 9.8% of professors are women; compared to this poor result, Humboldt University has a remarkable share of female professors with 15% of all professors (excluding medicine). The university still seeks to raise this proportion with the Harnack Programme, by which outstanding female scientists of all disciplines can be recommended for a professorship. This year, up to three professorships will be offered with the programme.

Junior researchers are another focus in the strategy to hire the best scientists available. The most prominent initiative recently was the appointment of Junior Professors (see section *"Promotion of junior researchers"*).

Thus, the remarkable results of Humboldt University's research performance can be traced back to a successful recruitment policy, with numbers and quality enforced by unique historical circumstances. With the active pursuit of this policy in future, Humboldt-University seeks to ensure an excellent quality of research and teaching.

Setting scientific objectives

By the mid 1990s, the renewal of staff was complete. A phase then began during which Humboldt University used the newly recruited staff to set scientific objectives. The Collaborative Research Centres (*Sonderforschungsbereiche*) financed by the *Deutsche Forschungsgemeinschaft* were a significant means to sharpening the university's research profile. These centres form a programme of long-term cooperative research in universities and neighbouring academic research institutions. Collaborative Research Centres are designed to enhance the research profile of those universities successful in constituting highly qualified, cooperating research communities in their midst. They are usually located in one place, with special Trans-regional Collaborate Research Centres establishing local and trans-regional networks of interdisciplinary research and material resources in two or three locations. In the humanities, the Collaborative Research Centres have an interdisciplinary approach and promote international cooperation and the internationalisation of research.

The first two Collaborative Research Centres were established at Humboldt University in 1994. Presently, the university acts as coordinator for nine Collaborative Research Centres. In addition, Humboldt- University participates in a further 11 Collaborative Research Centres headed by partner universities. This is a good result considering that there are altogether 299 Collaborative Research Centres in Germany.

The success of the Collaborative Research Centres is mirrored by the development of funding expenditure. In 1993, only shortly after the reunification, only EUR 16 million of third-party funding was spent, but this figure grew significantly over the years. In 2001, third- party funding amounted to EUR 92 million. Of these, 20% was attributed to human and social sciences, 17% to natural sciences, 63% to medicine. The remarkable results of the human and social sciences department at Humboldt University in the DFG research ranking mentioned at the beginning of the chapter reflect the outstanding performance of the School of Business and Economics, which received about 85% of third-party funding for the human and social sciences.

The natural sciences only improved their performance after 1998. The major increase of funding at the science departments was due to the Institute of Physics, which more than doubled its expenses on research funding between 1997 and 1999. The same development is expected at the Institute of Biology, where a new Collaborative Research Centre on "Theoretical Biology" began in 2002.

A recent success story is the Berlin initiative "Mathematics for Key Technologies". This research centre financed by the *Deutsche Forschungsgemeinschaft* brings together the research strengths of the three Berlin universities as well as two non-university research institutes, the Weierstrass Institute for Applied Analysis and Stochastics and the Berlin Konrad Zuse Centre for Information Technology. This new research centre, which began work in 2002, concentrates on modelling, simulation and the optimisation of real world processes and makes Berlin the centre of applied mathematics.

Many current research problems can only be solved by involving several disciplines. A promising example is the Hermann von Helmholtz Centre for Cultural Technology. It brings together scientists from philosophy, art history, cultural science and literature as well as mathematics and computer science with the objective of investigating the interactions between scientific or cultural upheavals and technical innovations. Its innovative approach may serve as an example to other disciplines.

In future, Humboldt University seeks to set scientific objectives by founding several new centres, such as a centre on life sciences combining research in the fields of medicine, biology and chemistry or a centre on the Old World, bringing together historians, philologists and cultural scientists.

Ensuring scientific quality

Within its departments, Humboldt University seeks to enhance the emphasis on research by developing an internal quality and performance culture. The two methods most relevant with this respect are performance oriented budgeting and research evaluation.

The concept of research evaluation was established with regard to the recent internal quality management system at Humboldt University. An integrated concept of internal self-assessment and informed – peer review, the latter carried out with an external visiting committee, was created in 2001 to ensure, monitor and develop the research output and the structure of 35 disciplines at Humboldt University. The first, now completed, assessments were made of three disciplines, which in general coincide with departments. The experience of evaluating the history, chemistry and biology departments has been used to improve the concept and procedure for the assessment of the other

32 disciplines. It is planned to complete the first assessment cycle within the next 5 years.

The major subjects of research assessment are:

1. to evaluate the research output and services in reference to the internal and external research environment, with the objective of strengthening the profile of each discipline by employing a new appointment policy and enhanced facilities and equipment;

2. to set up a reference for output-focused funding and to create individual terms of reference between the university and each department to support future development;

3. to facilitate public transparency of the University's research quality and to use the results for public relations purposes.

In the long run, step by step improvement of the research evaluation concept and its procedures toward best-practices for universities is expected, which will lead to an integrated quality management approach to combine teaching and research evaluation in a single concept.

Furthermore, in 2001, university-wide performance-oriented budgeting was introduced as another incentive to research. This internal system is based in principle on the same criteria as the external performance-oriented budgeting within the State of Berlin. Within Humboldt University, 20% of flexible funds are dealt out to faculties and institutes for basic equipment, 60% are distributed according to performance criteria in teaching and research, another 20% are reserved for innovative projects. 5% of the distributed funds go towards gender mainstreaming measures. The distribution parameters for performance-oriented budgeting correspond to the principal goals of the university. For research, three indicators for performance are taken into account:

- third-party expenditure relative to the average third-party expenditure of each subject in Germany

- number of dissertations and "habilitations"

- internationalisation measured by the number of Alexander von Humboldt Scholars.

Funds for innovative projects in research are available as start-up capital for innovative research, by ensuring basic equipment for research projects and to start research evaluation. It is important to mention that in Humboldt's spirit, both the innovation fund and the performance- oriented budgeting consider teaching and research on equal terms.

These quality measures will ensure the standard of research performance Humboldt University has achieved during the last decade and guide the university to promising new directions of research in the future.

Promotion of junior researchers

The strategy of recruiting the best scientists makes the promotion of junior researchers a key issue for Humboldt University. Placing this policy second on the 12-point programme summarising the main tasks for the term of the presidency's office emphasises the fact that Humboldt University regards this policy as the most important investment in future research talent. The need to identify early the best talents among young scientists is underlined by the fact that, in the coming decade, a great change in generation of university professors will take place in Germany.

Humboldt University has made a variety of efforts to invest in its scientific future: on a basic level, young scientists are supported and supervised in writing their dissertations and "habilitations"[42.] In 1997, just under 400 dissertations were successfully completed. In following years, this number grew to over 500 dissertations a year. The number of "habilitations" completed has continuously increased: in 1997, 58 "habilitations" were completed. In 2001, this number rose to 104[43].

In Germany, doctoral education is traditionally fairly unstructured. It generally relies on a one-to-one basis between the doctoral candidate and his/her supervisor and is subject only to minimal control mechanisms or general quality standards.

However, Humboldt University has been very successful at improving the structure of graduate and postgraduate education. The research training groups financed by the *Deutsche Forschungsgemeinschaft* are a very promising means of graduate education. These groups are institutions established at universities for a limited period and are aimed at promoting postgraduate young researchers. They offer doctoral candidates the opportunity to carry out their work in the framework of a coordinated interdisciplinary research programme supported by several university faculty members. This is intended as an additional means of integrating them into the research activities of the institutions participating in the research training group whilst being supervised by individual advisors. The offer of an accompanying and systematically organised study programme ensures a sound introduction to, and a broader understanding of, the field work being conducted. A special sub-program, international research training groups, aims to encourage bilateral cooperation in research training between German universities and graduate programmes abroad.

In the 1990s, at a very early stage in its reform process, Humboldt University fostered the establishment of these research training groups. With the respectable number of 18 *Deutsche Forschungsgemeinschaft* research training groups, it now takes the leading position in Germany.

A long-term task is to found a Humboldt Graduate School. The aim is to establish an umbrella organisation for all Ph.D. courses at the university to ensure structured Ph.D. programmes and supervision of international standards. A first step in this direction is the International Humboldt School in Berlin Adlershof, with the participation of three non-university research institutes and the WISTA-Management GmbH, a company promoting and managing the Adlershof science park. This graduate school distinguishes itself by an interdisciplinary approach, a set curriculum and business-related modules.

A strong means to promote scientists on the postdoctoral level are career development groups. These groups enable young scientists who are not yet employed at universities to engage in independent scientific work in all disciplines. The sponsoring organisation finances the positions of three junior scientists and universities only have to pay for the support structure. Humboldt University is proud to host seven out of 58 career development groups financed by the VW Foundation, and is the leading university in Germany in this respect. In total, twelve career development groups carry out research at Humboldt University.

The most important step at present to promote junior researchers of a postdoctoral level is the introduction of junior professors. In a pilot project of the Federal Ministry for Education and Research, Humboldt University was the first university in Germany to offer 50 positions as junior professors to promising young scientists. These positions enable young researchers to carry out independent research and teaching after their dissertation. Afterwards, they should be entitled to apply to ordinary professorships without having to write a "habilitation" as was previously requested in Germany.

This approach is completely new in Germany, where traditionally, junior scientists depend on their professors until they themselves become professors. As an innovative project, Humboldt University used the junior professorships to promote female scientists: out of the 40 junior professorships so far offered to successful applicants, 32.5% were given to women. Throughout Germany, the introduction of junior professorships is seen as a big move towards international compatibility and worldwide mobility.

Besides these institutional ways to promote young scientists, there are also some measures of individual support. Both the Division of Research Matters and the university Career Centre offer courses on a range of scientific 'soft'? skills, such as scientific writing, scientific journalism, career development for female scientists and management of third-party funding. In the Division of Research Matters, a specialised counsellor supports junior researchers in the application for grants.

A future project for the promotion of junior researchers will be the foundation of a Humboldt Centre for Junior Research Fellows uniting all career development groups. It aims to offer optimal conditions for scientific work and development to outstanding young researchers. As an institutional and organisational frame with both internal and external mentors, the Centre for Junior Research Fellows aims to foster independence, inter-disciplinarity and the internationalisation of research.

Internationalisation

For a first-class university, international exchange in research, teaching and students is a matter of course. In keeping with its geographical location, Humboldt University has developed close relationships with northern, central and eastern Europe. During the times of the German Democratic Republic, long-standing and intensive research and exchange links were developed with the universities in Eastern Europe and particularly with the former Soviet Union, as well as with institutions in Western Europe and the United States; many of these links are without parallel in Germany.

This network of links has been continuously extended to universities and research centres in other parts of the world, in particular to institutions on the periphery of the western horizon. At present, Humboldt University cooperates with 120 partner universities from all over the world.

This international orientation proves particularly fruitful in the area of student mobility. With just under 600 international exchange students as guests on the Erasmus Programme and 500 Humboldt University students out on Erasmus scholarships in 2000-01 (are there more recent figures?), our university is the first university in Germany regarding both incoming and outgoing students. The Teaching Staff Mobility Programme shows further positive results: with 69 members of staff sent to teach abroad, Humboldt University was the most active university in Germany.

In the area of research, international cooperation flourishes at the level of the faculties and is based on the initiative of individual researchers. In 2001, more than 450 scientists visited from abroad to teach and research at Humboldt University as guests for a period longer than a week.

The Alexander von Humboldt scholars represent a special group of guest scientists. The Alexander von Humboldt Foundation grants research fellowships and research awards to highly qualified scholars and scientists of all nationalities not resident in Germany, enabling them to undertake periods of research in Germany. As they are free to choose their host institution, Alexander von Humboldt scholars document the reputation of universities in Germany. As mentioned above, the number of Alexander von Humboldt Foundation scholars is taken as an indicator for the performance-oriented budgeting of how the individual departments engage in international research exchange.

Between 1997 and 2001, 228 Alexander von Humboldt scholars visited Humboldt University. Regarding their distribution throughout the faculties, one can note the strong initiative of the human and social sciences departments to attract foreign guest visitors receiving just over 56% of scholars. Between 1997 and 2001, and for philosophy, German literature and history, Humboldt University was even one of the top three institutions. On a general level, Humboldt University was also one of the most attractive places for Alexander von Humboldt scholars to stay. Between 1997 and2001, Humboldt University was among their five most popular choices as host institution amongst all German universities.

Other programmes to promote junior scientists also carry an international character. Several of the Humboldt University research training groups are by definition international, such as the Berlin Graduate School of Social Sciences. On the postdoctoral level, the Emmy Noether programme enables young researchers to engage in independent scientific work at an early stage in their career on an international level. This is accomplished over a six-year period involving a research stay abroad and subsequent autonomous research activities at home. At present, there are five groups of scientists working on the Emmy Noether programme at Humboldt University.

In the quest for the best scientists, Humboldt University seeks to recruit international staff. Since the personnel reforms started in 1992, 24 professorships have been successfully offered to international scientists. Of course, one should take into account that this number constitutes only 6.7% of all professors, but the university hopes to improve this figure in the near future. With junior professors, Humboldt University has done much better: out of the 40 positions matched so far, 25% are filled with scientists from abroad.

With regard to EU third-party funding, Humboldt University shows a comparatively low percentage of EU funding with regard to the total research budget. This is due to the specific size of the EU research programmes, which in the past supported mainly more technical or applied research projects. As the 6th Framework Programme provides a broader range of scientific fields, especially in the human and social sciences, and has shifted the support towards more basic research activities, Humboldt University has a good chance to perform better in applying for support from the European Union.

Last but not least, the international aspect will be reinforced by academic representative offices of Humboldt University abroad. In September 2002, such an office was opened in Moscow (is it confirmed now?) and its equivalent in New York opened in October 2002 (confirmed now?). The aim of these representative offices is to increase the international reputation of the university abroad and to strengthen its attractiveness for academic exchange as well as to support networking both for scholars and students. In the area of research, these academic residences will spread the results of research at Humboldt University internationally and support cooperation in research with these countries.

University-industry relationships

The exchange of knowledge and its application to business and industry is a further pillar of research activities at Humboldt University. Collaboration with industry and non-university research institutes takes various forms. The three most important fields of collaboration are joint professorships, the foundation of spin-offs and university-owned companies and, most importantly, the strong involvement of Humboldt University in the Berlin Adlershof science park.

The closest means of collaboration between the university and non-university research institutes is the exchange of scientists. Thus the head of a non-university research institute (or of a department of a non-university research institute) can be made professor at the university. At present there are 16 appointments linking Humboldt University to twelve scientific institutions. In this way, the exchange of knowledge is part of everyday communication. These appointments are mainly in the Faculties of Mathematics and Natural Sciences and in the Faculty of Business and Economics.

Another important vehicle for collaboration is the placement of professors who are partly financed by donations (*Stiftungsprofessur*). Industry or private persons contribute a specific amount of money allowing the university to fund the professor and/or its equipment for a given time. The university is obliged to commit to the follow-up of the appointment. At present, Humboldt University has eight professors funded by donations in the Faculty of Medicine and the Charity, and a further eight in other faculties.

Promising, though less well established, are joint research projects with industry. The reason for this is partly linked to the history of Humboldt University. After the reunification, the economy of the former GDR broke down. Industry in western Germany had at that time long-established ties with universities in West Germany. Therefore, the establishment of new contacts for Humboldt University took place mainly in combination with the appointment of professors from the western hemisphere.

Furthermore, the lack of money from industry is due to the fact that two-thirds of the academic staff works in the field of humanities. It is therefore remarkable that the amount given by industry was increased from EUR 1.4 million in 1998 to EUR 3 million in 2001. This tendency is expected to continue in the coming years. The main reason to support this view is the fact that by 2007 all the Departments for Mathematics and Natural Sciences will move to the Adlershof Science and Technology Park.

In 1991, the State of Berlin took the far-sighted decision of creating a science and technology site in Berlin Adlershof. The Humboldt University enthusiastically joined this venture and made it its strategically most important project to date. Great synergies are expected both for cooperation with industry and for the setting of research objectives between the disciplines within the university.

The science and technology park encompassed a site for Humboldt University, a Media City, a technology park and a residential park with related services and a social infrastructure. The concept envisages the academic teaching of the natural sciences, research and development linked to industrial, media and service companies as well as recreation and housing. This gives Berlin Adlershof a unique position compared with other technological sites. The close spatial and specialist proximity offers diverse opportunities for dialogue.

Today, with approximately 570 small and medium-sized enterprises, Adlershof ranks among the 15 largest science parks worldwide. It has acquired a reputation for its research results, products and services that extends far beyond the borders of Germany. With 13 non-university research institutes and the Departments of Computer Science, Mathematics and Chemistry of Humboldt University there are strong academic partners already on site. The Department of Physics of Humboldt University joined in the spring of 2003.

The close links between science and business provide an ideal setting for the development of new products, new technology and intelligent services. This also applies to the development and testing of forward-looking forms of university teaching, research and further training. One of the first examples of new forms of collaboration originating in the proximity to industry is the establishment of the International Humboldt Graduate School on Structure, Function and Application of New Materials founded in 2001.

Another point of intersection between university and industry, teaching and research in Adlershof is the Ernst Schrödinger Centre, a unique combination of a classical library and a computer and multimedia centre. Here, a modern free-access library, the university computer centre, the multimedia department and recording studios are combined. To date, no other German university has a centre with a similar concept, and even on a worldwide scale there are very few comparable facilities.

But the Schrödinger Centre is not only designed for academic work, but also as a means of communication with non-university research institutes, the small and medium-sized businesses on the site and other organisations. It will be shared by the university, the WISTA-Management GmbH and the Igafa e.V., the Joint Initiative of Non-University Research Institutions in Adlershof.

Berlin Adlershof also provides a sound infrastructure for the setting up of research-related companies to members of the university. The Innovation and Business Incubator Centre (IGZ) offers start-ups, young companies with innovative, technology-driven projects, and companies with fixed-term innovation projects, a broad range of support services including consulting, a technical-organisational infrastructure and adequate premises for start-up and corporate development.

Not only its members but also Humboldt University as a whole are now able to set up companies. Two laws initiated this opportunity: in 1999, universities were offered the right to act as entrepreneurs; in 2002, a law was passed that the rights of an invention were now owned by universities and no longer personally by the inventor.

As a result of these laws, the company "ipal" was founded by the universities of Berlin and the state-owned Bank for Innovation Berlin. Whereas in the past, the results of Humboldt University's academic research excellence were usually disclosed to industry without receiving any adequate recompense, the aim of "ipal" is to protect and to make use of the intellectual property rights of the university. This will further encourage researchers to collaborate with industry and to become equal partners.

A future project is to set up a private limited company to market the University´s research results commercially. This company is expected to be able to act flexibly according to market demands and to be an active partner in cooperation with industry.

Conclusion

Humboldt University was set up as an autonomous institution in a crisis situation in order to facilitate outstanding scholarly and scientific achievements and to promote the debate on established bodies of knowledge for the benefit of society. After nearly 200 years, this legacy still stands. As a prominent home for research, Humboldt University sets great store by the preservation of its range of disciplines and research institutes. It is only through the interaction of the sciences and the humanities, of medicine as well as the social sciences and the arts, which the indispensable inter-disciplinarity can be guaranteed.

During the last decade, Humboldt University has undergone extraordinary development. Completely changing its structure and exchanging much of its scientific personnel, the university managed to reach important goals on the road to a prosperous scientific future: a new team of outstanding scientists and the setting of innovative scientific objectives. This process was based on four factors:

1. a strong emphasis on individual researchers. The strategy to win and keep the best scientists started with the Structure and Appointment Commissions in the early 1990s and continues today to promote young researchers and research evaluation.

2. the identification of future talent in research. The support of young scientists means innovation in research as well as continuous scientific excellence for the future. Humboldt University drives towards this goal with numerous supportive programmes.

3. international cooperation. Humboldt University has long tradition of fostering international contact in teaching and research. This ensures lively scientific exchange as well as up-to-date scientific standards.

4. local networks with industry and research institutes. The Humboldt University is keen to cooperate productively with its scientific, cultural and economic environment for the benefit of its own objectives. Berlin's rich scientific background as well as active support structures make this cooperation fruitful.

Humboldt University has evolved out of the traditional German university system into a modern scientific institution. With many of the strategies outlined in this chapter, Humboldt University is among the first universities in Germany to put reforms into action. However, as outlined in the sections, there are still many projects to ensure scientific success for the future. Humboldt University will continue to pay tribute to its reform-oriented foundation history by planting innovative ideas into study, research and organisation.

NEW WORKING CONDITIONS OF RESEARCHERS: UNIVERSITÉ LIBRE DE BRUXELLES

V. Cabiaux and F. Thys-Clément

Introduction

The University is undergoing major changes, as it is faced with several challenges, whilst the expectations of its partners about the missions it should pursue are rising. It is also undergoing major changes in management and governance methods imposed by financial restrictions from the public sector (F. Thys-Clément, 1995). Consequently, the University as an institution is facing a major paradigm transformation expressed in particular by the notion of "academic capitalism" stressed by the American scholars L. Leslie and Sh. Slaughter (1997).

The French-speaking Belgian universities are in the midst of reorganising the way they operate because they are confronted with financial restrictions brought about by the implementation of budgetary federalism (B. Bayonet and F. Thys-Clémént, 1998) which effects mainly the French speaking community – Brussels.

Our paper deals with the organisational arrangement of contractual research at the (French-speaking) Université Libre de Bruxelles (ULB), the financial volume of which has virtually tripled in the last fifteen years. (R. Tollet, 2002).

The first part of this article will briefly cover the integration of research in Belgium in an international context. The place of the ULB in the Belgian academic landscape and, in particular, that of the Communauté française de Belgique (here after referred to as French speaking community) will then be broached, followed by the specific organisational arrangements of contractual research. The conclusion will underscore the need for a strategic implementation of this modus operandi for the University.

Belgian Research in an international context

A recent study by the Federal Ministry of Scientific Policy (BRISTI – 2001, 2002) summarises the characteristics of research in Belgium by presenting a table with its main indicators for science, technology and innovation, and by comparing it with its main trading partners.

Table 2 reports this work, with a slight change in presentation.

Table 1 shows the ranking of Belgium in comparison to the average values of the EU Member States (15 countries). This ranking was compiled using 1 as the highest value indicator, with 8 as the lowest value.

Table 1. **Ranking of Belgium according to scientific indicators**

	Rank
A. Input indicators of science and technology activities	
Public budget appropriations on R & D *In% of GDP*	7
Public budget appropriations on R & D – Civil R & D *In% of GDP*	5
Public budget appropriations on R & D *In% of total government expenditure*	7
Gross domestic expenditure on R & D *In% of GDP*	5
B. Output indicators of science and technology activities	
Scientific publications *Per 1000 inhabitants*	3
EPO patents – inventor's country *Per 1000 inhabitants*	4
EPO patents – country of filing *Per 1000 inhabitants*	4
USPTO patents – inventor's country *Per 1000 inhabitants*	5

Note: EPO (European Patent Office); USPTO (United States Patent Office); EU15 = Index 100 – Countries compared: Belgium, Denmark, France, Italy, Pays-Bas, United Kingdom, United States, Japan.

Table 2. **Comparison of results obtained in science, technology and innovation (most recent years available: 1997-2000)**

	BE	DE	FR	IT	NL	UK	EU15	US	JP
A. Input indicators of science and technology activities									
Public budget appropriations on R & D (1)	0.58	0.80	0.99	0.58	0.79	0.67	0.74	0.77	0.66
	78	*108*	*134*	*78*	*107*	*91*	*100*	*104*	*89*
Public budget appropriations on R & D – Civil R & D (1)	0.58	0.73	0.74	0.56	0.77	0.44	0.63	0.39	0.63
	92	*116*	*117*	*89*	*122*	*70*	*100*	*62*	*100*
Public budget appropriations on R & D (2)	1.36	1.86	1.96	1.38	1.88	1.85	1.99	2.90	1.80
	68	*93*	*98*	*69*	*94*	*93*	*100*	*146*	*90*
Gross domestic expenditure on R & D (1)	1.98	2.46	2.17	1.04	1.94	1.87	1.85	2.62	2.91
	107	*133*	*117*	*56*	*105*	*101*	*100*	*142*	*157*
Gross domestic expenditure on R & D by companies (1)	1.41	1.63	1.35	0.56	1.06	1.20	1.15	2.01	2.17
Total R & D staff (3)	1.13	1.16	1.23	0.61	1.10	0.95	0.94	-	1.29
Tertiary education in % of the 20 – 29 age bracket	26.2	19.4	25.2	21.6	20.2	22.9	22.7	38.8	20.8
Total number of researchers in companies (3)	0.38	0.34	0.27	0.12	0.23	0.32	0.25	0.59	0.63
C. Output indicators of science and technology activities									
Scientific publications (5)	0.80	0.67	0.67	0.45	1.00	0.96	0.61	0.74	0.48
EPO patents – inventor's country (5)	0.13	0.24	0.12	0.06	0.17	0.10	0.13	0.13	0.13
	131	*110*	*110*	*74*	*164*	*157*	*100*	*121*	*79*
EPO patents – country of filing (5)	0.10	0.22	0.10	0.05	0.24	0.07	0.11	0.09	0.12
	101	*195*	*94*	*49*	*136*	*76*	*100*	*104*	*101*
USPTO patents – inventor's country (5)	0.08	0.12	0.07	0.03	0.09	0.07	0.07	0.31	0.25
	91	*200*	*91*	*45*	*218*	*64*	*100*	*82*	*109*
	114	*171*	*100*	*43*	*129*	*100*	*100*	*443*	*357*
D. Innovation indicators									
Number of people who have started a business in the last three years (6)	2.4	4.7	2.2	5.7	-	5.2	-	12.69	1.26
Informal venture capital, number of people who invested in a start-up created in the last three years by a third party (6)	1.15	3.94	1.91	2.14	-	3.07	-	6.97	1.37
Formal venture capital (1)	0.27	0.13	0.13	0.06	-	0.21	-	5.27	0.22

Note: EPO (European Patent Office); GDP (Gross Domestic Product); USPTO (United States Patent Office); BE (Belgium); DE (Denmark); FR (France); IT (Italy); NL (Netherlands); UK (United Kingdom); EU15 (European Union 15); US (United States); JP (Japan). *in% of GDP, in% of total government expenditure, in% of the working population per 1000 inhabitants, per 1000 inhabitantsper 100 adults*

These tables show that Belgium's ranking varies widely depending on the indicators used. Its best ranking is in terms of scientific publications. The ranking for patents puts the country in the middle of the results obtained for the international sample considered; conversely, in terms of public appropriations on R&D, Belgium occupies the penultimate position.

The French-speaking Université Libre de Bruxelles – a particular case of Belgian University

Belgium is a federal state with several components: the federal state, the language-based communities, and the regions (M. Uyttendaele, 1991). Since 1989, Belgian universities have been run mainly by the Flemish Community and the French-speaking Community. The Belgian population comprises nearly 10 million inhabitants, of whom nearly 40% are part of the French-speaking Community and 60% of the Flemish Community.

B. Bayenet *et al.* (1998) provide a description of how Belgian universities are funded to carry out their teaching mission. Research funding, which comes from the various public authorities, has not been the subject of a full inventory, but rather of several studies, in particular two volumes published recently by the Federal Departments of Scientific, Technical and Cultural Affairs (BRISTI, 2001 and 2002).

We shall discuss the complexity of how research funding is organised by analysing the difficulties encountered by researchers, and the different financing available to the universities.

Development of doctorates in Belgium

There are no official data on the number of doctorates presented in Belgium, the data are based on sources from Flemish and French-speaking universities.

Tables 3 and 4 show developments by field, gender and ratio of number of foreign doctoral candidates, in relation to Belgian students.

A different development in the distribution of scientific and health sciences can be gauged between Flemish and French-speaking universities. Unlike the latter, the Flemish-speaking universities show an increase in dissertations in health sciences.

Figure 1. **Development curve of the number of doctorates per language community**

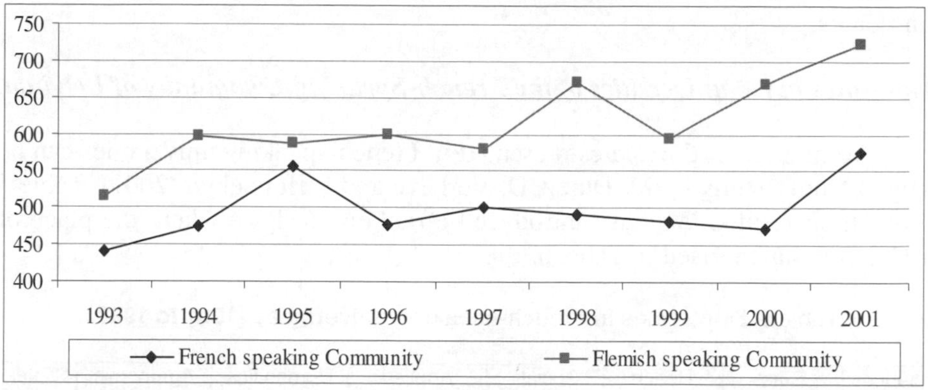

Figure 1 shows the detailed quantitative development in each of the language communities. It is striking to note the comparable production in each of the areas studied in 1995. After that point, a deliberate policy on the part of Flanders led to a considerable increase in the number of doctorates. The French-speaking Community however registered a clear decline from 1995 to 2000, before resuming a more sustained rate in 2001.

Table 3. **Number of doctorates in Flemish-speaking universities**

	1993	1998	2001	1993 – 100 1998	2001
Total	514	672	723	1.30	1.40
% humanities/social%	21.8	20.8	23.9	0.95	1.09
sciences	63.8	56.9	58.1	0.89	0.91
% health sciences	14.4	22.3	18.0	1.54	1.25
% women	27.2	33.2	32.2	1.22	1.18
% foreign nationals	19.5	26.8	25.86	1.37	1.32

Source: Vlaamse Interuniversitaire Raad (VLIR) [Flemish Inter-university Council], compiled I. Beuselinck and J. Verhoeven (1998) – Data produced by VLIR up to 98-99 and by the Departement Onderwijs, Ministerie van de Vlaamse Gemeenschap [Department of Education, Ministry of the Flemish Community] as of 99-00. We would like to thank D. Gilliot for providing us with these data.

Table 4. **Number of doctorates in the French-speaking universities**

	1993	1998	2001	1993 = 100 1998	2001
Total	440	491	575	1.11	1.30
% humanities/ social	25.3	27.1	29.0	1.07	1.14
% sciences	57.0	58.0	57.7	1.01	1.01
% health sciences	17.7	14.9	13.3	0.84	0.75
% women	26.8	32.8	31.3	1.22	1.16
% foreign nationals	37.3	35.6	34.6	0.95	0.92

Source: CREF – Conseil des Recteurs des Universités francophones de Belgique, 2002

In terms of gender, each of the Communities awards more than 30% of degrees to women, and each hosts a large number of foreign doctoral candidates.

Doctorates in the universities of the French-Speaking Community of Belgium

The number of doctorates presented in French-speaking universities can be gauged from a study by M. Durez, D. Verheve and I. Hondekyn (2001). Table 5 shows their results. We have introduced a ranking analysis where the place of the ULB is summarised in Table 6.

Table 5. **Doctorates in French-speaking universities (1991 to 1998**

Sciences	Exact		Health		Socials		Applied		Humanities		Agronomic		Total
	R	N	R	N	R	N	R	N	R	N	R	N	
UCL	2	384	1	231	1	300	1	233	1	232	1	156	1536
ULB	1	528	2	216	2	109	3	78	2	127	3	29	1087
ULg	3	362	3	197	3	72	2	130	3	72	4	0	833
FUNDP	4	175	4	1	5	9	5	0	4	0	4	0	185
UMH	5	84	5	0	4	34	5	0	4	0	4	0	118
FSAGx	7	0	5	0	7	0	5	0	4	0	2	105	105
FPMs	7	0	5	0	7	0	4	73	4	0	4	0	73
FUL	6	3	5	0	7	0	5	0	4	0	4	0	3
FUCAM	7	0	5	0	6	2	5	0	4	0	4	0	2
FUSL	7	0	5	0	7	0	5	0	4	0	4	0	0
Total		1536		645		526		514		431		290	3942

Source: CReF, "Les étudiants et le personnel des institutions universitaires francophones de Belgium. Données statistiques." Data compiled by M. Durez *et al.* (2001). Legend: UCL : Université catholique de Louvain ; ULB : Université libre de Bruxelles ; Ulg : Université de Liège ; FUNDP : Faculté universitaire Notre-Dame de la Paix à Namur ; UMH : Université de Mons-Hainaut ; FSAGx Faculté universitaire des Sciences agronomiques de Gembloux ; FPMs : Faculté polytechnique de Mons ; FUL : Fondation universitaire luxembourgeoise ; FUCAM : Facultés universitaires catholiques de Mons ; FUSL : Facultés universitaires Saint-Louis à Bruxelles. R = ranking, N = number.

Table 6. **Ranking by field and by the number of doctorates in the ULB**

	Exact sciences	Health sciences	Social sciences	Applied sciences	Humanities	Agronomic sciences	Total
ULB Rank	1/10	2/10	2/10	3/10	2/10	3/10	2/10

As the table shows, the ULB ranks first in doctorates in exact sciences, and second in three other fields, *i.e.* health sciences, social sciences and the humanities. It ranks third in applied sciences and agronomic sciences.

M. Durez et al (2001) have also analysed the difficulties of producing a doctoral dissertation that was analysed in greater detail in a study they conducted among 356 people who earned a doctorate (1992-1998) in the universities of the French-speaking Community of Belgium. This sample covers 122 dissertations in exact sciences, 47 in applied sciences and the humanities, 41 in medical and dental sciences, and the rest spread across the other fields. The study stresses the double difficulty faced by Ph.D. candidates in the French-speaking Community, owing to the low funding of scientific research, but also to the fact that this situation leads to a plethora of different statuses and forces researchers to obtain additional funding, as shown in Table 7 below.

Our Flemish sister institution, the "Vrije Universiteit Brussel" is the top ranking university in terms of the academic career of women. The ULB ranks second for this category, and first for the categories of professor, instructor and lecturer.

Table 7. **Financial difficulties and variety of statuses of Ph.D. candidates in the French-speaking Community of Belgium**

Status	Number of people		
	Beginning of dissertation	With additional funding	% in difficulty
University assistants	78	13	17
Grants:			
- Industrial and Agricultural Research Fund	75	33	44
- National Scientific Research Fund	52	7	13
- University Heritage	22	10	45
- Federal Departments of Scientific, Technical and Cultural Affairs	18	4	22
- Others	14	5	36
- Partially private	10	1	10
- Foreign	10	5	50
- European	9	7	89
- Collective Basic Research Fund	8	-	-
- Concerted Research Action	5	4	80
Total	**301**	**89**	**30**

Source: M. Durez, D. Verheve and I. Hondekyn (2001)

Gender differences concern researchers as well as international officials of scientific policy

A study by G. Kurgan-Van Hentenrijk (2000) helps to place the ULB in terms of the number of women in its academic personnel.

Table 8. **Women in Belgian university teaching**

Women professors in Belgian universities (in% of the total number of professors)											
French-speaking universities						Flemish-speaking universities					
UCL		ULB		Ulg		KUL		RUG		VUB	
1992	*1998*	*1992*	*1998*	*1992*	*1998*	*1992*	*1998*	*1992*	*1998*	*1992*	*1998*
Full and special professors											
2.5	2.9	10.3	11.4	3.8	7.0	2.1	2.3	6.5	8.8	10.7	12.7
Professors 6.1	7.0	16.9	18.3	8.1	7.0	8.7	11.8	5.8	8.6	15.6	15.9
Instructors 12.0	21.0	16.9	21.6	12.9	10.8	6.4	16.3	7.3	15.0	12.7	20.9
Lecturers 9.1	20.2	17.7	22.2	-	-	-	-	-	-	-	-
Assistants 24.7	32.2	19.4	20.5	9.7	-	-	-	-	-	-	-
Total professoral body 6.2	11.3	14.5	17.6	7.8	8.4	4.3	9.7	6.6	12.1	12.3	17.5

Source: G. Kurgan-Van Hentenryk (2000)
Acronyms: UCL: Université Catholique de Louvain; ULB: Université Libre de Bruxelles; Ulg: Université de Liège (French-speaking); KUL: Katholieke Universiteit Leuven; RUG: Universiteit Gent; VUB: Vrije Universiteit Brussel (Flemish-speaking).

Table 9: **Rank in terms of the number of women professors in Belgian universities (in% of the total number of professors)**

French-speaking universities						Flemish-speaking universities					
UCL		*ULB*		*Ulg*		*KUL*		*RUG*		*VUB*	
1992	*1998*	*1992*	*1998*	*1992*	*1998*	*1992*	*1998*	*1992*	*1998*	*1992*	*1998*
RANG											
Full and special professors											
5	5	2	2	4	4	6	6	3	3	1	1
Professors 5	5	1	1	4	5	3	3	6	4	2	2
Instructors 4	2	1	1	2	6	6	4	5	5	3	3
Lecturers 2	2	1	1								
Assistants 1	1	2	2	3							
Total professorial corps 5	4	1	1	3	6	6	5	4	3	2	2

Recruitment of Belgian researchers

Recruitment is hindered by high social security charges and taxes, as shown by F. Thys-Clément (2002). This situation was illustrated by ranking European countries according to the take-home pay (also known as net pay) of the recipients of Marie Curie Grants. This analysis shows that, on the basis of a comparison of 31 countries in Europe made in 1991, Belgium came out on top in terms of gross salary. In terms of take-home pay, however, it ranked eighth, far outstripped by Switzerland, and to a lesser extent, Denmark, the United Kingdom and Norway. Furthermore, salaries are higher in the Flemish-speaking Community than in the French-speaking Community, under which the ULB falls geographically. Finally, comparisons with the pay of foreign researchers (B. Bayenet and F. Thys-Clément, 2002) pose many methodological problems.

These include, in particular, the correct assessment of the cost of living and the differences entailed by the burden of taxation and parafiscal charges.

A comparison of ULB salaries with those of the Henri Poincaré Nancy 1 University is indicative of the difficulties encountered. The ULB reports gross and semi-gross incomes after withholding direct income tax at the source. The Henry Poincaré University can only provide the gross income, because taxes are not withheld at the source in France. It is therefore useful to indicate that the comparison between the highest gross income of tenured academics in each of the universities shows a 20% difference in favour of the French salary.

Comparisons with the private sector are rare. Nevertheless, such a comparison was made for the particular case of economists. It shows that young assistants and researchers rank last in terms of average income compared with the range of occupations accessible to individuals with this type of training.

Quite recently, the federal government (which is responsible for social security and income tax of citizens) addressed the issue (*Le Soir* 2003). The Council of Ministers of 8 October 2002 actually approved the partial elimination of the pay-as-you-earn or wage tax (withholding at the source) for assistants and researchers in universities. This measure will cost the government about thirty million euros a year. The gain for the ULB will amount to more than one million euros per year, and for the National Scientific Research Fund, which is also concerned by this measure, to EUR 2 230 000 a year (*Le Soir*). Measures to promote mobility have also been taken. They pertain to the social security system for foreign researchers. In concrete terms, doctoral and post-doctoral researchers who are not nationals of the European Economic Area (EEA) will be partially covered by the social security system and be granted protection adapted to their needs: health – disability insurance, family allowances, occupational accidents and disease. Researchers who are EEA nationals will be fully covered by the social security system and thus entitled to unemployment benefits and a pension (*La Libre Belgique* 2003).

Management of contractual research at the ULB

The need to manage research on external funds is linked to the funding difficulties of Belgian universities and to the specific nature of the research. More specifically, in a certain number of cases, research does not fall directly under the two main missions of the University, *i.e.* teaching and research, but rather in the implementation of its third mission, *i.e.* services to the community.

As is well known, research funding comes from various sources depending on the different missions of basic research and applied research:

- From the general funding of the university and special, usually public, research funds, with research assignments and grants;

- From occasional research contracts for the short and medium term.

These sources must be examined separately because they have different consequences on the management of the career of researchers.

General funding and special funds

The first source comes from funding allocated legally, according to pre-defined distribution keys, to the universities of the French-speaking Community or the Belgian federal authority (M.C. Lenain, 2002).

The basic allocation for a university (see B. Bayenet and F. Thys-Clément, 1998) is calculated in proportion to the number of students registered at the university, with different coefficients depending on the fields of study or the origin of the student. The calculation is carried out on a "capped budget" basis, *i.e.* fixed for all of the French-speaking universities. Consequently, a university's operating subsidy will be increased only if its number of students increases proportionally more than that of the other universities. The ULB's operating subsidy has gone from EUR 91.175 million in 1991 to EUR 111 million in 2002, a very small increase compared with the cost of living. The part of the operating subsidy earmarked for research is evaluated at 25%. Eighty percent (80%) of this overall allowance is used to pay the salaries of the academic and scientific staff of the institution. These include administrative, technical and managerial staff, as well as academics.

The special research funds are those provided by the French-speaking authority and by the federal authority. Consequently, for the French-speaking Community, Concerted Research Actions (CRA) are distributed each year among university institutions accredited to award undergraduate or graduate diplomas or degrees. The aim of these subsidies is to develop centres of excellence in particularly important fields for the advancement of knowledge and its application in the medium- and long-term. They constitute sufficient sizeable, multi-year inducements to reinforce a team and are likely to be repeated. They are intended for teams that have already proved their scientific value, so as to give them sufficient means to establish their authority in their field of expertise.

Ideally, these research programmes should bring together several teams from the same institution to pool their multidisciplinary and complementary skills and knowledge to fully cover all the fields of the proposed research.

These research funds are attributed among the universities on the basis of a distribution key defined in 1976 with the following criteria:

- the number of students registered in the last year of the undergraduate and graduate cycles in each institution (weighting factor of 2);

- the number of researchers at the institution (weighting factor of 1);

- the part of the funding granted to each institution in the first generation of concerted research actions (weighting factor of 2).

Criteria "a" and "b" translate the "potential" of the institution; whereas "c" is a stability criterion.

The distribution between universities is established on the basis of these criteria according to Table 10 below, where the amount for the ULB for 2002 is EUR 3.5 million.

Table 10. **Distribution of the CRA funds among the French-speaking universities of Belgium**

UCL	37.75%
ULB	30.60%
Ulg	27%
FUSAGx/FUNDP/UMH	4.65%

Acronyms: see Table 5

The CRAs are financed for a maximum period of five times twelve months in accordance with Article 3 of the French-speaking Community Decree of 13

April 2000. When the duration is shorter than 60 months, it must be duly justified; it may never be shorter than 48 months.

The federal authority funds inter-university attraction poles with a fixed amount per university, calculated according to two distribution keys:

1. A distribution key between the French-speaking and Flemish-speaking Communities of the country. For the latest phase of the Inter-University Attraction Poles (IAP) – (Phase 5 started in 2002), the distribution key was 44% French-speaking and 56% Flemish-speaking. This key depends on the following criteria:

   – Belgian, EU, non-EU primary basic cycle students (1999-2000)

   – Undergraduate basic cycle students (1999-2000)

   – Master's degrees in specialised studies (DES) and in pre-doctoral studies (DEA) (1999-2000)

   – Ph.D. degrees (1998-1999)

   – Academic and scientific staff (1999-2000)

   – Scientific staff on secondment (1999-2000)

   – Researchers at research centres

An intra-community distribution key is defined as follows:

   – The number of fundable cycle students (weighting: 37.5%);

   – The number of fundable Belgian undergraduate and graduate cycle degree holders(weighting: 12.5%);

   – The number of full-time teaching and scientific staff (weighting: 50%).

The distribution among universities of the French-speaking Community is given in Table 11 (the amount for the ULB: more than EUR 12 million):

Table 11. **Distribution of the IAP funds among the French-speaking universities of Belgium**

UCL	35.67%
ULB	25.98%
Ulg	22.34%
FUNDP	5.19%
UMH	3.96%
FPMs	2.13%
FUCAM	1.98%
FUSAGx	1.89%
FUSLO	0.86%

Acronyms: see Table 5.

The IAPs are awarded every five years (for a five-year period). They entail the participation of at least three Belgian universities - two of which belong to the French-speaking and one to the Flemish-speaking communtities – and one foreign national university.

It is worth underscoring that these two types of funding impose no constraints on the research to be carried out and, in particular, on the obligation to apply the research. In general, they are used to carry out basic research in the humanities and the exact sciences. The research staff under CRA and IAP contracts usually work on their doctoral dissertation or a on a post-doctoral project.

Finally, we must discuss the special research fund, which is a subsidy given to French-speaking universities with the sole obligation that it be used for research.

The subsidies granted are distributed among each university in proportion to the number of Belgian undergraduate and graduate degree holders.

To qualify for such subsidies, each institution draws from its resources, including the operating subsidy, a minimum sum equivalent to a given percentage (17.5% in 2001, and since) appropriated from the general operating budget. The percentage for the ULB has developed as shown in the table below (ULB amount in 2001: more than EUR 2 million).

Table 12. **Special Research Fund**

YEAR	% ULB
1997	26.74
1998	24.65
1999	23.85
2000	24.36
2001	23.88

Funding of scientific projects submitted to external funding sources

Chapter *"General funding and special funds"* describes the funding part of research linked to "predefined" amounts, whether through the operating allowance of the university or external funds pre-distributed between the universities. There is a second type of funding through submitted scientific projects or invitations to submit projects, both of which are geared to external sources.

On the basis of the projects submitted, the National Fund for Scientific Research awards a certain number of positions either for a specified period: doctoral grants of twice two years or post-doctoral contracts of three years, or for an unlimited period (qualified researcher). The latter are integrated in to the academic body of the university. This fund also distributes research funding through several programmes. There are no constraints as to the nature of the research. The positions are obtained through a competition between all the universities of the French-speaking community.

Funding provided on invitation to submit projects is the most diversified and most complex to manage. It comes from a wide variety of sources both Belgian and international and amounted to EUR 36 million in 2001 (Table 13). The contracts are obtained on the basis of replies to the invitations to submit projects, and the criteria, attribution procedures and administrative management of the projects are at times highly diverse. In fact, there is little in common between the amount and the implementation of a "framework programme" of a European project and a study financed contractually by a region. The terms of these contracts can also vary widely, from 2 to 3 months for a targeted research study, to 4 years for some European projects. The packaging and monitoring of these projects are provided in the research department through what is known as an "interface" unit which also deals with all problems to do with intellectual property (application for patents, distribution of royalties, conclusion of licensing agreements, etc.).

Table 13. **Development of funding by external contracts of the Université Libre de Bruxelles**

	In% of the annual amount 2001					In millions of euros
	1996	1997	1998	1999	2000	2001
Federal (except IAP)	110	125	112	120	109	3.9
Wallonia-Brussels Community (except CRA)	30	46	39	51	55	2.8
Walloon Region	62	61	65	88	108	10.4
Brussels-Capital Region	59	54	72	67	70	3.7
German-speaking Region			40			pm
EEC + Erasmus Tempus	131	138	109	42	118	7.3
International	95	71	155	78	101	1.2
Not-for-profit organisations and foundations	91	139	105	148	123	1.7
Industrial	82	103	86	101	105	5.0
Donations and sponsoring	95	94	100	113	207	0.2
TOTAL	73	79	74	69	87	36.2 = 100

Source: ULB Research Department Database. The precipitous drop of European funding in 1999 corresponds to the interval between two framework programmes.

European, regional, and even more so, private funding entails multiple and varied constraints on the degree of applicability of the research, as some contracts are purely of an industrial nature. We will not discuss further here European funds, of which the rules are identical for all the participating partners. But the analysis of regional funds does illustrate the complexity of the management and its sources of funding: owing to the distribution of powers in the Belgian state, projects must contain sophisticated development plans that, in certain cases, go as far as forming spin-offs or start-ups. In these cases, we are no longer in the strict framework of academic research. This is all the more true when the research consists in developing an industrial prototype. The results then belong to the company that has funded the research and it may discontinue the cooperation with the university at any time, thus generating more fluctuation on staff management. Staff taken on under such contracts are not necessarily required to produce a doctoral dissertation.

Research staff

If we consider that the academic and scientific staff of the university devote half of their time to research, with the other half being devoted to teaching duties, and not taking administrative tasks into account, the "labour force" devoted to research is made up in equal parts of tenured teachers-researchers and of researchers whose status depends on the availability of funds outside of the university. The academic staff consisted of nearly 1 000 full-time equivalents (FTE) in 2001, representing therefore 500 FTEs in research, with the same number of researchers hired through external funding!

This development requires a serious analysis of the management of this specific category of staff paid with external funds with widely disparate statuses.

Highly different career paths can be observed at times. Some obtain a doctoral dissertation followed by a post-doctoral position during which they try to join the tenured faculty. Some do not succeed, and continue to pursue their career through this type of funding. Others do not write a doctoral dissertation, but concentrate on research work, often in response to questions put by outside organisations or authorities.

The existence of researchers paid from external funds raises several questions of comparison with the status of researchers on the university staff: can the university align their wage brackets, or leave the greatest freedom of choice in salary for researchers who depend on external funding? Should the university encourage a career that is independent of academic criteria such as obtaining a doctoral dissertation? Should the fact that there is a difference between public and private statuses mean that the significant difference in the pension at the end of the career needs to be compensated? Should researchers be involved in the teaching or the administrative activities of the university? If the source of funding dries up, should one manage either the research's career or the burden of her/his notice, which weighs increasingly heavily on the university's budget as the average age of people depending on external funds increases? How is the end of the career of such employees to be managed? Finally, should these people be subjected to the same evaluations as researchers on the university staff?

All of these questions have led the university to undertake a series of reflections which are still in progress at this time. We shall go over them briefly in the chronological order in which they were applied and discuss the advantages and disadvantages of the decisions taken.

Management of staff depending on external funds: the ULB approach

In 1993, the university created a structure to promote and manage contractual scientific research, *i.e.* to act as an interface between the university and its external partners and to manage the research contracts. In this context, the University found it advisable to take on some experienced researchers on a more permanent basis by offering them prospects of a career at the university.

To access these statuses, researchers must meet three conditions, summarised as follows:

1. Have at least six years of scientific seniority;

2. Belong to one or more research units prepared to remunerate the researcher and to contribute voluntarily to the fund established to cover any severance pay claims;

3. Have been selected by a scientific evaluation board chaired by the Rector. This board will consider the specific aspects of the research conducted under external contacts, both in terms of the publications and the activities carried out.

The stages of a career in a scientific unit are as follows:

- Researcher

- Qualified researcher

- Senior researcher

- Director of research

At each of these stages, the candidate's promotion is subject to an evaluation of his or her qualities, conducted in comparison to the career of researchers on the ULB staff.

This decision reflects the university's desire to recognise the importance of research carried out with external funding as well as the importance of appreciating the individuals concerned. We should point out that in terms of the status that could be obtained the completion of a doctoral dissertation is only required for the top level, *i.e.* director of research.

The question of pay scales is clearly raised and the salaries of researchers under contracts were brought in line with equivalents defined by decrees of the French-speaking Community for staff paid by the university. It seemed desirable however to leave some room for manoeuvre in negotiating the salary to the sponsor and the researcher under contract, and it was proposed to fix the maximum equivalent scale of the salary paid to a researcher under contract at 130%. This would provide a certain flexibility but could also enable the researcher, if she/he wanted, to create a sort of savings plan that would compensate the difference in the pension that she/he would received if she/he had pursued his or her career at the university.

The adoption, by the university of the rules described above also raises the question of managing the redundancy notice. The proposed status does not provide for the termination of employment and presupposes that no effort will be spared to continue getting contracts that would stabilise the researcher's employment situation. It is nonetheless possible that a source of funding dries up, and that notice will have to be served and be paid for by the university. To make the sponsor liable, and to limit the impact on the university of having to pay such notices, a solidarity fund was created, and is fed by each department paying EUR 5 000 into it for each researcher who attains the proposed status.

In order to limit such services of notice, which are discouraging for researchers carrying out quality work for which the funding is renewed, the university has pursued a policy that distinguishes three categories of researchers:

- Those hired for a specified period: these individuals are hired until a specific date, usually connected to the end of the contract for the research project in question.

- Those hired for an unspecified period "with notice", these individuals have already had several successive contracts for a specified period at the university, and are hired up to a specific date defined by the notice that is generally connected to the end of the research contract. The notice may be protective, since the person in question can be hired under a new contract for a specified period "with notice," financial resources permitting.

- Those hired for an unspecified period "without notice", these individuals have had several successive contracts for a specified period at the university, for which the sponsor can guarantee, with minimum risk, that the contracts in progress and new contracts will make it possible to avoid dismissal.

Affiliation to the second or third category occurs through the research sponsor's proposal and is assessed by a management committee for "staff on external funds". This committee analyses all the research teams, both regarding the financial volume they generate and the specific situation of each of its members. Given the precariousness and multiple sources of funding, the committee concluded that in the case of a team of a certain size, it is possible to limit the number of notices served by tending towards an equitable distribution

(1/3) of each of the three categories of researchers described above. For small-sized teams (1 or 2 researchers), for whom the volume of the contracts is less sizeable, the risk of serving a notice is higher. The research sponsor is regularly sent a summary table of the people who depend on him including precise information on their situation. The sponsor informs the personnel department as soon as a new development is likely to change this situation. In addition to better management of the personnel files of those hired under external funds, the existence of the committee and its operating mechanism has raised the awareness of research sponsors about the management of this type of staff, and has boosted constructive contacts between the sponsors and the University's central administration.

The university improved these procedures in June 1997 by singling out certain experienced researchers hired under external funds with a remarkable scientific track record: these researchers will be designated below by the term "ULB researchers".

Their candidacy for this title must be backed by the sponsor. The candidacy file must show the value of having the researcher permanently at the university, and demonstrate his or her aptitude to generate and manage new contracts. The candidate must have a doctorate and at least six years of scientific seniority, including at least two at the ULB. The ULB researcher has the same prerogatives as members of the academic body of the university. In this capacity, she/he takes part in faculty voting, can have a financial account and apply for teaching positions for which there is an internal vacancy. In terms of pay, the ULB researcher obviously accedes to the various pay scales provided by the French-speaking Community.

It is worth pointing out, however, that she/he is not given tenure and that his or her situation and salary will depend on contracts. Nevertheless, the sponsor undertakes the moral commitment to do everything possible to keep the researcher in the team and, in case of difficulty, to grant him or her priority over other researchers.

These procedures are different from the previous situation in the essential ways:

- The ULB researchers are integrated in to the academic body and their designation criteria are similar to those of the academic body, in particular regarding having a doctorate. Researchers with the 1993 status who have a doctorate, moreover, now automatically have the title of "ULB researcher";

- The way the notice is handled is defined by the management committee for staff on external funds and the guarantee of EUR 5 000 requested from the sponsor is cancelled.

The June 1997 document provided for limiting the number of people who could obtain the status of ULB researchers to four persons per year. In fact, this number has never been attained, and at present one or two applications are filed annually, essentially from faculties in the exact sciences (sciences and medicine). This situation is therefore based on the fundamental question of the degree to which researchers under contract can/must be integrated in the academic body, as well as the degree to which criteria, such as having a doctorate, reflect the reality in the field, especially in the humanities. The question of the evaluation of applications and the criteria used must also be reconsidered. Furthermore, the average age of the population of researchers under contract (Table 14) leads the university to recognise, with increasing frequency, the situation of researchers between 45 and 58 years serving notice. This precariousness can be explained by many causes, such as the drying-up of the source of funding, the retirement of the sponsor or the increasing difficulty to find contracts to cover increasingly higher salaries.

Table 14. **Number of agents under external contracts: researchers, administrative, technical and managerial staff (2000)**

Age	Number of agents
20-29	240
30-39	270
40-49	123
50-59	53

The strategic need for a new organisation of research under contracts

Such a reorganisation is needed for many reasons, which relate both to the external environment and to the ULB's desire to properly shape the position of researcher.

The external reasons stem from the reduction of the operating subsidies granted by the public authorities within the overall revenues of the University, which have gone from more than 80% in 1980 to about 60% in 1995 (R. Tollet, 2002). It is well known that revenues from temporary contracts have taken over, be they public (European, national, EU, regional, and even municipal!), or private.

A proper shaping of the profession of researcher has become necessary both for the adequate management of the university as a whole and in order to enable it to meet the researchers' increasing desire for mobility, as well as for the sake of the excellence of European research (Ph. Busquin, 2002). The reasons for the mobility of researchers are known (F. Thys-Clément, 2002) to be numerous, as they cover salaries, but also prerequisites such as being a member of a centre of excellence, working on a promising research topic, having control over the operating appropriations and equipment, etc.

Conclusions

The new working conditions of researchers reveal the transformation of the paradigm that links scientific knowledge to societal development: the establishment of a globalised world where local knowledge and skills are essential. The scientist is at the centre of the process, called upon by all sides, both for his or her contribution to the progress of knowledge and his or her role in economic growth, as was underscored by the European Commission (2001a) during the launch of the European Research Area.

This recognition is accompanied by a recent increase in research appropriations in Belgium (see also Cincera M. *et al.*, 2001, 2002) and in particular for the ULB, as shown in Table 13 of this paper, which also shows the wide diversity of sources of external contracts. This diversity leads to a plethora of different statuses awarded to people hired by the university.

This development has led the ULB authorities to try and accommodate the career of the persons concerned, so as not to create excessive disparities between temporary researchers under external contracts and those linked regularly to the general operation of the university. Adjustments have been made to the precarious nature of the working conditions of researchers funded by such external contracts, but they have to be reviewed in the light of the increasing number of people concerned as well as the stakes raised due to the desired mobility of research in Europe.

The specific nature of research conducted with external funds must also be taken into account, as it falls, in part, under the university's third mission: services to the community. The interface between such research and society is far more direct than that of research, including the applied purpose, conducted under the ordinary operation of the university. This is why evaluation criteria for research geared towards services to the community may vary widely from those used for academic research. It is a matter then of reconciling these two modes of thinking, which though different may prove quite complementary and certainly deserve a place in the institution. This is a challenge that the university, as an organisation, must take up if it wishes to continue to be a major source of knowledge within its local social and economic environment.

Acknowledgement

The authors would like to thank Mrs P. Dekie, Secretary at the Centre of Education Economics of the ULB for her help in preparing this text, and the National Scientific Research Fund (known by the French acronym FNRS) for its support on the research project on education and science economics. We thank also Professor M. Gassner for her careful reading and their helpful comments.

REFERNCES

Case study instructions

Bayenet B. and F. Thys-Clément (2002), Research Report: "Gestion du personnel scientifique et académique en Communauté française de Belgique: premiers aspects d'une mise en perspective européenne" - Fonds National de la Recherche Scientifique.

Bayenet B. and O. Bosteels (1998), *Le financement des universités en Belgium,* S. Bodson and F. Thys-Clément (Eds)Collection "Education", Editions de l'Université de Bruxelles.

Busquin P. (2002), "L'organisation de la recherche en Europe", in *European Universities: Change and Convergence*, M. Dewatripont, F. Thys-Clément and L. Wilkin (Eds), Collection "Education", Editions de l'Université de Bruxelles.

BRISTI (2001 and 2002), Cincera M., Clarysse B., Kalenga-Mpala R., Monard E., Nauwelaers C., Spithoven A. and Teirlinck P., *Belgian Report on Science, Technology and Innovation*, Federal Office for Scientific, Technical and Cultural Affaires, Brussels.

Commission des Communautés européennes – *Proposal for a Decision of the European Parliament and of the Council concerning the multiannual framework programme 202-2006 of the European Community for research, technological development and demonstration activities aimed at contributing towards the creation of the European Research Area., /*COM/2001/0094 final – COD 2001/0053*/ Official Journal C 180 E, 26/06/2001 P. 0156-0176.*

Communauté Wallonie - Bruxelles, Article 3 de l'Arrêté du 13 avril 2000, about financement of concerted research actions between the belgian french community an the Universities allowed to deliver second and third cycles diplomas.

CRE – Programme d'évaluation institutionnelle (1996-1997), "Rapport d'auto-évaluation", Université Libre de Bruxelles.

Durez M., D. Verheve and I. Hondekyn (2001), « De la thèse à l'emploi en Communauté française de Belgium », in M. Dewatripont, F. Thys-Clément and L. Wilkin (Eds) *The Strategic Analysis of Universities: Microeconomic and Management Perspectives*, Collection "Education", Editions de l'Université de Bruxelles.

Guillaume C. (2002), note interne ULB, Cellule Recherche, Département Recherhe.

Kurgan – G.Van Hentenryk (2000), « La féminisation du personnel académique en Belgium: processus progressif ou stagnation ? » in *Femmes de culture et de pouvoir*, Publication given to A. Despy-Meyer, Sextant, ULB.

Lenain M.C. (2002), note interne ULB « Evaluation de la part de marché de l'ULB dans les financements publics », Chef de service, Cellule Recherche, Département Recherche.

La Libre Belgique 22/01/2003

Le Soir 22/01/2003

Magerman F. (2002), note interne ULB "Pyramide des âges du personnel sur fonds extérieurs », Chef de service, Cellule de gestion financière de la recherche, Département financier.

OECD (1999), « University Research Financing », DSTI/STP(99)18.

Osterrieth M. (2002), note interne ULB « Brève analyse des statistiques du CREF sur l'effort de recherché des universités de la Communauté française », mars, Chef de service, Cellule Etudes et évaluation, Département Recherche.

Slaughter S. and L. Leslie (1997), *Academic Capitalism. Politics, Policies and the Entrepreneurial University*, the J. Hopkins University Press, Baltimore and London.

Thys-Clément F. (1995), "The crisis of university funding", *CRE-action*, n°106.

Thys-Clément F. (2001), « Research Management in the European Union Universities », paper presented at the OECD/IMHE/UNU experts meeting on "University Research Management: Learning from diverse Experience", Tokyo, 27-28 February.

Thys-Clément F. (2002), « Changes in Research Management: the New Working Conditions of Researchers », in *The Belgian Innovation System: Lessons and Challenges*, Vol. 2, Federal Office for Scientific, Technical and Cultural Affairs (BRISTI).

Tollet R. (2002), "La réforme comptable, budgétaire et financière de l'Université Libre de Bruxelles: 1996-2001", in *European Universities: Change and Convergence*, M. Dewatripont, F. Thys-Clément and L. Wilkin (Eds), Collection "Education", Editions de l'Université de Bruxelles.

Uyttendaele M. (1991), *Le fédéralisme inachevé – Réflexions sur le système institutionnel belge, issu des réformes de 1988-1989*, Editions Bruylant, Bruxelles.

BUILDING A RESEARCH PROFILE:
BOĞAZIÇI ÜNIVERSITESI, TURKEY

Oktem Vardar

This report reflects the personal views of the author as former vice-rector in charge of R&D and faculty member very much involved with research related issues at BU (Bogaziçi University). Most of the factual data may be taken as common perception but the interpretations and analyses are unavoidably subjective.

The Turkish higher education system[44]

Turkish universities are affected essentially by four types of factors: social, demographic, bureaucratic, and political.

Socially, education has always been an avenue to upward social mobility, that in turn has increased the demand for a "diploma". Society has looked upon higher education as a road to a profession certified by a diploma and has not fully internalised the meaning of "university". Thus, the emphasis has been on teaching at the expense of research. Moreover, training for a profession as opposed to education is the accepted norm.

The **demographic** pressure that Turkey has been experiencing since the 1950s has not helped either. Population growth rates have been close to 3% per annum. Demographers suggest that this upward trend has levelled off and was decreasing in the 1990s. Nevertheless, 50% of the population is currently aged 20 or below and universities are bound to feel the crippling effects of demand for "mass education at any cost". Various governments responding to this demand tried to increase the undergraduate intake of universities, overcrowding the campuses as well as overburdening poorly paid academic staff. A recent approach has been to create new universities, often in response to political pressure in different parts of the country. The number of state universities in 1992 was 28. As of 2002, the number of state and foundation universities has risen to 53 and 21 respectively, with almost no corresponding increase in budget allocations to higher education. With close to 97.6% of all students on their campuses, state universities carry by far the major portion of the higher education load.

The Turkish "state tradition" emphasizes over-centralized and monist as opposed to pluralist solutions. This tradition, naturally, has led to the emergence of a **bureaucracy** which likes to centralize and control and in turn puts universities - institutions that naturally thrive within a pluralist environment - in a straight-jacket.

The Turkish **political** system is a typical parliamentary system with a 550-member parliament, a prime minister, a cabinet, and a president of the Republic who is constitutionally neutral and above day-to-day politics. The higher education system is governed by the Council of Higher Education (CHE), the President of which is appointed by the President of the Republic. The Minister of Education may preside over the meetings of the CHE, if he deems it necessary; however, ministers of education, since the founding of CHE, have rarely done this. The Ministry of Education directs its attention to primary and secondary education, leaving the ground of higher education almost exclusively to the CHE. The Council of Higher Education acts as "board of regents" for all Turkish universities.

The major source of income for state universities is the funds allocated through the annual state budget. Income generated through revolving funds and tuition fees make up the rest of funds available to universities. On average, revolving fund revenues form up to 25% of their total income. However, this is not uniform across universities, as in those having medical schools and hospitals, revolving fund revenues often go above this average. However, non-medical universities like Bogazici University, often earn much less than the above-mentioned average from their revolving fund activities. Student tuition fees make up merely seven percent of the total income and are basically used to subsidize meals and lodgings provided for students. The allocation from the state budget per full time student fluctuates between USD 1000-1500. The annual government allocation to each university is determined by an indicative budgeting system. University administrators negotiate with related governmental agencies (the Ministry of Finance, and the State Planning Organization for investment) on the basis of the allocation and expenditure for previous years. This, naturally, leaves very little room for new policy development. The government centrally determines salaries, as academic and non-academic administrative staff are all government employees. An extremely non-flexible and bureaucratically controlled line item budgeting system dictates various lines of expenditure giving no freedom to university administrators to switch funds between these lines. In addition, the amounts allocated in the budget are made available (and at times reduced) at different intervals during the fiscal year.

The newly founded private universities enjoy full financial autonomy. Both student tuition fees and faculty salaries are at levels comparable to US standards. They are also entitled, theoretically, to a state subsidy of up to 45% of their budget, though subject to certain limitations.

The dominant features

Demand for higher education is very strong. Approximately 1.5 million students take the central university entrance exam and only 140 000 are entered in four-year undergraduate programs, 80 000 in two-year vocational programs as full time students and 20 000 in distance education programs. Similarly, the need for new faculty members is high. Most of the newly established universities do not have sufficient faculty members to pursue a meaningful curriculum. The older and established universities such as BU, the Middle East Technical University (METU), Istanbul Technical University (ITU), Hacettepe and newcomers such as Bilkent, Koc, and Sabanci (foundation universities), can concentrate on research and Ph.D. programs to supply faculty members to others. Such complementary roles should be clarified and the CHE seems to be moving in this direction with its emphasis on graduate programs in the above-mentioned universities but they could never explicitly identify different categories of universities.

All universities are unanimous in demanding the reform of the financial system of which they are prisoners. A "lump-sum" budget system instead of "linc-itcm" budgeting seems to be the most urgent need. Higher tuition fees, better salaries, the overhaul of the revolving fund system and freedom to generate and spend income are other issues on the agenda. There are no mechanisms to provide impartial assessments of the relevance, competence and performance of the programs at each university. Neither institutions nor faculties feel the need to be accountable. No input or output parameters seem to affect the state funding of institutions or individuals. Sharing the wealth equally represents a disincentive to institutions and individuals who are more productive than others. Subjective but transparent assessment is difficult to achieve within the Turkish culture. Once a professor is appointed to a state university, all universities must recognize the title. They may offer lower positions on recruitment, but this is rather rare. This centralized structure lowers the standards of promotion. All universities do not share the same quality culture but participate in this centralized process of faculty promotion.

The growing competition between state and foundation universities has generated tension within academia. Still in their infancy, these private universities have so far had to rely on the transfer of academics who have gained experience and prestige at state universities. The attractive salaries at these private universities, are based, however, on temporary but renewable contracts. A conscious effort is being made to establish a "publish or perish" environment on some of the private university campuses.

The institutional profile of Bogazici University

BU is unique both nationally and internationally in terms of its history and heritage. BU is the successor to Robert College, which was the first American institution of education established abroad (1863). It started as a missionary school, served minorities and ended up as a private institution favoured by the Turkish elite. Financial problems added to rising leftist sentiment in Turkey in the 60s, led the Board of Trustees in New York to hand it over to the Turkish government in 1971 on condition that the state establish a public university and take over the schools of higher education (including faculty members, administrative personnel, and academic infrastructure, *i.e.* library) granting bachelor degrees.

BU, officially founded in September 1971, has always been proud of this culturally and organizationally rich and diverse tradition. It tries to emphasize continuity and to go forward and build on this rich academic tradition. BU had to go through very rapid and painful growth in student numbers, from 1 000 in 1971 to 3 000 in 1982 and to 10 000 in 1991 in response to government pressure to provide more places for high school leavers. Those numbers stabilized in the 90s; an incremental reduction has even been achieved. BU takes in exceptionally good students. The average performance of the admitted students corresponds to the top 1100 in the central exam taken by 1.5 million candidates. In percentage terms, this means that to qualify for most BU programs, a student must be among the less than top 1% of 1.5 million students taking the central placement exam. No other university comes close to this figure. On the whole, the growth rate did not lower the quality of the students since the number of students coming from high schools grew at the same pace, if not at a higher rate. These growth figures created important problems for the institution at two levels: firstly, heavy use of the infrastructure and the consequent need to spend more than other universities on maintenance and repairs of historically important buildings; secondly, inadequacy of the classroom size to handle large numbers of students and insufficiency of science laboratories. The university very strongly resisted the increase of academic staff with a most orthodox commitment to the quality of its faculty members. This in turn meant, larger classes and heavier teaching loads for the faculty members, and difficulty in devoting time to research. The choice of the faculty members to maintain high standards in recruitment at the expense of their own convenience in teaching and research is an excellent indication of the esprit de corps that exists at Bogazici and the commitment of the institution to quality. This is perhaps the greatest strength of the institution.

Academic and administrative structure

The basic units of the academic structure are the departments. 24 departments are grouped into four faculties: Arts and Sciences, Engineering, Economics and Administrative Sciences, Education. Two Institutes administer graduate education, with the support of the above-mentioned faculties: Science and Engineering, Social Sciences. In addition, four smaller, specialized institutes offer graduate programmes: Biomedical Engineering, Environmental Sciences, Kandilli Observatory and Earthquake Research, and the Atatürk Institute of Modern Turkish History. The School of Applied Disciplines offers four-year applied programmes and the School of Foreign Languages concentrates heavily on English preparatory programmes. This school is highly specialized and experienced in bringing native Turkish speakers up to a level of English proficiency (a minimum of 213 and 4.5 on TOEFL) for study in an English-speaking university such as Bogazici.

The departments are chaired by a department head appointed by the dean, upon nomination by the department itself. The deans are also nominated by popular vote at Bogazici although the law gives the power of appointment to the rector. The dean and the executive board of the faculty run the daily business of the faculty whereas academic matters are taken up at the faculty council, which is a larger group of academics chaired by the dean.

The administrative structure of the schools and institutes is similar to those of the faculties. The rector appoints their directors.

The rector is the chief executive officer of the University. The appointment of the rectors in Turkey is a complicated three-tier process. The university rank orders six candidates by popular vote. This list is narrowed down to three by the CHE. Formally, the CHE is not required to respect the rank ordering of the university. The President of the Republic appoints the rector from amongst the three candidates nominated by the CHE. Normally, both the CHE and the President of the Republic respect the ranking order preferred by the university. However, there have been instances when both the CHE and the President felt free to make their own choices. The appointment of the rector at Bogazici is in line with this national process. So far, higher authorities in the case of Bogazici have always respected the preferences of the faculty members.

The rector is endowed with important executive and financial powers. He/she also presides over the Senate and the University Executive Board. The University Executive Board, composed of four deans and three members elected by the Senate, is the chief executive council. The principal academic body is the Senate. It is composed of the rector, the vice-rectors, the deans and the directors of institutes and schools as well as elected representatives from each faculty, making up a group of approximately 20 members. All members of the Senate and the University Executive Board are required to be full-time professors. The University Executive Board meets at least twice a month depending on the volume of business. The Senate meetings are less frequent.

Three vice-rectors, appointed by the rector, share the administrative duties of the rector. Most of the activity is carried out through committees, standing or ad hoc. Issues discussed and matured in committees and faculty councils are taken up at the University Executive Board or the Senate and finalized there. Most of the services (such as library services, registration, computer centre, student affairs, public relations, financial aid, health care etc.) are centralized and carried out by the rectorate rather than the faculties individually.

University statistics

The total student enrolment is 9 599 for the 2000/01 academic year. Undergraduate enrolment in faculties is 5 327, graduate enrolment is 1770. 338 professors are employed. The ratio of students to full-time academic faculty members (excluding the English Prep School) is about 23. The number of full-time staff and administrative personnel is 798. Details of these statistics are given below.

Table 1. **Student Enrolment for the 2003-04 Academic Year**

Undergraduate Students in Faculties	Graduate Students in Institutes	School of Applied Disciplines		School of Foreign Languages		TOTAL
		2 years	4 years	Trans.*	Prep S	
5668	2050	8	640	189	1687	10242

Source: *Department of Translation and Interpretation

Table 2. **Distribution of Students to Undergraduate Programs in Faculties(2003-04)**

Faculty of Engineering	Faculty of Arts and Sciences.	Faculty of Econ. And Adm. Sci.	Faculty of Education	TOTAL
1571	1488	1432	1177	5668

Table 3. **Distribution of Students to Graduate Programs (2003-04)**

Science and Engineering		Social Sciences		Specialized Inst.		TOTAL	
MS	Ph.D.	MA	Ph.D.	MS/MA	Ph.D.	MS/MA	Ph.D.
772	255	522	132	240	129	1534	516

Table 4. **Number of Faculty Members**

Professor (Full, Associate, Assistant.)	Instructor/ Lecturer	On Contract	Part time	TOTAL
378	193	48	229	848

SWOT Analysis

The following SWOT analysis taken unchanged from the self-evaluation report to CRE as the preliminary phase of the institutional evaluation scheme in 1999 is still believed to be valid:

Strengths:

- a very well-educated and qualified group of faculty members and a certain level of "*esprit de corps*" among them.

- BU has a very good reputation and attracts the best students in the country.

- strong demand in the labour market for BU graduates acts as positive feedback in attracting students of the highest calibre.

- the legacy of Robert College which is based on the appreciation of quality.

- vision and strategic planning.

- an American system of education at both the undergraduate and postgraduate levels.

- English as the medium of instruction.

- enthusiastic, well-disposed and responsible alumni and an increasingly supportive foundation (BUVAK) filling the gaps in university funding.

- a highly successful summer term increasing the number of academic terms to three per year and allowing the efficient use of university resources.

Weaknesses:

- increasing difficulty in recruiting new qualified faculty members due to very low salaries and the limited ability to offer non-pecuniary fringe benefits like low-cost housing.

- inability to recruit qualified administrative personnel due to low salaries. Furthermore, it is highly difficult to achieve administrative efficiency due to the stipulations of the State Civil Servant Law that assures job security.

- similarly, the civil servant status ensures job security for academic personnel making the imposition of high academic standards especially difficult for promotions.

- tight financial constraints due to an inflexible and centralized line item budget system further decrease the potential of an already low budget allocated by the state.

- small research volume measured against international standards: the transformation of Robert College, an excellent teaching college by international standards, to a fully-fledged research university, is still in progress.

- no tradition of institutional cooperation with industry or society at large.

- the exclusive social club atmosphere, legacy of Robert College, which at times may be in conflict with the announced aim of becoming a leading research university.

- complacency of some faculty members with the belief that BU is the leading university in the country.

Opportunities:

- increasing the level of international contact and a desire to measure performance according to international standards.

- creation by the Foundation (BUVAK) of a number of incentives to encourage academic research.

- increasing the number of continuing education programs.

- increasing the level of contact with the industry.

- increasing the level of consciousness and willingness among faculty members to transform the university in a radical manner.

Threats:

- looming competition by private universities for students, for faculty members, and for fresh Ph.D.s returning home from abroad. Private universities offer incomparably higher salaries and fringe benefits as a competitive edge in the recruitment of new faculty members. Aggressive full scholarship programs are aimed to challenge the position of BU as the most desired university by students.

- potential of the Council of Higher Education (CHE) to intervene in academic and administrative details, challenging university autonomy.

- being subject to the same rules and regulations in an over-centralized system including the other 53 state universities, some of which may hardly be called university.

Research initiatives

Since 1971, BU has aimed at increasing the scope and number of graduate programs. It was hoped that the transition from RC to BU would also be a transition from a teaching college to a graduate study-dominated institution. During the 1970s, graduates of RC were returning home, to BU; the faculty size increased from 36 to 78 during the 1971-1980 period. However, the system did not move towards a research environment. It was a period of transformation from a private institute to a state university and the university was busy adjusting to the national state system. One major problem was to develop an identity within the state university system while preserving the heritage of RC.

The military regime in 1980, followed by the Higher Education Law introducing the CHE, was the dominant feature of the 1980s. Like many other universities, BU went through a painful period of extreme central control, aimed at eliminating differences between Higher Education Institutions (HEI). This policy had the consequence of promoting mediocrity. The overall intentions may have been laudable, but specific applications, particularly in the case of BU, led faculty members to turn inward, minimize social contact and prioritise defending the trenches. The rector, appointed from outside the University, did not encourage the development of institutional objectives and strategies. The student population skyrocketed during this period, in line with the vigorous policy of the CHE to increase student enrolment at the universities, no matter what the cost to individual institutions may be.

The dominant character of the CHE eased in the 1990s and the opportunity to elect a new rector from amongst faculty members of BU in 1992 boosted morale and led to a new period of soul-searching. A strategic Planning Committee was formed in 1992 to discuss and develop strategic vision. The Senate adopted a mission statement in 1993 emphasizing that *BU is determined to transcend its current status and sophistication as a leading university in the country to become an institution of research and education aiming at taking scientific excellence of an international nature as a norm.*

In November 1995, the Senate approved the strategic plan worked out at the Strategic Planning Committee after several iterations with faculty members and departmental councils. The basic goal of the plan was to take all the measures necessary to ensure international levels of excellence both in teaching and in enhancing and developing research and knowledge creation activities. More specifically, the plan aimed before the year 2000 at a) increasing the number of faculty members (assistant, associate, and full professors) to 400 (from the existing 270); b) the number of graduate students to 1 800 (from 1 236); and c) decrease the number of undergraduate students to 5 000 (from

6 390). The plan was rather sketchy but the relative weights of the functions were there. The philosophy was to transform BU into a research university that Robert College had never been. BU was going to continue to excel in teaching but choose to put research on a par with teaching. Generating intense knowledge and experience in certain areas, BU aimed to be the reference point for society as well as for public and private enterprises. It is hard to claim that a large majority supported the plan but the administration, in any case, believed in the research-oriented university mission and tried to introduce measures to enhance research.

Research fund

Research Fund (RF) is a line item in the state allocated budget, which is administered through a committee of faculty members chaired by a vice-rector. It started in 1985 and has been a modest but sustainable support for researchers allocating funds through small projects proposed by faculty members. The established practice was to distribute available funds in the budget through a fair evaluation of projects. The connotation for fair included even, equal distribution without deliberate, publicly announced policies. Since 1996, RF operations have been streamlined as explained below; supports have been diversified and each category has been clearly identified, all being tied to projects. Record-keeping was improved. Unfinished projects have been closely followed up to be concluded in a final report.

The seed money allocation was a major program to help promising new faculty members begin research or to provide funds for more established faculty members for research in new directions. A typical allocation was about ten thousand dollars. The intention was to provide support in the initial stages of the research (*i.e.* 2-4 years) so that each faculty member could develop enough momentum in his/her project to then facilitate application to external funding agencies. **Travel fund** to conferences was included in this category.

Matching fund was adopted to reward faculty members who could bring external funding to the University and needed further support to make up for a deficit in his/her budget. **Infrastructure support** (funds for basic equipment for common use) was started to accommodate both equipment and software. A scanning electron microscope, a NMR, an X-ray diffraction unit together with popular codes (mathematica, matlab, spss, ansys) were procured through this program.

Multidisciplinary projects embracing scientific, technical and social aspects of a particular problem have been promoted in the hope that they will draw upon the social/ natural science mix of the University. To make them attractive, budgets of up to USD 25 or 30 000 were announced. The idea was to encourage mode II type projects.

Other Funds

Individual **applications to external funding agencies** were encouraged. Lists and addresses of funding sources were circulated (NSF, CNRS, Fulbright, ESF, WHO, Ford Foundation, Johan Jacobs Foundation, Social Science Research Council, National Endowment for Humanities, the Population Council, NASA); particular emphasis was placed on the Scientific and Technical Research Council of Turkey (**TUBITAK**) which is the Turkish counterpart of American NSF. Applications from BU have traditionally been low for TUBITAK projects; this problem not only reduces the chances of bringing in more funds but also downgrades the image of the University in national research circles. Little progress has been achieved in this issue even today.

Another source for research funding at BU the investment funds from the **State Planning Organization (SPO).** In 1990, the SPO began allocating project-based funding to well-established universities with the idea of developing centres of expertise in areas compatible with the Five-Year Plan. Although the idea was good, the implementation favoured human networks and personal relations, wasting a good share of the funds. Since SPO allocations were generous and were not distributed according to scientific grounds, TUBITAK tried to gain control of these funds. The BU administration had to fight on two fronts: it was explained to CHE and TUBITAK that it was healthier to have diversified sources of research funding. It had to be explained to BU faculty members that applications to SPO were not systematic but subject to review at University level since these funds were part of the university budget and that the total university budget was always limited with respect to other universities and the allocations of the previous year. Consequently, the SPO projects were limited to proposals in line with strong fields at BU based on expertise already developed and shared by 3-4 team members. Social and economic relevance were also among the considerations. These projects, which can amount to several hundred thousand US dollars, could be used to implement institutional research strategies, as opposed to initial stage (seed-money) RF support or completely individual TUBITAK/NSF support.

As one might expect from the cultural profile of BU, there was much opposition to the review procedure for SPO projects at University level through the Research Policies Committee. Implementation of the institutional research strategies may not have been achieved so far but the system has been operational since 1998, eliminating applications with no specific objectives, methodology, critical mass or previous performance.

In 1997, there was an attempt to upgrade the infrastructure relating to experimental studies in science and engineering through a SPO project. A ten-million-dollar project was approved but the foreign credit permit was waiting for governmental commitment. In the meantime, a central laboratory building for surface physics and chemistry was constructed, and a scanning electron microscope, a nuclear magnetic resonance and an x-ray diffraction unit, funded jointly through RF and SPO projects, were set up at the University in 2001, to no great excitement. Criticism of the location of the building was stronger than appreciation of the new facilities.

BU Foundation

All state universities in Turkey established non-profit foundations to bypass the rigidities of the higher education law and to supplement income. Usually, the rector of the university is also the president of the foundation; harmony and synergy can thus be established between the university and the foundation. A separate chairman with more free time to search for donations or commercial activities may seem more efficient and appropriate for an autonomous fund-raising institution such as the foundation. Turkish organizational culture, however, continually fails to promote teamwork and perceive the benefits to be derived from diversity.

BU foundation (BUVAK) was established in 1978; until the mid 1990s it had a simple structure, basically serving as a "petty cash" source. Since 1992, the new administration of the university has promoted a three-pronged fund-raising and income generation structure, the University, the Alumni Organization, and the Foundation (BUVAK). The resulting growth of BUVAK was not based on structural re-engineering or commercial success. The charisma of the rector played an important role in the growth measured in terms of funds raised. Nevertheless, BUVAK generated income and supported research at BU from 1992. A committee of academicians chaired by a member with no administrative duties was responsible for managing the research support.

Travel support for conferences to present a paper (limited to one person per year) and publication support (to boost BU publications) were the most extensive programs. Smaller ones were run to award outstanding research performance, to support local conferences, to invite scientists (for travel expenses and one per department only), to recognize BU faculty members who obtained an external award. The total support for the programs above increased from USD 12 500 in 1993 to USD 160 000 in 2001. The amounts may not be huge but the message they carry is clear.

Inefficiency at BU is blamed on low pay. This is sometimes the case. For six months, the strategic planning committee discussed how to measure merit and finally recommended to the administration initiating a widespread, annual award mechanism to supplement the salary of every faculty member who fulfilled an academic's minimum basic duties - teaching, research and service to the university. The key measure of merit was one refereed publication per year, since the others, teaching and committee work, were established and widely performed anyway. The proposal approved by the Senate was announced in 1997. The implementation of the program began in 1999 with academic activities in 1998 taken as a base. The Academic Incentive Award was the first open move at BU to make a distinction between those who do research and publish and those who don't. This was a message that the University favoured research over everything else. In an environment where 25% of the faculty members were active (see fig.1, a faculty member is considered active if he/she published in that year) this was a courageous move and especially good guidance for young faculty members. In 2001, the funds used for the Academic Incentive Award reached USD 163 000, which exceeded the sum of all other research supports provided by BUVAK.

Research Policies Committee

The Research Fund described in the previous pages is a structure defined through the Higher Education Law and deals with project assessments and approvals, mostly valuable but routine matters of research. To create a platform where more general policies of research can be discussed, a new committee was established in 1998, called the Research Policies Committee. Its mandate was determined as follows:

- to develop research policies;

- to encourage the transfer of research results to society and industry;

- to develop ideas and proposals to diversify research funding and to establish research infrastructure;

- to identify difficulties and deficiencies related to research;

- to encourage identifying strong areas, focused studies;

- to advise the University Executive Board on matters related to SPO projects;

- to develop joint strategies with the Research Fund, BUVAK, the Strategic Planning Committee, and the Research Centres Coordination and Evaluation Committee;

The Research Policies Committee held 25 meetings during the period 1998-2000. It was clearly pointed out that there were no attempts to regulate research activities. The differences between the social and natural science environments were shared. Critical mass, infrastructure needs, evaluation of research performance, publicizing the research capabilities and performances, post-doctoral research mechanisms, the teaching versus research duality, incentives versus disincentives and other related issues were addressed. Serious attempts were made to formulate strong areas in departments. Rather than leading to specific decisions, meetings served to share information, viewpoints, ideas and most importantly to help the vice-rector in charge of research to develop policies. Since 2001, the Committee has been working on SPO proposals and on editing the Research Section of the draft of the Strategic Plan, meeting less frequently and with less emphasis on policy matters.

Another committee, which is responsible for evaluating the Applied Research Centres, has basically worked as a quality assessment board. The number of applied research centres was reduced from 22 to 10 in the period 1994-2000 since they were inactive or just one-man operations. Centres may represent a powerful mechanism to push research, particularly multi-disciplinary activities and to create synergy. The Evaluation Committee of Centres could join the Research Policies Committee in this respect.

Documentation

One of the requirements for evaluation is the availability of information. Such transparency is also necessary for accountability. Research relevant issues are typically publications, projects, citations, graduate students and their theses. An inventory of published journal papers, conference proceedings and projects covering the period 1982-92 was published in 1993. To introduce an element of competition and to acknowledge the active researchers, this inventory has been made public every year since 1993. In addition to tracking the number of publications, the quality of such publications had to be emphasized. Peer review being difficult to quantify and not well-suited to Turkish culture, citations were adopted as an accepted measure of quality and an Inventory of Citations was started in 1996; the first volume covered the 1991-95 period, separate volumes were issued annually thereafter. A Handbook of Research Funds was issued every two years to announce various mechanisms; it spelled out all the details to apply to RF and gave information on how to use and spend the funding according to bureaucratic regulations. Facts and Figures about BU was another compilation of information published yearly after 1993 covering student numbers, faculty members, student-to-faculty ratios, university budget, Research Fund allocations, university facilities, etc. Intended for the guidance of young faculty members on research funding and useful as a source of references, a <u>Research Possibilities at BU</u> booklet was issued in 1998 and again in 2000. This 90-page booklet not only discussed the research policies currently in place; it also summarized recent Research Fund projects to help faculty members share information. A table from this booklet updated for 2001 and 2002 is given below to show the research income of BU over the years. The most valuable item should be the external sources, but unfortunately these cannot be determined since faculty members chose not to share information on research grants that they were able to secure through their own efforts.

Figure 1. **Active faculty (=publishing at least once in the corresponding year) and number of faculty receiving AIA**

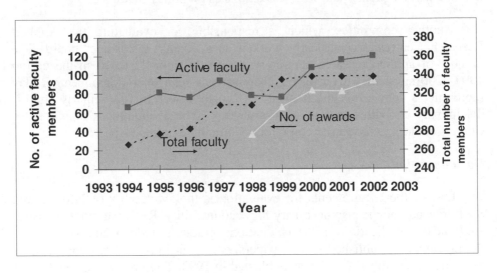

Table 5: Budget and resource funding trends

- in USD	1992	1993	1994	1995	1996	1997	1998	1999	2000	2001
University budget	25.8	29.5	16.5	16.7	22.7	24.7	26.4	26.7	26.3	16.5
Salaries	14.5	15.4	9.3	10.3	12.3	14.2	15.0	15.7	14	9.1
Research fund	800 000	700 000	450 000	400 000	550 000	750 000	850 000	900 000	1 000 000	950 000
SPO projects,	800 000	1 215 000	650 000	530 000	730 000	900 000	470 000	550 000	950 000	820 000
BUVAK support,	25 000	12 500	71 000	103 000	85 000	120 000	140 000	200 000	460 000	323 000
External sources	?	?	750 000	1 000 000	940 000	570 000	100 000	?	?	?

UNIVERSITY RESEARCH MANAGEMENT: MEETING THE INSTITUTIONAL CHALLENGE –ISBN-92-64-01743-7 © OECD 2004

Written messages at BU are less effective compared to, say, American institutions of similar sophistication. Oral culture dominates in the dissemination of information. Thus, research chat-sessions have been arranged to spread the excitement, to stimulate a larger share of the faculty members into promoting the idea of a research-oriented university. From March 1999, a chat-session was held every three months. Available mechanisms and procedures were elaborated upon. The development of an accountability and evaluation culture was emphasized. It was repeatedly evoked that "BU is a small university and is forced to remain small due to space limitation. Thus it should concentrate on quality rather than quantity. In areas where infrastructure and critical mass is needed, BU must decide on its priorities and focus on limited areas. Equally and thinly distributed capabilities coming from a teaching college heritage makes it difficult to become a research address in specific areas. Nor do faculty members in related fields have a tradition of cooperation. Even in disciplines requiring little infrastructure, developing niches specific to BU would be an illumined attitude in a competitive world. A small number of sophisticated researchers and the presence of equally strong science and social sciences point to the fact that the multidisciplinary and problem-oriented Mode II research developed since 1995 could be to BU's relative advantage. Mode I research confined to the disciplinary boundaries and the view that research is an individual responsibility have become subject to serious questioning lately. The new trend is prioritising research to serve the community through projects reflecting needs external to the university. Research performance cannot be measured by numerical indicators alone. The emphasis on SCI/SSCI publications should not be interpreted as the ultimate goal. Opening laboratories, developing expertise, establishing a living research environment, training researchers, transferring knowledge and technology to the community and industry are issues which are at least as valuable as publications".

The success of chat-sessions was limited, judging by the numbers they drew. Once it reached approximately 50 to 60 faculty members, but generally attendance was around 15-20 and after 2001, the new administration did not continue with them.

Industrial links

Interface structures between the University and the community were established in 1998 on the recommendation of the European University Association (EUA which was formerly known as CRE) following a management seminar held at BU. The Continuing Professional Development (CPD) office was planned to run lifelong learning activities and the Technology Transfer Office (TTO) was to provide the link between industry and University. Being the contact point for industry, this office was supposed to work two ways trying to match BU skills and industry needs, industry being a generic name to include banks, companies, etc. Both offices began with the appointment of a director who chose to run the offices by way of committees. However, by 2001, very little had been achieved in terms of developing a structure or service to society. The failure can be attributed partly to the wrong choice of directors and partly to the general culture of the university.

In 1995, the Technology Development Centre was set up jointly with the Ministry of Industry, Small and Medium Enterprise Organization as an 'incubator'. A building was constructed on campus and small companies with innovative and feasible projects were provided with space and financial support for up to three years; the hope was to give young graduates an opportunity to convert their research results into successful products and allow entrepreneurial faculty members to set up start-up companies. In four years since the beginning of the operation, 18 companies have been supported. Nine faculty members served as consultants to these companies.

How successful was it?

A new rector and administration were appointed in August 2000. The outgoing rector had served two four-year periods, the maximum allowed by law. After almost two years with the new administration, it may be the right time to assess the "research initiatives" introduced to boost research consciousness

Arrangements made between 1992-2000 and quoted above were necessarily top-down. Faculty members were not responsive to issues related to research; the environment was not conducive to a bottom-up approach to change. The hope was that a large enough group could be motivated to trigger change. There are promising signs, but on the whole, the system is prisoner to election-based governance, which feeds populism, and blocks change. The concepts of classical, collegial universities such as ceremonial leadership, primus inter pares, still dominate the minds of many faculty members. Deans and directors of institutes are mainly concerned with day-to-day business and survival and do not feel the responsibility to lead their units. Research is still the responsibility of the individual; neither department heads nor deans question research agendas, planning and achievements. The senate as the top academic body never meets to evaluate the research standing of the University.

External actors are not pushing in the right direction either. The public attitude to research is indifference, as described at the very beginning of the report. The typical cultural difference in orientation between the university and business, so common in less industrialized countries, also prevails in Turkey -

i.e. academics wish to pursue groundbreaking publishable research; businesses seek short-term profit from practical applications. University-industry cooperation is wishful thinking, limited to very few situations. An entrepreneurial attitude to commercialise research results has not materialized yet. CHE seems not to have research or research-related issues on its agenda. TUBITAK, the Turkish NSF, does not have any leverage on universities apart from offering some funds to individual researchers. Thus, there is practically no research manager for the country. Nevertheless, the growing scientific output (in terms of SCI papers originating from Turkey, for example) is promising. Based on Institute for Scientific Information (ISI) documents, Turkey ranks 25th in terms of publications. There is a large group of top-notch Turkish scientists, well respected in the scientific community, all representing individual efforts and responsibilities.

On the other hand, the emphasis on research is a major move towards changing the university culture. It is expected to evolve over a period of time and certain delays in response to adopted policies are understandable. In spite of systematic shortcomings, postgraduate student numbers at BU steadily increased in the 1992-2001 period from 12% to 20%. There is growing interest from faculty members towards postgraduate programs. More people now believe in concentration, focussing and niche-building. Ten years ago, it was looked upon as a restriction of academic freedom.

The departments themselves have always enforced personnel policies for recruitment. The Senate ruled out exclusive internal recruitment in 1992; the principle is carefully protected to this day. Recruitment by most departments is based on academic excellence alone. A few started to include strategic preferences. The number of PhDs awarded increased from 15 to 30 between 1992 and 2001, and most engineering departments began requiring a SCI journal publication before granting the degree. The requirement for hiring an assistant professor was set at a minimum of one refereed publication in 1993. The unwritten, but mostly followed rule, was that promotions to associate and full professor were each accompanied by at least one further refereed, citation indexed publication. By 2001, the Senate formalized the minimum requirements at a higher level than before. Social, natural sciences, humanities and engineering departments are difficult to manage through general guidelines; thus, many alternatives were developed for promotions in an effort to encourage research output and recognise the peculiarities specific to disciplines.

Ethics as relating to research and professional conduct has been put on the agenda. A sub-committee prepared a document, which is being circulated and awaits Senate action.

Strategic planning efforts restarted more rigorously in 2001, spelling out core values of BU as:

- a research-oriented university

- a university with multiple sources of income

- a university emphasizing quality assurance and quality culture

- a university having strong international links

- a student-centred and flexible university

The draft of the plan elaborates extensively on research functions and related objectives. However, it remains to be seen how the Senate will respond to this draft.

The university housing policy was completely changed between 1992 and 1994 from favouring senior faculty members for an unlimited period to five-year terms awarded to newly arrived PhDs in need of housing. This policy has been continued by the new administration even more enthusiastically by using every opportunity to build new housing. Housing proves to be a major fringe benefit to draw young faculty members. It may be relevant to add here that the government had to make an adjustment to the salaries of full professors after the economic crisis in early 2001 due to loud protests but omitted similar adjustments for younger faculty members (assistant and associate professors), which may be another sign of public indifference and misguided policies on behalf of the government.

The balance between teaching, research and community service is an issue only recently addressed at BU. For a long time, service to the community was not accepted as being one of the functions of a university. Ivory tower syndrome and elite university concepts prevented the faculty from reaching down to the community. Only in the last 3 to 4 years has some progress been made. The previously established Office for Continued Professional Development was not successful. The present administration made a point to improve it, and provided strong support to replace it this year with a Centre for Lifelong Learning. The excitement around this new centre may open up new possibilities to BU in diversifying income sources. As to the research versus teaching balance, the average faculty member still allocates most of his/her time to teaching but is aware that he/she should also devote at least the same amount of time and effort to research. A survey conducted at the engineering school in 2001 shows that faculty members are spending 22% of their time to research and 40% to teaching, but defines ideal time allocation as 40% to research and 30% to teaching.

As a crude measure of research activity, one can track the number of BU publications appearing in SCI journals. Papers of BU origin, shown in the figure below, increased at roughly the same rate as the national average. This achievement is quite good if one considers that BU lost about 40 experienced faculty members in the last five years to foundation universities or universities abroad. Roughly 15-20 of those members (half in science and half social sciences) were major contributors to the research environment at BU. The Turkish national publication rate was very dynamic between 1992-2001, moving the country's ranking from 38th to 25th. Similar charts for social sciences and SSCI/ A&HCI are available and give similar messages, except BU social science publications representing roughly 10% of the national total (as opposed to 2% in science) which emphasizes the relatively pronounced share of BU social science departments within Turkey.

Figure 2. **SCI publications of BU origin**

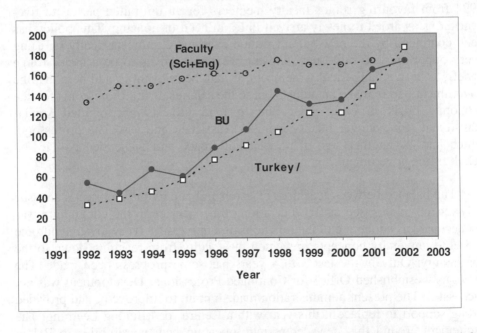

The publication support given by BUVAK to boost BU addressed articles was raised in 2002 to approximately USD 600 per publication, which is an all-time high and a clear indication of the research consciousness of the new administration. The dual character of the University in terms of sciences and social sciences presents problems in developing research policies. The needs, styles and appreciation mechanisms are very different. The cultural sensitivity to peer review leads to reliance on numerical indicators which are despised by the social science community. To even out the differences, publication support for SSCI or A&HCI articles are doubled. Salaries are the same in all state universities for a professor of a certain age and service since all faculty members are civil servants. There is tremendous job security and no incentive to perform. Foundation universities act like private universities in the United States; salaries and fringe benefits are offered case by case and there is no tenure. If a full professor is being paid USD 1 100 in a state university, he/she may receive USD 3 000 in a foundation university. The most lucrative arrangement is for experienced faculty members to retire from the state university, receive their pension - which is almost the same as the full salary - and integrate a foundation university. Hence, top performers have been attracted away by the foundation universities. Those who receive no propositions or those who value the collegial atmosphere, academic environment and above all, the quality of students rather than financial issues, continue with the state system. In spite of the unfair competition of which the state universities complain bitterly, foundation universities have brought in an element of competition which is very healthy for the overall system. However, the loss of faculty members to these universities may force administrators to resort to short-term policies, to provide rapid response to demand, which is unavoidably linked to teaching. There is a real danger of losing the Academic Incentive Award (AIA), a major policy tool, if administration relaxes the present journal publication requirement to please the voting body. Arguments emphasize distributing income among "responsible citizens" meaning those who support the established tradition of an excellent teaching college.

Conclusion

BU chose to become a research university, because

- Turkey needs research universities to keep up with accelerating scientific and technical progress and to continue training academics. BU with its qualified faculty members is one of the natural candidates

- it emphasizes the wish to continue to attract the best students. Severe competition from several state and foundation universities does not leave room for BU to neglect research

- the new generation returning home after receiving a PhD is in search of a "research environment". To maintain their advantage - marketability globally as well as to local foundation universities - the younger generation has a stronger motivation to pursue research.

BU had practically no graduate programs during the days of RC, no tradition of research, no laboratories and no infrastructure. Compared to other established universities today, it started from scratch and with no initial impetus (lump sum funds to boost the research environment) as some state or foundation universities did. Infinitely long periods of transition and adaptation will not be tolerated and a reasonable time has already elapsed.

The continued practice of one vice-rector being assigned to research and development is in line with the mission of the university. It can be hoped that it will be adopted by the coming administrations, as well as a clear message of growing the emphasis on research. One-to-one guidance and encouragement is important, be it by chat sessions or other means. The message needs to be given that a difference will be created between those who take academic life seriously and work along university policies and those who interpret their duties their own way. Promoting research centres and then assessing their performance; continuing with the Academic Incentive Award and increasing it, say, from USD 2 000 to USD 12 000; encouraging teams to look for serious research funds; making the rules of the game known, stable and global, may be decisive moves towards a research-intensive university. The protected and permissive environment of BU should be transformed into the competitive and professional milieu of a modern university.

These and many other supporting schemes not covered here may well be realized in the next five years at BU. However, the opposite is also possible. Even the limited accomplishments of the last 5-10 years may be abandoned. The initiatives have not taken root and policies have not been fully digested yet.

BU seems to be at a crossroad, having two options. Either it will push its research capacity to the limit and prove itself as a research university of international quality, or lose the best students to other emerging research universities and operate as a socially active, enjoyable, relaxed institution in the second league. The past advantage to which BU has been accustomed, of attracting the best students and best faculty members based on teaching and learning, is no longer an option.

RESEARCH MANAGEMENT
AT KEBANGSAAN UNIVERSITY, MALAYSIA:
TOWARDS THE MAKING OF A RESEARCH UNIVERSITY

Mohammed Yusoff Ismail, Mohd. Yusof Hj. Othman,
Ikram M. Said

Introduction

Kebangsaan University Malaysia, (UKM) a State university fully funded by the government of Malaysia under the Ministry of Education, was established on 18 May 1970. Originally set up with three faculties, UKM now has 12 faculties, 7 research institutes and 9 centres of excellence. The main campus is located in Bangi, with two branch campuses in Kuala Lumpur, the federal capital. Total student enrolment is 23 857 which includes undergraduate (16 946), postgraduate (4 961) and distance-learning students (2 400). While the majority of students are Malaysian, the university presently has 911 foreign students enrolled (including 61 undergraduates, 460 Masters and 390 PhDs), mainly from Southeast Asian, Middle East and African countries.

In 2001, the university was designated by the government as one of four research universities in the country. Although the criteria set for this designation is not very clear, UKM's record over the last 25 years has nevertheless proven that it meets standard expectations with regard to research and teaching. In order to fulfil its role as a research university and make a contribution well beyond this, UKM has taken various measures to ensure that a research culture becomes an integral part of its academic pursuit. This means that promotion exercises for its academic staff take into serious consideration active involvement in research as well as teaching, graduate supervision and publications.

The commitment of UKM to research has been outlined in its strategic plan that extends into the year 2020. According to this strategy, the university places emphasis on two kinds of research. Firstly, the university is committed to basic research befitting its role in expanding the horizon of knowledge. Secondly, the university is committed to conducting applied and experimental research as part of its contribution to building the nation. The university strongly believes in promoting research that has a very clear focus and sense of purpose. As such, preferences are given to funding for research projects that will eventually produce results which contribute to the university and the country as a whole in terms of increasing the nation's potential and the advancement of knowledge.

With a total number of 1 563 academic staff, UKM is expected to take the lead in conducting both basic and applied research projects, as shown by the fact that UKM is one of the recipients of various research grants from the government and the industry. In fact, more than 90% of research conducted in UKM is funded by the government, the most important of which is the special fund given by the Ministry of Science, Technology and Environment (MOSTE) under a drastically revised national research strategy known as Intensification of Research in Priority Areas (IRPA). Moreover, the university also receives a yearly allocation of research funding from the Ministry of Education which is equally distributed to all faculties. In order to encourage younger lecturers to conduct basic research projects, they are given preference when applying for these short-term grants. Individual academic members of the faculty and institutes also sometimes receive grants from industry to conduct joint research projects. Researchers at UKM have been involved in various research projects, networking with those from other universities, including those from overseas, as for example the collaboration between UKM and other domestic research and international institutes in Japan, the United Kingdom, and the United States.

Moreover, in 1999, UKM also established a joint research programme with the Malaysian Technology Development Corporation (MTDC) specifically aiming to enhance development activities in marketable technology, capitalising and making full use of university expertise and the entrepreneurial skills of the industry. One outcome of the collaboration with MTDC is the setting up of *Incubation Centres* within the university grounds to encourage and facilitate the formation and growth of new businesses based on knowledge generated by various research groups in the university. To date, there are seven companies that are involved with the incubation projects, covering various business ventures ranging from the development of computer software to developing vaccines and biotechnological products.

This chapter covers three main aspects of research management at Kebangsaan University, namely the procurement and allocation of research funding, the monitoring of research projects, and support services related to research activities. The bulk of the discussion will focus on how research activities are supervised and managed, especially those that receive direct funding from the Ministry of Science, Technology and the Environment under the Seventh and Eight Malaysia Plans. This chapter will also outline the role of the Research Management Centre at UKM in helping to shape and further consolidate the university as a research institution. In general, research activities in state universities in Malaysia have been prompted by the change in government policy regarding science and technology as reflected in the objectives stated in the last three national development plans covering a period of five years each, namely the Sixth, Seventh, and Eighth Malaysia Plans.

Policy Changes in Government Research Strategy

Within the national agenda known as Vision 2020, Malaysia expects to reach the level of a developed nation by the year 2020, with the establishment of a scientific and progressive society that is both innovative and forward-looking. Such a policy will help to change the country from being a mere consumer of imported technology to a contributor to scientific and technological knowledge in the future, hence improving its competitive edge in the global market. The 3rd Outline Perspective Plan (OPP3) which covers the second decade of development under Vision 2020, focuses on building a resilient and competitive nation. During this period, efforts will be made to raise the quality of development and generate high sustainable growth, bringing prosperity to all. The OPP3 has been formulated on a policy that will be called the National Vision Policy (NVP). The NVP will build upon the efforts initiated under the country's past development plans and strengthen the transformation of Malaysia into a fully developed nation as envisaged under Vision 2020. The key thrusts under the NVP include the development of a knowledge-based economy as a strategic move to increase the added value of all economic sectors and optimise the nation's brain power; strengthening human resource development to produce a competent, productive and knowledgeable workforce. Research and development is certainly the main area of focus within the umbrella of education in the implementation of the country's aspirations. To maintain the competitiveness of Malaysian industry and to benefit from the knowledge-based economy, it is crucial to strengthen the environment for innovation and knowledge. Attention will be given to improving the creativity and innovation of the whole process of training, enhancing R&D and S&T, and ensuring the availability of financial facilities. Efforts will be made to increase collaboration between public and private research institutions and the private sector for the effective development, dissemination and commercialisation of R&D.

In 1986, the National Science and Technology Policy was launched in order to provide guidelines for Science, Engineering and Technology (SET) development in the country. One of the strategies of the Sixth Malaysian Plan (1991-1995) was to promote and further enhance the country's effort to increase technological capability by transforming public sector R&D programmes in a drive to relevance in industry. However, this strategy was changed to a productivity drive when Malaysia introduced the Seventh Malaysian Plan (1996-2000), which set the thrust of SET development to meet the objectives of productivity-driven growth and to enhance competitiveness. The Eighth Malaysian Plan (2001-2005) also adopts the same strategy with some modification in certain areas of research.

The Second National Science and Technology Policy, officially launched in June 2003, provides a framework for the improved performance and long-term growth of the Malaysian economy. The goal of the second S&T policy is to accelerate the development of S&T capability and capacity for national competitiveness with the twin objectives of increasing the R&D spending of the country to at least 1.5% of the GDP and to achieve a competent workforce of at least 60 RSEs (researchers, scientists and engineers) per 10 000 labour force by the year 2010, so as to enhance the national capacity in R&D and the national capability in S&T. With these specific objectives, it is therefore not surprising to find that strengthening research and technological capacity and capability constitutes 2 of the 7 strategic thrusts of the second policy. The main thrust of the second policy emphasises, among other things, the intensification of a critical mass in terms of human resource capacity and capability necessary for the development of science and technology by increasing the ratio of students pursuing scientific, technical and engineering disciplines. It also stipulates the increase in number of postgraduate students to at least 60% of the total enrolment by the year 2005 and the establishment of science and technology postgraduate research universities.

In recognizing the importance of supporting R&D programmes for SET development in the country, the government, through the Ministry of Science, Technology and the Environment (MOSTE) has created R&D funding through an IRPA (Intensification of Research in Priority Areas) programme for state universities and government research institutes. Funding for the Seventh Malaysian Plan was RM1 billion, further increased to RM2 billion under the Eighth Malaysian Plan. Realizing that private sectors are not ready to invest money on R&D activities, the government has also introduced several incentive schemes that encourage the private sector to establish R&D collaboration with state universities and government research institutes. In comparison to other developing countries, the amount of money spent on R&D in Malaysia is only 0.5% of its GDP for the year 2000, while countries like Japan spent 2.8%, South Korea 2.9%, USA 2.5% and Germany 2.3%.

A direct benefit of the major shift in the national policy regarding science and technology is that universities and other research institutions are endowed with generous grants from the government on a competitive basis, thereby prompting these institutions to develop various strategies to bid for the government funding. Consequently, universities are forced to set up some kind of unit for a more systematic management of research activities.

R&D Initiatives at UKM

Although UKM is still a relatively young university, the research culture of the university has been embedded since its formation. During the development years, the administration put various initiatives in place for the sole purpose of imposing the importance of research and for the sustainability and high quality of the research activities carried out by the faculty. Even before the year 2000 and up to 2020, in accordance and in reaction to initiatives and policies set by the federal government, UKM produced a document *"Strategic Plan of UKM 2000-2020"* which contains 10 strategies for UKM to follow through to make all academic activities relevant and competitive in the twenty-first century. The plan was devised through input from all levels of the university, while at the same time considering other environmental factors (local and global).

The UKM Strategic Plan was formulated in view of the pervasive influence of local and global environments on higher education and our efforts to become the premier university of the nation. The document sets out the vision, mission, and strategic steps to be taken which include the plan of action and activities related to the strategy.

Vision   UKM is committed to being the leading university, pioneering innovations and creating a dynamic, knowledgeable and ethical society

Mission   To be the premier university that affirms and promotes the value of the Malay language while globalizing knowledge within the framework of the national culture.

Strategies related to R&D (directly or indirectly) are the following:

- to emphasize and intensify research;

- to upgrade the quality of our academic programmes;

- to raise UKM to international standing;

- to equip UKM as a leading agency of the ICT era;

- to provide the required physical infrastructure and environment for R&D.

In order to follow through the strategies that have been put in place to increase the capacity of our research programmes, UKM has also made sure that faculty members are given great encouragement to excel in research.

All faculty members are aware that research is an important component of their academic duties and their involvement in research will be taken into account (at least 20%) during each appraisal year and during the promotion exercise of the university. Thus, UKM has provided short-term research grants (mostly as seed money to a maximum of MYR 20 000.00 or about EUR 5 000) to each new faculty member, so that they can begin their research activities immediately. After a three-year term into their research, they would be expected to be competitive enough to bid for more substantial funding through the IRPA programmes under the Ministry of Science Technology and the Environment.

In order to prepare the faculty members for their careers as effective and contributing members of the academic staff at UKM, the university established the Centre for Academic Advancement which, among other functions, is responsible for providing courses to upgrade the skills of lecturers in most (if not all) aspects of their career. Some of these courses include: teaching university students, the use of ICT in teaching, effective supervision, writing research proposals, writing skills for international journals, evaluation and grading, time management skills, etc.. It has now become a compulsory requirement of the university for the academic staff to follow certain critical courses before they can be considered for any promotion. This is to ensure that UKM provides quality education and at the same time produces quality research. Other incentives for the faculty members to enhance their research capabilities include: paid sabbatical leave of nine months after five years of continued service, a three-month research leave taken after three years of service, awards for researchers, postdoctoral appointments or research assistants.

To manage the activities of R&D, the university also established the Research Management Centre.

The Research Management Centre at UKM

The centre was set up in January 1995 as a five-person unit. On 13th January 1999, in line with the availability of larger amounts of research funding from the government, the unit was expanded in response to the increased number of research activities. The research management centre now comprises 22 people, including 4 academic staff, 3 administrative officers and 15 support staff.

The centre reports directly to, and is placed under the responsibility of, the Deputy Vice Chancellor of Academic Affairs, while a Board of Advisors for Research is appointed by the Vice Chancellor to advise the university in matters regarding the philosophy, policy and direction of research in UKM. The centre is headed by a Director assisted by two Deputy Directors together with a head of the Instrumentation Unit (see Appendix 1).

One of the centre's main functions is to coordinate the management of (a) R&D funding applications, and (b) monitoring and assessing the progress of the projects at institutional level. Basically, its role is to provide accountability for the research funds received from the government by ensuring that researchers complete their projects during the stipulated period and deliver their interim and final reports on time. The centre also helps in the registration of products and innovative ideas accomplished at the end of respective projects. This includes the filing of patents and the dissemination of research results and products for the purpose of commercialisation. In addition, the centre also coordinates multiple usage and the maintenance of highly specialised scientific equipment purchased through grants provided by the funding agencies. Over the years, the university has accumulated a wide range of expensive and sophisticated scientific equipment bought and used for various research projects. The Instrumentation Unit, established in 2002, coordinates the usage of these instruments, their maintenance and repair.

Altogether there are nine committees directly involved in research management at UKM :

- the Research Advisory Board

- the UKM Research and Development Planning Committee (JPPP).

- the IRPA Sector Panel.

- the Research and Development Planning Committee of the Faculty (JPPPF).

- the Committee for the Transfer of Technology.

- the Advisory Committee for Research Management.

- the Committee for the Exhibition of Innovation and Invention.

- the Committee for the Instrumentation Unit.

- the Committee for Conferences and Exhibitions.

The Research Advisory Board

- advises UKM with regard to trends in R & D and their relationship with the economic development of the country.

- advises UKM in R & D with respect to domestic and international industrial development.

- advises UKM on the latest developments in research and their bearing on the academic curriculum.

The UKM Research and Development Planning Committee

- to evaluate, formulate and suggest changes to R & D policies of UKM;

- to determine priorities and main research thrusts for UKM;

- to suggest to the university the setting up of various centres of excellence and infrastructures for R & D;

- to decide on the amount of short-term research grants allocated by the university to the various faculties;

- to monitor all research activities by the departments, centres and institutes through the research committee of the respective faculty, centre or institute.

IRPA Sector Panel

Since the bulk of research funding also comes from the Ministry of Science, Technology and the Environment, the university formed a special committee to deal with research policy and issues under the IRPA programmes. The IRPA Sector Panel is given the following objectives:

- to suggest to the UKM Research and Development Planning Committee (JPPP) research priority areas and programmes to the IRPA for the attention of the government.

- to give a final evaluation on research projects and determine the success and impact of the projects on the development of the country as a whole.

- to evaluate all research projects under each IRPA programme and decide on the projects that should be given funding.

- to ascertain that there is minimum overlapping between projects and to suggest the amalgamation of projects that have common objectives.

- to make various recommendations to the UKM Research and Development Planning Committee which will then be forwarded by the research management centre to the IRPA Secretariat at the national level for further consideration.

The Research and Development Planning Committee of the Faculty

- to decide on the general policy and guidelines to be used by the faculty with regard to the delivery of research grants, the monitoring and evaluation of progress and final reports of all research projects;

- to re-allocate short-term research grants given by the Ministry of Education;

- to receive applications for IRPA research grants, to evaluate the proposals, to monitor the progress of the projects, and to endorse progress reports and final reports at faculty level;

- to receive proposals for outside grants other than short-term research grants and IRPA;

- to evaluate and monitor the progress of such projects.*Committee for the Transfer of Technology*

- to plan programmes for the transfer and commercialisation of intellectual property;

- to promote joint research between UKM and industry;

- to give necessary information regarding intellectual property and its protection to researchers, academic staff and students;

- to identify and give advice on intellectual property derived from research;

- to assist the university in updating the policy on intellectual property.

Advisory Committee for Research Management

- to give advice on the management and administration of the Research Management Centre;

- to give advice on relevant research focus according to sectors and in line with the vision of the university and the country's needs;

- to give advice and coordinate research priorities for each faculty;

- to prepare concept papers related to research in order to promote and intensify research activities in UKM.

Committee for Exhibitions of Innovations and Inventions

- to serve as the secretariat for exhibitions of innovations and inventions by UKM;

- to prepare the budget plan and the participation of UKM in exhibitions on research innovations and inventions;

- to prepare working papers for participation in various exhibitions at national and international level;

- to disseminate information on forthcoming exhibitions which will involve the participation of UKM;

- to coordinate preparation for organising exhibitions;

- to prepare the necessary infrastructure for exhibitions;

- to organise the logistics for the transportation of exhibits and equipment, and for the travel and accommodation of participants involved in exhibitions.

Instrumentation Unit

Established to serve as a "one-stop centre" to assist research activities that requires instrumentation facilities available at UKM (see Appendix 2 for an inventory of major instruments).

- to serve as a centralized unit of instrumentation for the whole university;

- to secure funds for the maintenance of major equipment at UKM under the "new policy" financial allocation;

- to prepare a computerized control system for major equipment to ensure optimum use of instruments;

- to make recommendations to the university regarding requirements for space and buildings for the safe storage of the equipment that is acquired;

- to train the necessary support staff to operate and maintain major equipment at the Instrumentation Unit.

Research Management Centres in Public Universities

Most of the public universities in Malaysia have some sort of research management unit within their administrative structure, although not all have been organised into a fully-fledged centre. The structure may vary between universities, but the main purpose of such a unit is to monitor and account for the public funds delivered by the government to the universities for research purposes. Some of the research centres operate under a consultation bureau while others are placed under the Registrar's office.

An interesting point is that all the research management units of the 17 public universities and colleges meet annually under a national council organised by one of the universities acting as the secretariat. The meeting aims at sharing experience and coordinating matters pertaining to research procedures in each university, in order to form a general guideline and uniform administrative policy that applies to all researchers in state universities.

Apart from the annual meetings, research management units are in constant contact with one another to reach a standardised procedure with regard to research management and solving various administrative problems involving researchers, research assistants, funding agencies and the university bursary.

The more established research management centres often help the new state universities to set up their own research management centres by giving them training and other necessary assistance.

Another major activity of the research management centres is to organize the joint bi-annual exhibition on research findings and innovative products involving all public universities sponsored by the Ministry of Education, one of the universities being given the responsibility of heading the secretariat of this national exhibition. The first exhibition was held in 2001 with Kebangsaan University acting as the main organiser. The exhibition planned for the second week of October 2003 was hosted by Putra University.

Procuring Research Grants

UKM has three types of research funding, namely the short-term grant (STG), the Intensification of Research in Priority Areas (IRPA) grant and the private sector grant (PSG). The first two are given by the government under the revised policy on research strategy, while industry funds the third. Briefly, under the Seventh Malaysia Plan (1996-2000) UKM received a total of MYR 88 620 993* for 341 research projects in various sectors allocated under IRPA funding. The amount of the IRPA allocation under the Eighth Malaysia Plan received by UKM was MYR 125 024 788 as of August 2003 (see Appendix 2 for further details).

Research for IRPA projects is categorized under the following sub-categories:

- **Experimental Applied Research** - research towards realising national potential and knowledge building to capitalise on the opportunities from the economy with strong potential for commercialisation.

- **Prioritised Research** - interdisciplinary research to address the immediate needs of the country with clear objectives and commercial outputs.

- **Strategic Research** - interdisciplinary research for future global competitiveness with clearly targeted commercial output.

Yet another type is categorized as "Main Stream" (*Arus Perdana*) research, in which the university appoints a group of scholars to do research on specific problems or issues using special funds derived from funds provided by the

Ministry of Education. To date three major projects have come under this category.

Distribution of Research Grants

Short-term research grants

The short-term grant received from the Ministry of Education is distributed annually to the faculties and institutes based on a very simple formula. Faculties with a large number of academic staff receive a larger portion of this research funding compared to the smaller ones.

Lecturers who are interested in conducting basic research projects are required to submit application forms and proposals to their respective faculty. At the faculty level, applications are appraised by a committee comprising departmental heads or their representatives, professors and senior lecturers appointed to sit on the committee. After the applications have gone through the evaluation process by the committee, the applicants are informed whether the proposals have been accepted in entirety, with some modifications, or have been totally rejected.

In most cases, applications are seldom rejected in their entirety since they have already gone through some kind of screening procedure at the departmental level. The decision made by the evaluation committee is governed by the fact that the general spirit is to encourage young researchers to embark on basic and fundamental research leading to the presentation and publication of original research findings as part of their ongoing training. The actual amount of funding given is determined by the faculty research committee. Short-term research projects come under the purview of the faculty. The Research Management Centre is informed of the number of projects and amount of money assigned by the faculty to individual projects. Information regarding the research projects that have been approved and are currently being carried out is also available on-line on the university's integrated information system.

IRPA grants

The procurement of IRPA research grants is very competitive among state universities and research institutes. The screening process for the application for the fund goes through departmental, faculty and sector levels before they are forwarded to the Ministry of Science, Technology and Environment for approval. The most rigorous process takes place at the sector level where the Research Management Centre has the responsibility of gathering experts from the respective fields of specialization to evaluate and make recommendations on the proposals. The evaluation committee also includes experts from outside the university, including industry and other state research agencies.

Even after the rigorous screening process by the sector committee, the rate of rejection by the ministry can be very high. The record of rejection for proposals submitted by UKM is around 45 to 50% on average, although some faculties are known to have a high success rate, as high as 90%.

The Research Management Centre's role with regard to the application procedure is to mediate between the researchers and the ministry. Regular workshops are also conducted by the centre to help guide potential researchers in preparing proposals that meet the requirements of the funding agency. It is during these workshop sessions that young researchers are given guidance and advice by the more experienced researchers who have worked successfully under IRPA grants. Representatives of the ministry are also called to the sessions and are consulted regarding the latest requirements and conditions set by the funding agency. Participants go through various stages of proposal preparation – identification of research problems and statement of objectives, justification for the research, literature review, methodology and the calculation of expected expenditure covering man-hour costing, purchase of equipment, travel expenses and other special needs.

Moreover, each faculty, centre and institute also organizes its own internal workshops in which researchers are given assistance in formulating their proposals and fulfilling the necessary requirements when applying for research grants. The whole process of application is shown in Appendix 3.

The following steps represent a typical process of grant application at UKM, particularly one that involves IRPA funding:

Step 1: the researcher or a group of researchers holds a discussion to formulate a proposal. Application forms which have been duly filled are sent to the faculty with endorsement and approval by the respective centre or department.

Step 2: the applications are evaluated by the faculty through its Committee for Research Management and Development. Applications that have been approved by the committee will be forwarded to the Research Management Centre.

Step 3: the Research Management Centre will then make arrangements with the committee at the sector level, chaired by the head of the sector to evaluate the applications. Proposals that have been approved by the sector panel will be sent to IRPA Secretariat in MOSTE.

Step 4: the IRPA Secretariat will inform the Research Management Centre of successful applications.

Step 5: the Research Management Centre will inform successful candidates of their applications. The Bursar's Department at UKM will also be notified of the approval so that an account will be opened for the research project. A code given by IRPA Secretariat of MOSTE will be used for the account.

Step 6: financial details of the research project will be downloaded by the Computer Centre into *UKM Research Online*, a website specially constructed to help researchers keep track of their research expenditures and financial status.

Step 7: the Computer Centre will issue a password to the researcher so that he can access the system for the purpose of monitoring online the financial status of the project.

Monitoring Research Activities

Monitoring of research activities by the Research Management Centre is done at various levels:

Level 1: monitoring is done by means of evaluating research project proposals at the departmental, centre and faculty levels.

Level 2: monitoring is done at the sector level of the Research Management Centre through the following mechanism: for projects that are categorized as 'Experimental and Applied' (EA), the proposals are discussed and evaluated by the Panel Sector Committee. If necessary, researchers are called to present their case in person to the committee. For projects classified as Priority Research (PR) and Strategic Research (SR), researchers need to present their case directly to the Panel Sector Committee.

Level 3: presentation of progress reports. The Research Management Centre organizes a special seminar called Seminar for Monitoring of IRPA Projects, which is held towards the end of each calendar year. The first seminar of this kind was held in 1999. The seminar will involve the following activities:

– presentation of technical and progress reports by researchers.

- presentation of an overall report by the head of each research project.

- evaluation by IRPA Sector Panel on the presentation. Normally the Sector Panel will give various suggestions regarding the research problems and take into consideration the views expressed by researchers.

- poster presentation of research findings.

  - To facilitate the evaluation process, researchers are required to prepare their presentation according to a set format, while papers are compiled into a report that is made available to all participants of the seminar. Every member of the Sector Panel is required to prepare a written report on the achievements and shortcomings of the research projects and submit the findings to the Research Management Centre. Copies of the reports are submitted to the IRPA Secretariat at the Ministry. Comments by the head of Sector Panel are also forwarded to respective researchers for further action.

<u>Level 4</u>: for IRPA projects that have been completed or stopped, monitoring is done by evaluating findings that have potential for commercialisation by industry. Researchers involved are encouraged to prepare and submit a proposal for product commercialisation to the Committee on the Transfer of Technology, UKM. The committee evaluates the proposals in terms of their commercial viability or decides whether the findings ought to be registered in the form of intellectual property (patent, trade mark, copyright, registered industrial designs, circuit board layout designs, etc.).

As for IRPA projects under the Eighth Malaysian Plan, UKM has suggested that the monitoring seminar for Experimental and Applied projects (EA) be separated from that for Priority Research (PR) and Strategic Research (SR). PR and SR programmes of research are comprised of separate projects that are carried out at different institutions. Heads of the research programme are report directly to the IRPA Secretariat in MOSTE in terms of financial accountability and the submission of progress and final reports. Thus, the Research Management Centre of UKM suggests that every research programme organize a periodical review (every three or four months) in order to self-monitor the progress they have so far achieved. If necessary, it is also suggested that an external assessor (national or international) should also be invited to evaluate and give suggestions on problematic areas of the research programme.

The IRPA Secretariat and the Research Management Centre are expected to be informed of the findings and remedies deliberated during the review.

It is also suggested that every year there should be a monitoring seminar for each programme in collaboration with other programmes. Thus, the monitoring process could be improved by the availability of post-seminar summary documentation.

Online monitoring of financial expenses and commitments of IRPA grants

Researchers can keep track of their expenditure records and financial commitments through a website dedicated to research activities in UKM. All that needs to be done is to go to UKM main web site http://research.ukm.my/ppp/penyelidikan/akaun.asp. By clicking on 'Research Account Online', researchers can access information on their account – how much money has been spent and how much still remains in the account. Online accessibility to research accounts is offered in three modules, one for researchers, one for the Research Management Centre and one for the Bursar of the university.

Dissemination of Research Findings

Research findings are disseminated in various ways. As mentioned above, the Research Management Centre is also involved in publicising research findings through the Committee for Exhibitions of Innovations and Inventions which is headed by the Director. The centre regularly participates in various exhibitions held at the national and international levels, including those held in Europe and Korea. Many of the exhibits tendered by UKM researchers at these exhibitions have won various awards and prizes.

Another unit of the centre, which deals with the public and tries to promote industry-university cooperation, is the Innovation Unit. The unit was originally established in the commercial section of the university, but was transferred to the Research Management Centre as of 1st January 2001. Its main task is to manage 'contract research' projects, the registration of intellectual property rights, and the commercialisation of IRPA research output and products. In general, it forms a bridge between researchers in UKM and outside bodies that have an interest in joint research projects and commercial ventures with UKM. The Innovation Unit is accountable to a university level committee responsible for formulating policies regarding the transfer of technology. The table in Appendix 5 lists typical activities of the Innovation Unit.

The Making of a Research University

According to the *Carnegie Classification of Higher Learning Institutions,* from a total of 3 941 institutes of higher education in the United States, only 6.6% or about 261 of them could be categorically defined as research universities. The classification divides research universities into two main types: (a) extensive research universities and (b) intensive research universities. The former are institutes of higher education that produce no less than 50 PhD graduates per year in no less than 15 fields of study. The latter are institutes that produce no less than 10 PhD graduates per year in no less than 3 fields of study or an overall number of 20 PhD graduates per year.

Based on this categorisation, UKM has fared well in terms of producing graduates at doctoral level and in terms of meeting the requirements of a research university. For example, the number of PhD graduates increased steadily from 44 in 2000 to 71 in 2003. The expected number of PhD graduates for 2003 was 80.

The criteria of a research university can also be measured by the number of postdoctoral positions offered by the institution. In 2003, only 5 such positions were held at UKM.

UKM's researchers have participated in many exhibitions held at both national and international levels. Many have also won awards and prizes in various categories UKM has so far won 11 national awards for the year 2003 at the MINDEX/INNOTEX/ITEX exhibitions and 11 international awards, 5 in Korea in 2002 and 6 in Geneva in 2003.

Conclusion

As UKM endeavours to meet the expectation of becoming a research university, two things can be said about the university's contribution to knowledge advancement. First, like other state universities in the country, UKM has set up various infrastructures to support research activities, including the purchase of equipment and software. The Research Management Centre is only one of the many facilities established by the university to coordinate and manage research activities involving academic staff, students and outside collaborators who also provide the university with technical assistance and training programmes.

Second, obtaining research grants has never actually been a major hindrance in developing a research culture in the university. This can be seen by the fact more than 50% of grant applications by researchers from UKM were successful in winning the approval of funding agencies, especially from the two ministries.

The setting up of the research management centre in UKM has definitely brought about a more conducive climate towards making research culture a core business of the university. As monitoring of the research activities is now centralised, the university can hope to be more competitive in procuring more research grants from the funding agencies. However, one of the problems faced both by the university and the funding agencies is the non-delivery of research reports at the end of stipulated period. While this problem is not particularly widespread at UKM, the setting up of a more centralised monitoring unit also means that the university can introduce proactive measures to reduce the problem. A centralised monitoring unit can also help to keep track of what has been achieved in terms of major research breakthroughs, while their dissemination can be organised in a more systematic and effective way.

The next step to be taken by UKM is to expand the enrolment of postgraduate students and postdoctoral positions to reflect the commitment of the university towards research.

APPENDICES

APPENDIX 1

Organization Chart of Research Management Centre
Kebangsaan University

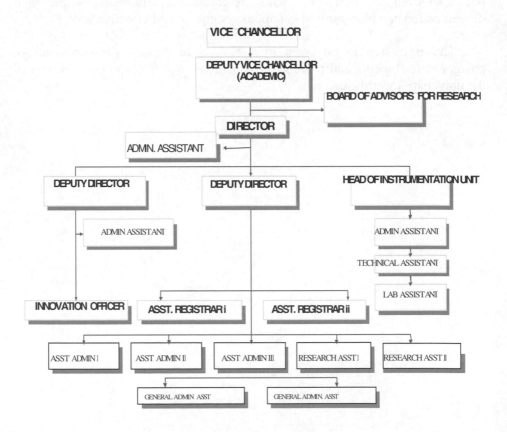

APPENDIX 2

Table 1. Types of research grant

Grant (type)	IRPA (7ᵗʰMP)*	IRPA (8ᵗʰMP)*	STG*	PSG
Duration	1996-2000	2001-2003	2000-2002	2000-2002
N° of projects	365	186	610	77
Amount (MYR)	88 295 995	125 024 788	4 178 994	4 948 867

(*Government funding)

Table 2. IRPA grant received under the Eighth Malaysia Plan

Categories	N° of projects	Amount (MYR)
Experimental & Applied	162	28 880 212
Priority Research	8	48 220 664
Strategic Research	1	38 207 048
Biotechnology	15	9 716 864
Total	186	125 024 788

Table 3. Distribution of IRPA grant according to sectors under EAR (Experimental and Applied Research)

Sector	N° of projects	Amount (MYR)
Agro-Industry	5	953 000
Energy	6	1 282 696
Manufacturing	7	1 235 540
IT/Services	35	7 297 383
Economy	1	183 490
Health	15	2 495 047
Social Science	15	2 195 834
Environment	8	1 723 166
Science & Engineering	70	11 514 056
Total	162	28 880 212

APPENDIX 2 (CONTINUED)

Table 4. **Distribution of IRPA grant to faculties under the 7th and 8th Malaysia Plan**

Faculty/Institutes	Seventh Malaysia Plan	Eighth Malaysia Plan
Economy	695 000 (3)	183 490 (1)
Engineering	25 794 818 (59)	74 334 396 (20)
Medicine	13 286, 31 (75)	13 609 151 (18)
Science and Technology	34 499 362 (153)	25 368 346 (85)
Allied Health Sciences	3 947 979 (21)	1 785 896 (11)
Science and Information Technology	3 744 502 (14)	6 867 835 (33)
Law	460 000 (1)	--
Education	789 900 (14)	620 412 (5)
Social Science and Humanities	1 611 424 (8)	1 785 896 (11)
Islamic Studies	62 600 (1)	314 000 (2
Business Management	--	122 670 (1)
ATMA (Institute of Malay World and Civilisation)		455 200 (3)
Lestari (Institute of Environment and Development)	2 717 377(7)	679 840 (3)
IKMAS (Institute for Malaysian and International Studies)	520 000 (4)	--
Biotechnology	--	9 716 864 (15)
Total	88 584 993 (364)	125 024 788 (186)

Number of research projects in parentheses.

APPENDIX 3

Application Process UKM - MOSTE

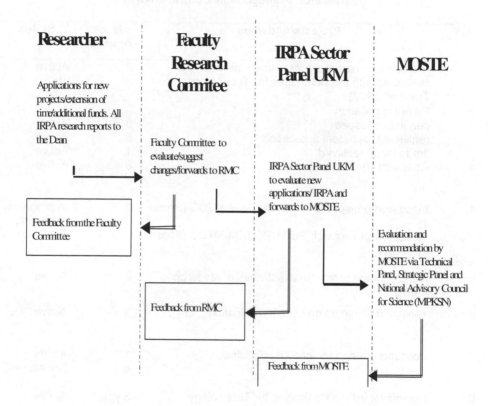

Researcher

Applications for new projects/extension of time/additional funds. All IRPA research reports to the Dean

Feedback from the Faculty Committee

Faculty Research Commitee

Faculty Committee to evaluate/suggest changes/forwards to RMC

Feedback from RMC

IRPA Sector Panel UKM

IRPA Sector Panel UKM to evaluate new applications/ IRPA and forwards to MOSTE

Feedback from MOSTE

MOSTE

Evaluation and recommendation by MOSTE via Technical Panel, Strategic Panel and National Advisory Council for Science (MPKSN)

APPENDIX 4

Activities of the Innovation Unit

Research Management Centre, UKM

No.	Projects/Activities	N° of projects	Status
1.	Projects with potential for commercialisation (as registered with the Committee for Technology Transfer, UKM)	9	Active
2.	Patent application		
	certificates issued	3	Active
	registered for patent application	5	Active
	'trade-mark' received	1	Active
3.	Research contract projects	9	Active
4.	Incubation project with PUSTEK UKM-MTDC (Phase 1)	3	In progress beginning
	Incubation project with PUSTEK UKM-MTDC (Phase 2)	-	Feb 2003
5.	Marketing and promotional activities of research products	8	Active
6.	Talks and seminars on commercialisation	3	Active
7.	Accounts opened for innovation projects	11	Active
		8	Not active
8.	Secretariat for the Committee for Technology Transfer, UKM	3 years	Active

APPENDIX 5

List of Research Institutes and Centres of Excellence at Kebangsaan University

Research Institutes

- Institute of the Malay World and Civilisation (ATMA)

- Institute for the Environment and Development (LESTARI) Institute for Malaysian and International Studies (IKMAS)

- Institute for Micro-Engineering and Nano-electronics (IMEN) (established November 2002)

- Institute for Bio-molecular Medicine (UMBI)

- Institute for Space Research (ANGKASA)

- Institute for Occidental Studies (IKON)

Centres of Excellence

- Centre for Advanced Engineering

- Centre for Genetic Analysis and Molecular Technology

- Centre for Insect Systematic Studies

- Unit for Research in Food Quality

- E-Community Study Unit

DEVELOPING RESEARCH IN A HEI
DUBLIN INSTITUTE OF TECHNOLOGY, IRELAND

Ellen Hazelkorn

Background[45]

The Dublin Institute of Technology (DIT) was formally established by legislation in 1992 from the merger of six colleges of technology whose individual origins date back to 1887. Today, it is the second largest HEI in Ireland. A multi-level institute, DIT provides full-time and part-time programmes across six faculties: applied arts, business, built environment, engineering, science, and tourism and food. Currently there are some 20 000 students pursuing more than 400 different programmes at apprenticeship, certificate, diploma, degree and postgraduate level.[46] It has developed a strong reputation for a practical, career-related approach with strong links to industry and the professions. While DIT has full degree-awarding powers it has not yet gained university status; rather it sits uneasily in Irish higher education between the Institutes of Technology and the universities.[47]

Research is relatively new at DIT, as it was not officially recognized prior to 1992. While this represents a significant change in mission focus, there had been some research activity, particularly linked to industry and in those former colleges of technology dedicated to science and engineering, since the 1970s. That latter period, marking the first phase of research development, had seen a number of initiatives to encourage and support postgraduate research, expanding the industrial liaison function to provide greater support and developing policies for the development of research.[48]

The International Study Group on Technological Education, which reported to the Minister for Education in 1987, stated that it "was impressed by the work of the colleges" and recognised the high standing which the colleges hold in their special fields of study. [Its] research activities…are wide ranging, as would be expected in an Institute of such diverse character. Collaboration with other researchers and institutions both nationally and internationally is a common feature of much research carried out by the Institute.[49]

The report recommended that statutory provision be made for the Institute to engage in research, and to make its expertise and facilities more widely available, as considered appropriate, to industry and business. Such provisions were enshrined in the DIT Act 1992 which permitted research, consultancy and development, either on its own or with other institutions, and services in relation to such work including participating in limited companies and the exploitation of such work. 1992 marked the beginning of the second phase of development (1992-1995) which can be considered a period of expansion and diversification.

DIT's third phase of research development, 1995 – today, has been coincidental to mounting Irish government acknowledgement of the role of research and knowledge production as critical factors for a knowledge economy. *A Comparative International Assessment of the Organisation, Management and Funding of University Research in Ireland* argued for a reciprocal commitment from both government and the universities/higher education to "redefining and reshaping the knowledge base of Irish society".[50] At that time, Ireland was one of the worst supporters of HERD of all OECD countries. A consequence of Ireland's low GERD [total R&D expenditure] and HERD [total HE R&D expenditure] as a percentage of GDP, which is itself low, is that the absolute expenditure on R&D in Ireland is much lower than in the other countries listed.[51]

In contrast, Ireland experienced significant economic growth beginning in the mid-1990s which led to a dramatic increase in and commitment to national funding. The *National Development Plan, 2000-2006*[52] has, for example, designated EUR 2.4 billion[53] for research and development via various agencies: Higher Education Authority, Science Foundation Ireland, Enterprise Ireland and the Research Councils for the Humanities and Social Sciences, and Engineering, Science and Technology. A special, albeit small, head-start fund of EUR €38 million was designated for the thirteen Institutes of Technology to enable them to build up the requisite research expertise and portfolio to compete for other external funding.

While these commitments contributed significantly to the growth of a research agenda at DIT and other Irish HEIs, [54] it remains to be seen how the recent economic slowdown will impact. During 2003, there was a noticeable decrease in total available funding, and a re-balancing of available funds towards Science Foundation of Ireland (with its focus on biotechnology and ICT basic research) and away from more broad based funding via the Higher Education Authority, the Department of Education and Science and the research councils; some of the latter funding will be restored in 2004. At the same time, the government, in line with EU commitment to increase research funding to

3% of GNP (unlike elsewhere, GNP is used given Ireland's high level of multinational output), has just introduced tax credits to promote R&D investment and abolished stamp duty on transfers of IP[55]. Nevertheless, the message is clear – research which facilitates and underpins economic growth is most likely to receive funds.

Today, DIT has a small but relatively considerable research profile with over EUR 26 million secured for research and innovation between 2001 and 2004. Over the past number of years the Institute has established a number of specialised centres, which provide services such as research, development, problem solving, consultancy and specialised training specific to various industries and the public sector both in Ireland and abroad. DIT Centres include: Digital Media, Environmental Health, Food Product Development, Industrial Control, Logistics and Transport, Maintenance, Optoelectronics, Social and Educational Research, Radiation & Environmental Science, Timber Development, Tourism Research, and Project Development.

Table 1. **Research Data, 1999-2003**[56]

Total Number Academic Staff	870	2002-2003
% Active Researchers	22.07%	1 106*
% Experienced Research Supervisors	8.39%	29.11%*
Total Number Postgraduate Research Students	119	10.22%*
% PhD students	25%	142
External Research Funding Earned	EUR 789,794	24%
Number of Patents	2	€10 939 449**
Number of Publications in Refereed Journals	49	1
Number of Books	13	123
Number of Refereed Conference Papers	49	12
Number of Exhibitions/Performances	6	167
Number of Industry Projects	10	14
Number of Postdocs	11	2
		16

* figures available for the year 2001-2002 only
** the figures relative to the year 2002-2003 are obtained as follows

- outside research revenue in 2002 = EUR 10 023 956 – of which a third (EUR 3 341 319) represents the period from September to December

- outside research revenue in 2003 = EUR 11 397 195 – of which two thirds (EUR 7 598 130) represents the period from January to August

Strategy, Management and Support of Research within DIT

Research Strategy

The mission statement in DIT's Research and Scholarly Activity Policy, published January 2000, states:

The Dublin Institute of Technology is committed to the provision of quality Research and Scholarly Activity including consultancy which serve the needs of society - including the enterprise sector - locally, nationally and internationally whilst enhancing the professional development of students and staff. These activities will integrate with the overall mission of the Institute and Ireland's economic and social development so as to ensure that the Institute plays a full and interactive role in academic, industrial and socio-economic affairs.

Research is defined broadly, although a distinction is made between research and keeping abreast of one's discipline, the latter of which is considered a normal part of an academic's role (see below):

- *Basic or fundamental research*: experimental or theoretical work undertaken primarily to acquire new knowledge without any particular application or use in view.

- *Strategic research:* work which is intended to generate new knowledge in an area, which has not yet advanced sufficiently to enable specific applications to be identified.

- *Applied research:* work which develops or tests existing knowledge and is primarily directed towards either specific practical objectives or towards the evaluation of policies or practices. Work, which involves the routine application of established techniques on routine problems, is unlikely to constitute research.

- *Scholarship:* work which is intended to expand the boundaries of knowledge and understanding within and across disciplines by the analysis, synthesis and interpretation of ideas and information, making use of a rigorous and documented methodology.

- *Creative work:* the invention and generation of ideas, hypotheses, images, performance or artifacts, including design, leading to the development of new knowledge, understanding or expertise.

Included in Research and Scholarly Activity when particular conditions are met (*e.g.* some form of peer review) are:

- *Consultancy:* which involves the deployment of existing knowledge and the application of analytical and investigative skills to the resolution of problems presented by a client, usually in an industrial, commercial or professional context.

- *Professional practice:* Some of which overlaps with consultancy when conducted at an advanced level. In certain subject areas and professions, the theorisation and effectiveness of professional practice are advanced by academic staff who practice and participate in it; this could include research into the teaching process, teaching and learning practice, student progress and related matters.

DIT accepts, as a matter of course, that all teachers are required to keep abreast of developments both in their subject areas and in methods of teaching. Therefore, activity mainly concerned with keeping abreast of new developments in subjects is not regarded as 'research'.

Two factors underpin this definition:

- Given DIT's origins, its educational focus, orientation of its staff and its late-development status, definitions of research has been kept purposely wide. Many of DIT's staff are research novices with expertise in disciplines with a poor or new research lineage (*e.g.* architecture, marketing and creative arts). Likewise, academic research has tended to be less significant than professional practice or consultancy, or teaching.

- Despite embracing this wide definition, the emphasis is purposively and disproportionately on applied research, and particularly that which is industry-focused (including national/local government and service sectors).

In the early 1990s, the Institute identified fourteen research priorities based upon national priorities and perceived academic strengths. They were supplemented by a number of specialised Centres and other units to engage in R&D or training and other services to industry, seed funded under the 4th Framework Programme and national agencies. Between 1993 and 1996, thirteen Centres were established, each with industrial representation on its Advisory Board. By 2000, two Centres had been closed, another was floated as a separate company, and a fourth established with substantial external funding.

In late 2001, DIT adopted a two-pronged strategy to extend the range of research activities within the Institute while also focusing on a small number of research strength. Seven pillars underpin this approach:

1. Development of both quality and quantity in postgraduate training.

2. Increasing the number of postdoctoral research fellows.

3. Promotion of a small number of selected areas identified in each faculty by the Faculty Research Strategy.

4. Joint research initiatives to seed new areas/new collaborations particularly in relation to cross-disciplinary and cross-faculty themes.

5. Development of applied research for industry through industry centres.

6. Development of existing and emerging areas of core strength to a level of European and International recognition.

7. Attraction of world-class researchers in areas of strategic importance to the Institute through appropriate schemes.

The first four of these are associated with the broad-based approach. The last two are aimed at establishing centres of excellence while the fifth pillar recognizes the importance to the Institute of a strong link with industry. While DIT initially promoted three areas of established research enterprise (Information Technology, Biotechnology and Food, and Engineering and Materials) the reality is a broader approach based on a combination of internal competence, available funding, national priorities, competitive advantage and pressure for relevance.

This two-pronged research strategy aims to encourage as wide as participation in research as possible. It openly favours collaborative, cross faculty research activity, co-ordinated by the centre with activity taking place at both faculty and research centre/unit level. The difference between the locus of current research activity and the strategic preference is indicated in Table 2 below.

Table 2. **Locus of Current and Strategic Research Activity**[57]

Unit of Research Activity	Current Distribution (%)	Strategic Preference (%)
Individual		10
	40	
Academic Faculty/department		20
Research Centre	30	20
Centre of Excellence		20
Industry Centre	30	30

The development of HEI research strategies in Ireland is a relatively new phenomenon. The HEA is unashamedly driving this approach via the Programme for Research in Third Level Institutions (PRTLI) which gives significant weighting to the institutional research plan. In this context, DIT's story is not unique.

Research Organisation and Management Structure

The public debate on the role of R&D within DIT goes back to the beginning of the 1980s when approximately 60 staff were considered to be involved, with an estimated annual external funding of EUR 254 000. A DIT Research and Development Committee was established, and an Industrial Liaison Officer (ILO) appointed. In 1983, the Project Development Centre was set up to facilitate the entrepreneurial activity of graduates. A Research Committee was established, and, beginning in 1986, it began to distribute small amounts of seed funding and develop a strategy for research.

In 1996 the newly appointed Director of External Affairs (henceforth Director of Research and Enterprise as of autumn 2003) was given primary responsibility for the promotion and conduct of R&D. The Director of Academic Affairs has complementary responsibility for the associated academic framework. The Head of Research and the Head of Industry Development report to the former; they are individually and jointly responsible for developing research within the Institute, developing links with industry and other external partners, and encouraging the commercialisation of IP (see below). Centre Managers or Faculty Deans have responsibility for encouraging and facilitating research within their remit, although the operational control of the centres remains in some instances with the Director of Research and Enterprise. The Head of Postgraduate Studies and Research, who is responsible for all research that leads to postgraduate degrees, reports to the Director of Academic Affairs.

Faculties have been encouraged to develop research committees and produce research strategy plans. Faculty strategies and priorities are developed via an iterative process signed off by the Faculty Executive consisting of the Faculty Dean and the Heads of School. These are reflected in the overall DIT strategy. For a short time, each faculty seconded a member of staff as Research Co-ordinator, with varying degrees of success – this role is likely to be reconsidered as part of the Institute's review of research strategy and policy (see Conclusion below). A Head of Industry and Innovation Services has been appointed to each Faculty to develop external funding and commercialisation opportunities, and to exploit IP. Research management structures at Faculty level vary; some have rolled this process out and have well-established research committees and school research coordinators while others are at an earlier stage of development. The recent establishment of a Research Support Unit is an attempt to bring all the players into one place to underpin research initiatives.

DIT is placing considerable emphasis on the creation and transfer of knowledge through training, collaborative and commissioned research, consultancy and the development of campus and non-campus companies. The Project Development Centre (PDC) is an incubator providing enterprise development programmes, incubator space and facilities, business counselling, funding and access to R&D expertise. The *Hothouse* programme is a year-long programme that provides knowledge intensive start-ups with expertise, networks and tools, needed to develop highly successful businesses capable of competing in global markets. There is also a pre-start-up programme called *Prospect* which helps academic researchers commercialize their work; the Fast Growth programme helps owner-managers of fast growing companies deal with the challenges associated with rapid expansion – to date, 50 entrepreneurs have been through that programme.

There are two Institute committees concerned with research:

- The Postgraduate Studies and Research Committee is a sub-committee of Academic Council. It has several sub-groups including taught post-graduate programmes, postgraduate research, ethics, and finance.

- The Directorate (President plus ten Directors covering Academic Affairs, Research and Enterprise, Finance and the six faculties), which is the Institute strategic management team, deals with research, scholarship and knowledge and technology.

The latter group is concerned with policy and strategy while the former is focused on academic issues including quality assurance matters and research administration.

Research Culture

The promotion of research and a research culture and ethos across DIT has been both difficult and long-term. Like many new and emerging HEIs across the OECD, DIT is subjected to many of the same problems and challenges of starting late into research from a poor resource base (see below for a discussion of the issues). Its history is such that research is not firmly embedded in the academic workload or ethos of the Institution, albeit the Faculty of Science has both the longest history and largest number of active researchers.

Throughout the Institute both attitudes and performance remain diverse with each area at a different stage of development. With the exception of the Faculty of Science, where involvement in R&D has an established legitimacy and a successful tradition, the situation in the other Faculties is generally characterised by sporadic and isolated activity. From a somewhat disparate base of R&D, DIT is faced with the complex problem of raising the general level of involvement and of identifying and promoting relevant areas across the Institute where competitive advantage may be created and sustained with the attainment of a critical mass.[58]

Side-by-side with the growing emphasis on research, the Institute is also the largest provider of apprenticeship training in the country. These two cultures are the source of further tensions which also need to be managed as the Institute grows and matures.

Not surprisingly, many staff consider themselves teachers first and only; while this is changing and has changed quite significantly over recent years, it nevertheless has had an over-determining influence on academic and trade union behaviour and attitude. For example, academic contracts and procedures for academic appointment and progression are nationally negotiated; the academic trade union has sole-negotiating rights and has exercised significant influence, from time to time, on the Department of Education and Science and DIT's Governing Body on behalf of its members. The academic year formally ends on 20th June, and lecturers are not required to undertake any work between then and 1st September. There are salary scales rather than a career structure normally associated with universities. Recent senior lecturerships were 'officially' made on the basis of contributions to teaching, research and the community; while effectively all eligible candidates were appointed, the appointments did set, for the first time and with agreement with the trade union, excellence in research, teaching and service as criteria for promotion. New appointments continue to show a significant shift in the qualifications profile of lecturing staff, and there is increasing pressure that appointment boards appoint research active individuals – albeit there is no agreed definition of 'research active' and given the range of course provision, there is no (and perhaps there can be no) uniform implementation of this approach.

DIT is geographically dispersed across the city of Dublin, occupying 39 buildings in 10 major locations on approximate 10 acres. This geographical dispersal means that researchers do not have the same opportunity to meet which they might otherwise have, *e.g.* often no designated school/department area or staff common room. Computer facilities, laboratories and office accommodation within specific buildings range from poor to good; most lecturers share office accommodation, often with more than four people. Formal classroom space predominates, a consequence of which is the absence of smaller seminar or tutorial rooms. Library resources are limited, albeit growing, while research space within libraries is perceived as student space. Access is a further difficulty; buildings operate according to normal business hours and there is very limited provision for 24/7 entry. There are limited staff or postgraduate research seminars, guest lectures, conferences, etc.

These difficulties have done little to help promote a research culture, and have combined to undermine DIT's ability to attract and retain high quality research-focused staff. To address these problems, DIT is developing new dedicated research facilities; the first such building is for physics and chemistry (FOCAS, a state-of-the-art spectrometry and microscopy Facility for Optical Characterization and Spectroscopy), and for optometry – both of which will open in 2004.

Funding Issues

Unlike the universities which are free to allocate resources according to their needs, DIT is restricted in how it can allocate its budget. Accordingly, it has 'diverted' funds and resources from other areas (primarily teaching) and supplemented this funding with research funding earned competitively. Against this background, DIT secured approximately EUR 8.89 million (3.6%) of the total EUR 244 million of total Higher Education R&D funds (HERD) during 1988-1991. From 1991-1995, there was, however, little or no real increase in core R&D funding; the net increase was principally associated with the establishment of the research centres. This deterioration in the funding ratio (income/employee) was indicative of predominance of low-level, peripheral, research activity and of growth in low-funding-intensity areas. The only exception was the Strategic Research and Development (SRD) fund, the first officially registered Department of Education and Science funded MSc programme, which was started in 1991 thereby enabling DIT to support the research postgraduates.

Over the period 1995-1999, DIT expenditures, other than that arising from the new funding initiatives, showed an annual increase of 25%. It was providing 30% of centre and 20% of other research support funds or 23% of overall funding. Compared to the higher education sector generally, (where the equivalent figure is 16%), DIT was subsidizing research in 1999 at a level approximately 50% higher than the universities.[59] In 1999, DIT was awarded EUR 10 million in the HEA's PRTLI programme to construct a facility for optical characterisation and spectroscopy to support research across science, engineering and food science. Today, approximately 7% of DIT's non-pay budget is applied to research. Table 3 below indicates income sources for research funding as a percentage of overall funding.

Table 3. **Income Sources for Research (as a percentage of overall funding)[60]**

Funding Source	%			
	1997	2000	2002	2003
Institutional funding	12	41	5.65	1.98
Grants (e.g. from research councils or similar agencies)	29	13	66.44	89.80
EU Contract or project funding from external sources	49	4	4.28	1.76
Funding from industry[61]	10	42	23.63	6.46
Other types of income (e.g. private non-profit, patent licenses)			n/a	n/a
Total	100%	100%	100%	100%

Similar to other OECD countries, Ireland is experiencing a decline in institutional funding from government. Increasingly, the bulk of DIT's research funds will have to be won in open competition. Accordingly, DIT is developing strategies in relation to what is regarded as third-tier research activities and is planning for participation at international/EU level and in major national programmes where funding notionally exceeds EUR 1 million. The main sources of funds are Higher Education Authority of Ireland, Enterprise Ireland, European Union, Industry and more recently 'Technological Sector Research grants' through the Department of Education and Science. Within the Institute, DIT has introduced a range of schemes to fund and support research, including seed funding, postgraduate scholarships, postdoctoral fellowships with special tax concessions, time-release for research and research supervision and sabbatical leave.

When applying for significant, competitive research funding DIT involves researchers in an internal screening process in the first instance. This internal process includes external representation and ranks projects accordingly. This has had a positive effect both on the quality of submissions which are subject to a number of iterations before being approved for sending to the funding authorities and has afforded the Institute opportunities to bring research groups together in co-operation.

There is a particularly strong focus on growing postgraduate student numbers, both taught and research; the latter are actively recruited via DIT scholarship programmes, which require research students to present twice yearly reviews, workshops and seminars where they must present their work. A seed fund, c. EUR 160k per annum, is distributed via the Directorate of External Affairs and Faculty Research Committees; it seeks to encourage new entrants and projects which are capable of attracting external funds. Cross-faculty and collaborative proposals are actively encouraged. External consultants review the impact of these mechanisms periodically.

Research Training and Recruitment

In 1999, it was estimated that 3 000 FTE persons were involved in research in the higher educational sector in Ireland.[62] Approximately 60% of these were in science and engineering. Corresponding figures for DIT suggested approximately 250 FTEs or 12% of the national total, 50% of who were involved in scientific and engineering research. Academic staff represented 50% of the total (FTE) numbers involved in research nationally; at DIT, the number was closer to 10%. Today, DIT's figures for active researchers and research students are relatively small but growing.

Concern about this fragility was reflected in an international review of DIT which was considering the Institute for university status.[63] The reasons cited were a major factor in recommending that DIT was not ready to become a university, a view endorsed by the Higher Education Authority. The report noted that:

- In some areas, academic staff are not appropriately involved in research.

- The number of post-doctoral researchers is low.

- The profile of the qualifications of the academic staff undoubtedly impacts on the Institute's research capability.

- Staff development and training in research methodology and research supervision should also be given a priority.

- The existence of an authoritative and self-sustaining system of monitoring research standards in the Institute will be a sine qua non of the grant of University status. There is a need to review the Quality Assurance and Peer Review processes in the postgraduate research areas.

Several strategies have been adopted by DIT to help overcome these research deficiencies:

- *Staff Development:* In recent years serious attention has been given to staff development initiatives to help boost staff qualifications, with particular emphasis on PhD's or other research qualifications. There is a significant staff development budget which financially supports staff pursuing higher degrees; a special relationship between DIT and Trinity College Dublin provides places for ten members of staff.

- *Research Training:* Research training at DIT has two foci: for postgraduate students and for staff. Regarding the latter, DIT is unique in Ireland in having a training programme for research supervisors. Postgraduate students receiving scholarships from DIT are required to participate in a research training programme organised by the Office of Postgraduate Studies and Research. In both instances, seminars and workshops in research methodology, academic writing, project preparation, funding opportunities, ethics, supervision, etc. are also held. A Diploma in Research Management is offered by the Faculty of Business

- *Recruitment:* While there has not been an open policy to align appointments to research strategies/priorities, appointment boards are looking much more carefully and closely at research capability/experience and not only teaching. There is also likely to be an increase in dedicated researchers, including post-doctoral and visiting, and researchers 'bought-in' or 'head-hunted'.

Balance between Research, Teaching and Community Missions

The overwhelming majority of academic staff consider themselves teachers first and foremost despite their contract requiring involvement in teaching, research and community service – the latter of which includes participation in DIT committees. Many academic staff officially accept the need and virtue of integrating teaching and research but teaching remains largely didactic and includes substantial class contract hours.

DIT's commitment to wider access and the community underpins its applied and practical teaching and research focus. For example, courses offered at access, foundation and sub-degree level are targeted at students who may otherwise fail to gain a university place. In addition, teaching release is offered to academic staff who involve themselves in some of the programmes offered by the Community Liaison Office, the Access Programme, the Disability Office and the Mature Students Programme. Moreover, staff are actively involved in a range of innovative programmes with both primary and secondary schools, including after-school mentoring and music teaching.

Yet, despite these various activities, there is no formal mechanism for balancing or varying academic activity or responsibilities across the myriad school/departments functions or across one's career. The academic trade union, which has members at both second and third level, has a particularly traditional view of teaching. Changes or negotiations occur within a national context, via the Department of Education and Science, and are not within the exclusive purview of management and decision-makers at DIT. Boyer's 'the creativity contract' has been raised but there has no agreement on it conceptually.

Intellectual property and legal issues

DIT has recently formalised its policy on Intellectual Property, which in which universities in the US and EU, assigns intellectual property and copyright to the employer, *e.g.* DIT. Moreover, it states:

"Any IP generated by the academic staff, the technical staff, undergraduate and postgraduate students of DIT, in the course of their duties and/or activities either directly or indirectly and/or which relates to their discipline, teaching, research, training or consultancy activities, is the property of DIT".

Current policy is likely to be revised in favour of greater sharing of benefits between DIT and the inventor. This arises in response to a growing realization that while DIT needs to raise consciousness among all staff about IP issues, policy or its potential value, it also needs to actively encourage and facilitate innovation and research activity across the Institute. The forthcoming review is likely to reflect the following:

- That DIT will take on certain obligations in respect of that IP to ensure that it can be commercially exploited via clear policies on licensing and spin-off activities;

- That clarity exists between ownership and distribution of benefit to incentivise researchers and ensure good income return;

- That the net benefit to the inventor is greater by disclosing than by not disclosing;

- That DIT will actively protect the IP in the future.

Moreover, given the level and range of research and scholarship across the Institute, including musical composition, artistic work and film-making, the policy needs to be able to traverse these dimensions in a manner which will encourage disclosure and compliance, and innovation.

Commentary and Analysis

There is little doubt but that while the advent of significant sources of research funding is a welcome development in some areas, it has effectively widened the gap or, in betting language, lengthened the odds. The forthcoming years will be increasingly difficult as research becomes the new fault-line cutting across higher education systems in Ireland and internationally.

As aforementioned, DIT suffers a range of problems associated with new and emerging HEIs:[64]

- Poor institutional infrastructure (limited accommodation and requisite equipment) and technical support.

- Underdeveloped institutional support mechanisms, *e.g.* project preparation, development and management, identification of funding opportunities, IP and commercialization services,

- Many academic staff were hired originally to teach, often with an emphasis on industry or professional experience. While they have the ability to engage in consulting and development work, they often lack 'traditional research skills', *e.g.* a research postgraduate qualification, and the necessary research experience. It could also be argued that barriers to research may be due to 'lack of realization of ability' rather then 'lack of ability'. Great efforts have been made to address this deficiency but this emphasis has created the difficult challenge of ensuring a balance between quality and quantity.

- Academic workloads are significantly greater than among university colleagues, and hence research is being built on the back of relatively heavy teaching commitments. These conditions are compounded by salary and career differentials.

- Many of DIT's strengths are in disciplines which have little or no research tradition as such it faces particular difficulties achieving recognition and funding for this activity.

These issues highlight the challenges of growing research and building a research culture. Moreover, they provide part of the explanation for the level of internal disharmony and tension, and morale difficulties which have afflicted the Institute from time to time over the past years, and which inhibit faculty-building strategies. These problems underlie and highlight other issues about research strategy and management.

- No recognition of research under the former legislation has been a critical historic legacy shaping the Institute's development and growth. While current legislation recognises that DIT may undertake research, there is no direct annual allowance from the parent Department of Education and Science nor targeted head-start funds. Indeed, there are strong pressures, not always explicit, to retain and rebuild the binary higher educational system, and thus contain DIT's activities. In this context, DIT's desire to grow research has caused certain strains within the organization particularly given its educational reach, from apprenticeship to doctorate. While there is strong mission support for all these endeavours, competitive national, global and financial pressures, and realignment within higher education may inevitably intensify these tensions.

- Territoriality is another problem facing DIT; because there are six Faculties, there is a great and perhaps easy tendency to divide resources accordingly. This creates problems not only for priority-setting but also has an adverse effect on inter-faculty co-operation. In line with international comparisons, it is usually easier to get inter-institutional co-operation.[65] To some extent, research centres overcome these problems but not to any significant degree. This may be changing and in recent times there has been a number of examples of cross-faculty co-operation leading to successful research funding.

- The definition of what constitutes research and where the Institute should place its emphasis contributes to these tensions. The Institute's commitment to develop strong industry-based or applied research is strong, but there is a tension between how this should be done. The Institute inherited a dichotomy between academic and industry research, expressed via school/faculty and research centre. Sometimes this is expressed as a distinction between academic and applied research. Many questions are asked about these distinctions, not least the notion that there are clear separating lines rather than a porous continuum.

- Relatedly, the definition and role of the research and development centres requires clarity and review, not least because evidence suggests that more research actually takes place in faculties rather than in 'centres'. Perhaps not surprisingly, internal tensions have been aggravated by a view that the centres have received an unfair share of insufficient funds. Moreover, the value, role, administration and viability of these centres have also the subject of ongoing debate. While they have "represented an important external interface mechanism and a means of providing opportunities for developmental involvement of a broader range of academic staff than conventional research…it has been difficult to establish adequate levels of viability, to effectively manage both the external and internal interfaces and to overcome the perception that such involvement is a distraction to, and an unnecessary burden on, core activities".[66]

Their line-management relationship has also remained unclear: is it to faculties, to the Director of Research and Enterprise or a combination of the two? Confusion on this issue has, in turn, undermined academic support and willingness to participate in centres (and vice versa).

- These issues manifest themselves in the existence of two committees which have aroused tensions between researchers, faculties and central management. The forerunner to the current Postgraduate Studies and Research Committee had been a very active and relatively cohesive group; it had led the development of research activity, including industrial linkages, from the mid 1980s. The role of the current committee is less clear, not least because of confusion as to where the emphasis in its title lies. Is it the *postgraduate* studies and research committee or the postgraduate studies *and* research committee?

The source of these difficulties is three-fold:

1. *Late Development.* DIT faces numerous barriers-to-entry due to its status as a late developing HEI. Among the most significant issues are undemonstrated capacity, poor resource base, HR and IR tensions, and limited scale. Despite the significant increase in national research funding, the gap is widening and is likely to widen further, not least

because of factors described in No. 2 below. Late development, however, can also be seen as a benefit, affording DIT the opportunity to learn fro successful strategies elsewhere.

2. *Government Policy.* Policy instruments are explicitly or implicitly being used to reinforce the position of older institutions. Moreover within the current binary system, DIT sits uncomfortably in a 'never-never-land' between the Institutes of Technology and the Universities due to its own legislative and developmental status. Accordingly, while DIT is to come under the umbrella of the Higher Education Authority, it is currently 'managed' by the Department of Education and Science. For example,

    – A close relationship has developed between policymakers and the universities,

    – Government policy appears to favour the established universities,

    – Criteria and rules for research funding are antipathetic to DIT's position as a late-developer and its particular discipline expertise,

    – Insufficient regard is given to DIT's infrastructural and other requirements,

    – Government policy facilitates operational differentiation.

3. *Institutional Management.* The process of developing an effective and broad-based research policy across the Institute has been difficult, albeit many of the outstanding challenges arise from failure to decisively champion the research agenda at all levels. International reviews have been critical of the apparent absence of an integrated research strategy expressed in terms of corporate significance given to research across the Institute as a whole. In particular, the link between research and teaching is both unclear and unstructured.

    "Nationally it is expected that major third-level institutions maintain a cultural, technical and strategic base of knowledge supported through involvement in research. Research is expected to help maintain the relevance of the teaching function and develop the knowledge and creative skills upon which modern economies depend. For serious institutional players research is a necessity and an opportunity, not an option."[67]

Conclusion

Despite structural impediments and deficiencies in strategic development, DIT has demonstrated remarkable growth in research activity.

- Individual research actively is growing and is well motivated.

- Development type activities, including industry centres, have been a defining and unique characteristic of DIT.

- International high quality research exists in two or three important fields.

O'Sullivan estimates that DIT was responsible for 50% of all development activities within the Institute of Technology sector and 3.5% of all HERD in 2000.

While this performance is credible, it has not been without cost and effort. DIT has chosen to commit a significantly higher proportion of its limited discretionary resources to the promotion of research than in the case of the Universities and, if further expansion is to be achieved, difficult choices will have to be made under conditions of increased selectivity and alternative support arrangements investigated.68

Across DIT, academic staff are currently involved in a process of developing an Institutional strategy for 2000-2015; fundamental to the various strategic and scenario planning exercises is the role of research and development, and the distinction between them. These deliberations are set against a background of increasing national urgency. In formulating its proposals, DIT must plan for growth. Involvement in national and international/EU research programmes, intra-institutional and inter-institutional collaborations, targeted support for research active staff, and increasing emphasis on externally-validated research outcomes are increasingly taking centre-stage. DIT needs to convince government that its role and future is critical to building the Knowledge Economy in Ireland.

Following the appointment of a new DIT President in September 2003, a review of research strategy and policy is underway. It is likely that the following issues will be addressed, thus marking the fourth phase of the development of research and scholarship at DIT.

- Definition – in place of a narrow definition, strategy/policy will equally embrace research, scholarship, and knowledge and technology transfer as part of a dynamic, interactive and often porous process;

- Engine of growth – academic schools will become a primary driver/facilitator of research and scholarship, via research centres forming interdisciplinary teams across the Institute;

- Intellectual Property – greater emphasis will be given to share the benefits of IP with the inventor, with active promotion of spin-off ventures and paths to market;

- Infrastructure – existing disparate functions will be brought together via a one-stop shop Research Support Service, and clear decision-making processes, involving researchers, will be established;

- Support and recognition for researchers and scholars will be introduced via varying mechanisms, *inter alia*, professorships, full-time research posts, sabbatical leave and awards for academic excellence;

- Funding – increasingly competitive and strategically driven interdisciplinary teams are likely to receive funds to encourage, facilitate and grow research and scholarship.

Over the next years, DIT will need to face up to the challenge of increasing its expenditure in real terms and significantly expanding staff involvement and quality of output in circumstances which will increasingly be more competitive and financially more difficult. Despite significant progress to date, there is a qualitative leap that now must take place. The message is clear: DIT must strive for excellence but be prepared to excel in only a few areas.

CONTRIBUTORS

Dr. Véronique CABIAUX
Vice-Rectrice à la Recherche et à la Coopération
Université Libre de Bruxelles
Brussels
Belgium

Dr. Helen CONNELL
Director
Connell Skilbeck Pty. Ltd.
Victoria
Australia

Professor Jean-Pierre CONTZEN
Chairman
Institute of Advanced Studies
The University of the United Nations
Tokyo
Japan

Chair Professor
Instituto Superior Tecnico
Lisbon
Portugal

Ms. Janet DIBB-SMITH
Director, Research Policy and Support
Adelaide University
Adelaide
Australia

Dr Ellen Hazelkorn
Faculty of Applied Arts
Dublin Institute of Technology
Rathmines Road
6 Dublin
Ireland

Dr. Mohammed Yusof ISMAIL
School of Social, Development and Environment Studies
Faculty of Social Sciences and Humanities
Universiti Kebangsaan Malaysia
Bangi, Selangor
Malaysia

Professor Maria Alice LAHORGUE
Vice-President Planning
Universidade Federal do Rio Grande do Sul
Porto Alegre
Brazil

Professor Lynn MEEK
Director
Centre for Higher Education Management and Policy
University of New England
Armidale, New South Wales
Australia

Professor Maria Helena NAZARÉ
Rector
Universidade de Aveiro
Aveiro
Portugal

Dr. Mohammed Yusof Hj OTHMAN
School of Applied Physics
Faculty of Science and Technology
Universiti Kebangsaan Malaysia
Bangi, Selangor
Malaysia

Profesor Hans Jürgen PRÖMEL
Vice-President for Research
Humboldt-Universität Berlin
Berlin
Germany

Professor Ikram SAID
Deputy Vice-Chancellor
Universiti Kebangsaan Malaysia
Bangi, Selangor
Malaysia

Professor Françoise THYS-CLEMENT
Former Rector
Université Libre de Bruxelles
Brussels
Belgium

Professor Oktem VARDAR
Former Vice Rector
Member of the Council of Higher Education
Boğaziçi Üniversitesi
Istanbul
Turkey

Professor. Fiona Q. WOOD
School of Professional Development and Leadership
University of New England
Armidale, New South Wales
Australia

---

[1] Germany is an exception here.

[2] The German university has been seminal in the development of the modern research university, from von Humboldt's ideal vision of the unity of teaching and research as the basis for the establishment in 1810 of the (then) new University of Berlin [now the Humboldt Universitat zu Berlin represented in this set of case studies], to the development of practical organisational structures which subsequently became funding units within the decentralised university – Liebig's research laboratory at Giessen; and Neumann's research seminar at Koenigsberg (Clark, 1995).

[3] As indicated in the widely accepted Carnegie classification of institutions.

[4] Krull (2003),Bonn seminar.

[5] In presentation to Paris seminar.

[6] For example, the Ernest Orlando Lawrence Berkeley National Laboratory at University of CaliforniaBerkeley.Steering and Funding of Research Institutions. Country Report: United States. 2003 OECD/ DSTI website.

[7] See references to Slaughter for Paris seminar.

[8] Thys-Clement and Wilkin, 1997

[9] Van Ginkel, 2001, Tokyo seminar.

[10] Ehrenberg, Rizzo and Jakubson, 2003.

[11] OECD/DSTI, 1999.

[12] Geiger, 2000, Paris seminar.

[13] Westbury, 2004.

[14] Ehrenberg, Rizzo and Jakubson, 2003.

[15] Steering and Funding of Research Institutions. Country Report: Norway. 2003. OECD/DSTI website.

[16] Geiger, 2000, Paris seminar.

[17] Geiger, 2000, Paris seminar.

[18] OECD/DSTI, 1999.

[19] Report of Paris seminar.

[20] Henkel, 2000, Paris seminar.

[21] Weill, 2001, Tokyo seminar.

[22] For example, depending on the researcher's inventiveness, available technical skills, and equipment and availability of appropriate supervision or leadership

[23] Weill, 2001, Tokyo seminar.

[24] Sifuna, 2001, Tokyo seminar. An extreme case was cited in the situation of Kenya.

[25] Steering and Funding of Research Institutions. Country Report:Germany, OECD/ DSTI website.

[26] See for a more detailed discussion Wood, F. and Meek, VL. 2002 Over-reviewed and underfunded? The evolving policy context of Australian higher education research and development. Journal of Higher Education Policy and Management. 24(1): 7-20.

[27] The following discussion is based on the DEST RTS Guidelines.

[28] Author of the report *Science – the endless frontier* commissioned in 1945 by the US government.

[29] Gétulio Vargas was President of the Republic during the periods 1930-1945 and 1951-1954. His first term in office came about as a result of coup d'état; for his second period in power he was elected by popular vote. The Vargas governments were noteworthy as periods of industrialisation as part of a nationalist and populist project.

[30] For more details, see www.mct.gov.br

[31] In 2001, the public sub-system accounted for merely 31% of the 3 million and more students in Brazil (2001 Higher Education Survey, www.inep.gov.br).

[32] See www.cnpq.br for the full data and time series. The 2002 version is the fifth version of the Directory of Research Groups.

[33] There is only one field of science where the coefficient of specialisation is higher than the national average, *i.e.* greater than unity, which is that of the exact and earth sciences (1.28 in 2002).

[34] The CAPES assessment criteria are as follows: quality of teaching staff, measured in terms of scientific training and performance; average time required for award of an MSc or PhD; interaction with other doctoral programmes; consistency of the research activities of teaching staff with the draft programme, etc.

[35] These areas correspond to CAPES level 7. The genetics research establishment includes the Brazilian researcher with the highest number of citations in foreign papers.

[36] Out-reach (supplying services to the community) is one of the missions of the University of Brazil under the Federal Constitution (in the chapter on teaching).

[37] An abbreviation of the Portuguese title *Pró-Reitoria de Pesquisa*.

[38] On a scale ranging from 1 (disagree) to 5 (fully agree), the average answer amounted to 4.59 (www.ufrgs.br/propesq).

[39] Wissenschaftsrat 2000: Drittmittel und Grundmittel der Hochschulen 1993 bis 1998, p. 15.

[40] Deutsche Forschungsgemeinschaft (DFG), 2000: DFG-Bewilligungen an Hochschulen und außeruniversitären Forschungseinrichtungen 1996 bis 1998, Bonn.

At present, the DFG ranking is the only research ranking of universities in Germany. With a share of ca. 40%, the DFG is the largest third-party funding source for universities. The next report by the DFG is to be published at the beginning of 2003.

[41] In view of recent history, all employees (as for all civil servants) had to demonstrate their former moral integrity.,An inquiry was initiated at the Gauck-Behörde, the public archive of documents of the former state security service,for all staff. Employees were assessed by a committee of honour, on whose recommendation 54 people were dismissed.

[42] "Habilitations" are extended pieces of scientific work on a post-doctoral level, qualifying scientists for the position of professors. The law making a "habilitation" obligatory for professorships was abolished in 2002, making German universities more competitive on an international level.

[43] The remarkable rise of these figures is due to the fact that many dissertations and "habilitations" were only begun after the formal conditions for these degrees were set and the institutional changes at Humboldt University had been

completed. These figures are expected to grow much more slowly in the coming years.

*Sections 1 and 2 are taken partly from a report to CRE available on the BU web site

* MYR *(Malaysian ringgits)* is the currency unit used in Malaysia. One US dollar (USD) is equivalent to MYR 3.80.

[45] Background information is drawn from 'Case Study of DIT Research' prepared for the OECD/IMHE study Processes and Strategies for Growing Research in New and Emerging HEIs (2002*), DIT Policy on Research and Scholarly Activity* (January 2000), and Brendan O'Sullivan, *An Evaluation of Policy, Strategy, Organisation and Performance in the Direction of research, Development and Related Activities*, A Report to the Office of the President of DIT (June 2000).

[46] There were 10 000 whole-time, 4 800 part-time and 3 000 apprenticeship, 1 000 CPD/CED, 1 400 junion music students during 2002-2003 academic year.

[47] See Tony White (2001) *Investing in People. Higher Education in Ireland from 1960 to 2000*. Dublin, Institute of Public Administration.

[48] Thomas Duff, Joseph Hegarty and Matthew Hussey (2000) *The Story of the Dublin Institute of Technology*, Dublin, Blackhall Publishing. p87.

[49] Report of the International Study Group to the Minister for Education (1987) *Technological Education*. Dublin: Government Publications Office.

[50] C.N. Lindsey, 'Statement by HEA', Report of the CIRCA Group Europe for the Higher Education Authority (1996), pp2.

[51] Ibid. p66.

[52] Government Publications Office, Dublin.

[53] All Irish punt converted to euro.

[54] White, op. cit., pp272-276.

[55] See Ed Micheau, 'Tax credits will promote R&D investment,' *The Sunday Business Post*, 7 December 2003, p11.

[56] 1999-2000 data drawn from 'Case Study of DIT Research' op. cit; 2002-2003 data.

[57] The Strategic Evaluation is taken from "Case Study of DIT Research" op.cit

[58] O'Sullivan, op. cit., p.12.

[59] O'Sullivan, op. cit., p.20.

[60] Changes in research funding need to be seen within a wider economic context. For example, significant funds for R&D have become available over the past years: (1) around €370 million was the allocation for R&D in the 1988–93 Sub-Programme of the Industry Development Programme; (2) €457 million was allocated for the R&D Sub-Programme for the 1994–99 period; whereas (3) an overall allocation of €2.47 billion was earmarked for research, technological development and innovation in the current NDP of which €698 million was to be dedicated to RTD and innovation in the education sector and €711 million to establish a Technology Foresight Fund to support the activities of SFI. During 2003, there was a significant decrease in public sector/government-sponsored research, and funding to HEIs. As national funding for research has become available, Irish researchers have been less inclined to seek EU grants.

[61] Industry is widely defined and includes the private and public sectors, and community/social organisations.

[62] *Making Knowledge Work for Us,* Report of the Science, Technology and Innovation Advisory Council (STIAC), Dublin, Ireland (1995) reported similar figures thus suggesting that the number of Irish researchers had not grown over the decade.

[63] *Report of the International Review Group to the Higher Education Authority.* Dublin, Higher Education Authority (1998).

[64] E. Hazelkorn (2004) 'Research Management Challenges for New HEIs', *Higher Education Management and Policy*, Journal of the Programme on Institutional Management in Higher Education, OECD; in press; Ellen Hazelkorn (2002) 'Challenges of Growing Research at New and Emerging HEIs', in *Enterprise in Universities: Evidence and Evaluation*, edited by Gareth Williams, London, SRHE/Open University.

[65] Ellen Hazelkorn (2002) 'Growing Research - Challenges for Latedevelopers and Newcomers', Keynote Address, New Generations University conference, Sydney, Australia.

[66] O'Sullivan, op. cit., p19.

[67] O'Sullivan, op. cit., p13.

[68] O'Sullivan, op. cit., p33.